PICTURE A PROFESSOR

TEACHING AND LEARNING IN HIGHER EDUCATION

James M. Lang, Series Editor
Michelle D. Miller, Series Editor

A list of titles in this series appears at the end of this volume.

PICTURE A PROFESSOR

LIBRARY OF
CONGRESS
SURPLUS
DUPLICATE

Interrupting Biases about Faculty and Increasing Student Learning

....

EDITED BY

JESSAMYN NEUHAUS

West Virginia University Press · Morgantown

ISBN 978-1-952271-67-0 (paperback) / 978-1-952271-68-7 (ebook)

Library of Congress Control Number: 2022016002

Cover and book design by Than Saffel / WVU Press

CONTENTS

. . . .

PART TWO

Making Connections: Strategies for Building Trust and Rapport with Students

PART THREE

Anti-Racist Pedagogies: Strategies for Increasing Equity

PART FOUR

*Teaching with Our Whole Selves: Strategies for
Instructional Authenticity and Pedagogical/Professional
Success*

....

EMBODIED IDENTITY, EMPOWERING PEDAGOGY, AND TRANSFORMATIVE LEARNING

....

Jessamyn Neuhaus

Look! Up at the lectern!

Is it a teacher? Is it an educator? No, it's . . . Super Professor!

More charismatic than a Hollywood heartthrob! Able to win over the most reluctant, resistant student with a single quip or impactful PowerPoint slide!

During class, Super Professor delivers Oscar-worthy performances, scribbling formulas theatrically on a chalkboard or eloquently reciting lyric poetry to entranced students agog at the expertise on display. Super Professor always lectures brilliantly and entertainingly, effortlessly elucidating the most obscure subject. Students hang on Super Professor's every spellbinding word, laughing at each joke and painlessly absorbing difficult academic material simply by listening to Super Professor talk about it. Students are routinely so overcome by admiration for Super Professor's lectures that they spontaneously burst into applause.[1]

Super Professor appears over and over again on our TV and movie screens, quite wrongly depicting learning as a purely top-down activity whereby knowledge is simply poured into students' heads by an irrefutable expert. He's also usually an able-bodied, cisgendered, heterosexual White man.[2] In this way, popular culture reflects and reinforces the myriad of political, social, and cultural discourses that gender intellectual authority as male and support what Resmaa Menakem terms "white-body supremacy" by racializing knowledge and expertise as White.[3] Socialized and enculturated by this imagery, all too often, Super Professor is who we think of when we picture a professor.

Every single person teaching a college class in any subject or modality must contend in some way with the narrowly defined, limited/limiting expectations of how a college professor should act in the classroom, what they should look like, and what identity markers they should embody. Anyone who doesn't manifest those traits—before saying a single word or interacting in any way with students— will not meet certain conscious and unconscious student expectations. And expectations shape learning.[4] Moreover, biases about professors impact students' ability to connect and build rapport with instructors and to fully engage in the course material. *Picture a Professor* takes as its starting point that the "socially imagined professor," as contributor Rebecca Scott terms it in her chapter, impedes effective teaching and learning.

Assumptions about what professors "look like" directly contribute to what sociologist Roxanna Harlow identifies as "disparate teaching realities."[5] White women, women faculty of color, faculty with physical disabilities, nonbinary faculty, and all Black, Indigenous, and People of Color (BIPOC) faculty must navigate different intersectional mazes of racial, gender, and other biases about embodied identity on an exhausting daily basis. Scholar of higher education Nichole Margarita Garcia explains that no matter what their intention, when students, colleagues, administrators, staff, or random strangers tell her "you don't look like a professor," the phrase is a verbal assault on her expertise and her academic authority.[6] It's a manifestation of racial hierarchies and systemic inequities in higher education, including white-body supremacy, because anyone who doesn't "look like" a professor is "presumed incompetent," in the unforgettable words of that trailblazing edited collection and its 2020 follow-up volume.[7]

"Before we even open our mouths," as contributors Jacinta Yanders and Ashley JoEtta write in their chapter, students question the very *presence* of any instructor who doesn't conform to the professor stereotype. Similarly, in their chapter about teaching as blind/seeing impaired professors, contributors Sheri Wells-Jensen, Emily K. Michael, and Mona Minkara summarize this deep-seated student skepticism: "What they want to know is whether we belong in the classroom." Importantly, such implicit or even explicit questioning, and instructors' subsequent feeling of "unbelonging," as contributor Jesica Siham Fernández terms it in her chapter, is never restricted just to the classroom. Ableism, sexism, ageism, racism, homophobia and heterosexism, transphobia, classism, and other systemic inequities are baked into all aspects of academia—inequities that are further exacerbated by higher education's exploitative contingent and non-tenure-track employment practices.

A wide range of scholarly books and articles, research studies, memoirs, and social media extensively documents these inequities and shows how prejudices manifest in different scholarly disciplines in different ways, such as additional biases against all women faculty in the STEM fields.[8] The sexism and racism of academic systems are particularly evident when it comes to student evaluations of teaching and the disproportionate power these evaluations hold over professional teaching careers.[9] However, published scholarship of teaching and learning (SoTL) and popular advice about college classroom management, learning assessment, and other teaching stratagems frequently fails to adequately address or even acknowledge this simple truth: embodied identity matters to college teaching and learning. As I've argued elsewhere, disparate teaching conditions are one of the very first realities of teaching and learning both in person and online that every SoTL book, article, and *Chronicle of Higher Education* advice column should acknowledge.[10]

SoTL needs to much more thoroughly and methodically grapple with all the ways that society and academia's systemic inequities and hierarchies traverse our individual classrooms and to better address the "implicit professor theory" described in contributor Reba Wissner's chapter. As contributor Chavella T. Pittman states in her chapter, "It is impossible to understand the best teaching practices without understanding their intersection with the bodies that are doing the teaching and learning." More scholars of teaching and learning need to offer actionable pedagogical approaches that recognize the significance of embodied identity and propose real-life teaching strategies—tools, means, activities, methods, and processes—for empowering a true plurality of professors in their teaching practices. This is the aim of *Picture a Professor*.

The authors in this book represent a diverse slice of the modern professoriate, not simply in terms of individual identities and personal experiences but also in terms of teaching contexts and scholarly disciplines (you can find a brief biographical statement for each author at the end of their chapter). However, I must note that this is not a comprehensive collection in that we do not claim to speak for or represent the experiences of every group of people working and teaching in higher education who face micro-aggressions, discrimination, and barriers because of their identity, ethnicity, disability, speaking voice/accent, sexuality, financial resources, or employment status. For example, this volume does not discuss how contingent employment in higher education impacts teaching practices. Nor does it address "hidden" disabilities, such as mental health issues or other chronic health conditions. The authors included here are instructors whose lived teaching experiences have been shaped by not *looking* "like a professor" (i.e., not looking like a White, able-bodied—at least, as visible to students—cisgendered man). The intersectional teaching strategies explicated in this volume have been tested, reflected upon, and adapted by instructors whose students' cultural and social expectations about a college professor are upended in the very first moment of meeting the instructor and then again in every subsequent interaction.

It's worth pointing out that even someone who may "look like" a professor in every way may also embody a disability or historically minoritized identity, and as such, teaching in higher education will include navigating systemic inequities. That said, instructors who appear to embody certain aspects of the professor stereotype are afforded an advantage when they enter the college classroom. Namely, White instructors benefit from systemic white-body supremacy, and White men benefit from systemic White patriarchy. No matter what other inequities and discrimination shape their daily work as educators and no matter what subsequent teaching strategies they use that will challenge student expectations, White, cisgendered, heteronormative men begin with a particular advantage over everyone else when it comes to teaching: their bodies appear to conform to the stereotype of an academic expert, and in this way, they initially meet conscious and unconscious student expectations about professors and college.

The authors in *Picture a Professor* all take as their starting point their own lived experiences of how powerful stereotypes about who a professor is and what a professor "looks like" shape students' expectations and influence teaching and learning. They advance the SoTL by offering clear, specific strategies—things readers can do right now—for effective teaching with this reality firmly in mind. But it would contradict the very premise of the collection to suggest that each teaching strategy described here can or will always work well for everyone. Every instructor's individual and unique teaching context matters hugely to how they might use any assignment, technique, or pedagogical approach. To take one important example, some of the authors in *Picture a Professor* describe how choosing to use professionally appropriate and relevant self-disclosure in the classroom setting has helped them build connections and rapport with students. Such self-disclosure can be a highly effective teaching tool, but student biases and preconceptions around issues such as race, gender, mental health, and sexual identity will shape how students perceive and respond to instructors' self-disclosure.[11] Additionally, course subject influences the context for instructor self-disclosure.

Similarly, many of the teaching strategies described in this volume build on active learning teaching methods, but research demonstrates that predictable initial student resistance to active learning—and, indeed, any "nontraditional" teaching approach—increases when the instructor doesn't fit the professorial stereotype.[12] When readers consider how to adapt the active learning strategies described here, they will have to take into account their own individual positionality and institutional teaching context to plan for factors such as student resistance. In every case, instructors' ability to try new teaching techniques and innovative classroom practices may be constrained by their employment status, class size, department demands, and so on. There is no such thing as a one-size-fits-all, works-every-time-and-everywhere "best practice" or failproof set of "tips and tricks" when it comes to college teaching.

Evidence-based teaching advice about methods to facilitate authentic student learning always matters and needs to be taken seriously by all educators. But when the rubber meets the road in the individual in-person or virtual classroom, the instructor's context, positionality, and personality always matter as well and need to be taken seriously. With this critical caveat that an educator's individual context is significant at all times when using classroom techniques, and taking into account the multiplicity of disciplines and course subjects represented in *Picture a Professor*, three widely applicable principles emerge from these chapters' range of strategies and approaches—three broad pedagogical practices for increasing student learning and interrupting student biases that will benefit all readers who want to be effective teachers.[13]

First, all of the authors in this edited collection have embraced the process of ongoing personal pedagogical learning and reflection. They understand that nobody is born an effective teacher but rather that we are all always learning and relearning how to help our students succeed. The authors describe or draw on their own trials and errors, referencing their lived classroom and teaching experiences, including their mistakes. They try new things, assess, reflect on what worked and what didn't, revise, and try again.

Second, they don't undertake pedagogical learning and reflection in a vacuum but instead look to the published research and SoTL to help them understand their own experiences and to develop teaching strategies. They don't try to go it alone in their daily teaching lives. Rather, as contributor Celeste Atkins recommends in her chapter, they "find their people" or in contributor Sarah Mayes-Tang's words, their "cheerleaders." Finding and building support for teaching in your own unique context means engaging in conversations about teaching and learning, both in terms of the scholarly conversations in the SoTL and at teaching conferences and engaging with your own personal pedagogical learning network. These authors demonstrate that we can significantly further effective teaching and learning when we share rather than hoard our "funds of knowledge," as Atkins writes. These chapters illustrate one of the most valuable messages at the heart of the best SoTL and educational development: you are not alone.[14]

Third, these authors lead us to rethink and remake the role of the professor in teaching and learning. More than just diversifying the stereotypical *image* of a professor, the chapters in this collection argue for reimagining the function of "the professor" itself in teaching and learning. Their strategies and approaches actively redistribute power in the classroom, facilitating authentic learning by building class communities to support and encourage students as full and active participants in their learning. Unlike Super Professor, the educators in this volume don't hog the spotlight and suck up all the air in the classroom but instead view themselves as members of a classroom learning community. They engage students as co-teachers, as Chanelle Wilson and Alison Cook-Sather elucidate in their chapter, and prioritize what Donna Mejia identifies as "mutuality" in class communities. They serve as "team leaders," writes Erik Simmons in his chapter, and they deliberately reposition the professor as a "collaborator and organizer," as described in Scott's chapter.

By using pedagogical learning and reflection, drawing on the research, building support networks, and rethinking and redistributing power in the classroom, these authors create, develop, revise, and implement empowering teaching strategies in their unique individual teaching contexts—strategies that empower *teachers* for pedagogical and professional success while navigating academic systemic inequities and empower *students* to engage in meaningful learning.

In part one, "The First Day: Strategies for Starting Strong," the authors tackle what the SoTL clearly identifies as a vitally important day of any college class: the first class meeting. No matter what your individual and unique teaching context, every instructor needs to think extremely carefully about and painstakingly plan for the first day of class. Too many experienced teachers fail to adequately plan for the first day of class. This is a big mistake. First impressions are incontrovertibly powerful in any interaction, which obviously includes first impressions between students and teacher, and not just in face-to-face courses but also in online classes. In many ways, the first five minutes of the first class meeting or the very first time a student logs on to an online class are the most important few minutes of the entire term.

Because experienced instructors always need to conscientiously prepare for the first day of class, the first section of *Picture a Professor* will be useful reading for anyone. But instructors at the beginning of their teaching career may find it an especially good starting point for classroom planning and pedagogical reflection. This section draws on themes and issues that can be of particular import to new teachers, such as ways that an instructor's youthful appearance or style expression may impede students' acceptance of authority and expertise. Though not a permanent aspect of anyone's embodied identity, and certainly not to suggest that it operates on the same level as entrenched inequities around racial and ethnic discrimination, looking "too young to be a professor" is a stumbling block that new instructors, particularly women, may encounter. Thus the "strategies for starting strong" in this section apply not just to the first day of class but also to the beginning of a career in the college classroom.

The first day is without question vital to laying the groundwork for authentic student learning, but what previous SoTL has not adequately addressed is that first impressions on the first day take place in the complicated intersections of identity and power structures in higher education, including conscious and unconscious student expectations and gendered, racialized, and ableist stereotypes about academic expertise and intellectual authority. All the pressures of the critical first class meeting are magnified and multiplied when the instructor doesn't "look like" a professor. But so too is the opportunity for counteracting such student biases about professors. English and linguistics scholars Sheri Wells-Jensen, Emily K. Michael, and Mona Minkara explain in their chapter, "How Blind Professors Win the First Day: Setting Ourselves Up for Success," that when student expectations about the professor's identity don't match the reality, carefully preparing well in advance for the first day of class is key to shaping the "class narrative." Their recommendations are excellent advice for any instructor, including grounding yourself firmly in your own unique teaching context (which may mean actually "ignoring the usual advice") and spending time before the first class familiarizing yourself with the physical space in which your class will be meeting.

The rest of the chapters in part one detail specific activities for interrupting student biases on day one and laying the groundwork for increasing student learning. In "Critical Reflexivity as a Tool for Students Learning to Recognize Biases: A First Day of Class Conversation on What a Professor Looks Like," Jesica Siham Fernández describes a first-day activity that was the direct inspiration for this volume's title. She calls it the "What Comes to Your Mind?" activity, and it asks students to close their eyes and reflect on what they think of when they think of a professor. Fernández uses "What Comes to Your Mind?" to spark an important first-day conversation in her ethnic studies classes about assumptions, stereotypes, and biases, including discussing her own pedagogical presence in the classroom as a contrast to the stereotypical professor. Kelly E. Theisen's chapter, "Commonalities and Research: A One-Two Punch to Combat STEM Fears and Biases on the First Day of Class," demonstrates how she uses research about growth mindset while sharing information about her own educational journey to connect with students on the first day of class, emphasizing her experiences as a dyslexic, first-generation college student who now holds a PhD in chemistry. While building rapport and increasing students' ability to succeed, she is, simultaneously, demonstrating her pedagogical skill and subject expertise. In "Where's the Professor? First-Day Active Learning for Navigating

Students' Perceptions of Young Professors," Reba Wissner details how she conveys expertise and experience that her young-looking appearance undermines for some students while also effectively drawing them into tactile, active learning on the first day of her music courses. Her activity, "The Object Petting Zoo," positively impacts learning and student engagement for the remainder of the semester. It could be adapted by both new and experienced instructors in a variety of disciplines who are seeking strategies for interrupting bias (with regard not only to a youthful appearance but also to any aspect of embodied identity) while simultaneously setting a positive tone for the class.

Part two, "Making Connections: Strategies for Building Trust and Rapport with Students," is organized around one of the most well-documented aspects of effective teaching: connecting with students by building trust and rapport.[15] As the SoTL has overwhelmingly shown for years and as the experiences of educators and students during the COVID-19 pandemic revealed even more starkly, sociality and connection are crucial to learning. Teaching and learning are never purely intellectual exercises but also always entail emotions.[16] Again, while the SoTL plainly indicates the value of making connections with students and helping students make connections with each other, with the instructor, and with the course content, scholars of teaching and learning have been slower to recommend clear takeaways for instructors who must additionally navigate student biases, assumptions, and expectations about professors' embodied identities. The authors in this section address this issue with a variety of proven, practical, and inspiring strategies.

In "Using Experiential Learning to Humanize Course Content and Connect with Students," Breanna Boppre shows how she uses tours and field trips, service-learning, and documentary films to facilitate learning in her criminal justice classes. She explains how experiential learning enables her to better connect with students who may question her authority and subject area expertise because of her gender and appearance. Fen Kennedy's chapter, "Collaborative Rubric Creation as a Queer, Transgender Professor's Tactic for Building Trust in the Classroom," focuses on assessment practices as a means to build trust and rapport. As a dance professor, Kennedy employs assessment rubrics co-created with students as a way of, first, empowering the students as learners and dance practitioners themselves and, second, demonstrating in a very concrete way Kennedy's commitment to fair and equitable classrooms. This process, Kennedy argues, helps mitigate students' skepticism or even fear about how Kennedy's identity may impact teaching practices.

In "Reflect to Deflect: Using Metacognitive Activities to Address Student Perceptions of Instructor Competence and Caring," Melissa Eblen-Zayas describes how after coming to terms with the ways students doubted and questioned her expertise as a physicist because of her gender presentation and appearance, she set out to find ways to "demonstrate deep caring for students and their success while also reinforcing" her authority and competence. She asserts that metacognitive activities offer a way to build student self-efficacy and trust, which in turn decreases student resistance and bias. Philosopher Rebecca Scott also uses metacognition as a pedagogical practice. In her chapter "From Absentminded Professor to Epistemic Collaborator: Reframing Academic Expertise through Vulnerability and Metacognition," Scott argues for "radically restructuring our very conception of academic expertise" by "acknowledging and modeling epistemic vulnerability" as instructors and by helping students to engage in metacognitive reflection about knowledge creation. She asserts that by "explicitly attending to the ways in which knowledge is produced and maintained in community with others," educators can empower students as learners and redefine professors as "epistemic agents within the learning communities of which they are a part."

In the final chapter of part two, "Black Man in a Strange Land: Using Principles of Psychology and Behavior Science to Thrive in the Classroom," Erik Simmons argues that a "humanity-first" approach to teaching—a recognition of each student's unique context in different "systems of influence"—can help instructors make stronger connections with students and to build trust. Drawing on his expertise as a social psychologist and his teaching experiences as a Black American in Australia, he urges other educators to "avoid the fundamental attribution error trap," create psychological safety in classes by serving as a "team leader," and cultivate a community of "we-ness" with students.

Part three, "Anti-Racist Pedagogies: Strategies for Increasing Equity," turns to one of the most pressing issues for all educators in the twenty-first century: cultivating anti-racist pedagogical practices. This imperative should be at the forefront of every teacher's reflective pedagogical learning today, particularly in light of increasing anti-Black, anti-immigrant, and anti-Asian racism and violence, and the enduring injustice facing native and Indigenous peoples. Any reader interested in working toward more inclusive classes and campuses and reducing systemic injustice and inequity in all aspects of higher education can learn from the chapters in this section. Because racism is inextricably entwined with expectations and assumptions about what a professor "looks like," anti-racism teaching practices are essential for combating stereotypes about professors and interrupting student biases, as well as facilitating increased equity, justice, inclusion, and learning for students in the college classroom.

Anthropologist and educational developer M. Gabriela Torres's chapter, "Beyond Making Statements: The Reflective Practice of Becoming an Anti-Racist Educator," gives readers a powerful, practical tool for getting past empty institutional or personal statements about diversity and inclusion and moving toward cultivating effective anti-racist teaching. Her "beginner's guide to fostering individual change in order to fuel institutional change" is available online.[17] With this open-access resource, Torres offers any educator who wants to develop anti-racist teaching practices eight questions for reflection and action. She argues that this process can empower faculty to "transform individual classrooms and institutional agendas" and will help educators "embrace anti-racism as a life's disposition."

In their chapter, "Rippling the Patterns of Power: Enacting Anti-Racist Pedagogy with Students as Co-teachers," scholars of education Chanelle Wilson and Alison Cook-Sather argue that "teaching and learning can be a partnership, not a performance; power can be shared, and we can work in community rather than in competition with one another." Their chapter describes how they enlist students as co-teachers for their course "Advocating for Diversity in Higher Education" and demonstrates ways that this model effectively supports five specific aspects of anti-racist pedagogical practices.

Finally, Jacinta Yanders and Ashley JoEtta critique common pedagogical practices of their scholarly fields—

English and second language studies—in their chapter "Beyond 'Good Writing': Enacting Anti-Racist Policies in Academic Writing." First, they pinpoint troubling links between racist gatekeeping and standard writing instruction in higher education, including its role in their own educational journeys. Then they give readers specific strategies for promoting an anti-racist writing classroom by validating and celebrating language and writing diversity, ensuring that syllabi and course materials reflect real commitment to language diversity, and reconsidering traditional grading and assessment practices for writing. Yanders and JoEtta persuasively conclude that "students deserve to be in a classroom where their whole selves are welcomed and celebrated, including their language choices."

The authors in the final section, part four, "Teaching with Our Whole Selves: Strategies for Instructional Authenticity and Pedagogical/Professional Success," argue that instructors too deserve to bring their whole selves into the classroom and, moreover, that doing so can empower them and their students. This section offers specific, proven strategies for disrupting student bias and increasing learning while always maintaining attention toward instructors' success both as educators and professionals in higher education. Donna Mejia details strategies for accomplishing this in her chapter "The Superpowers of Visual Ambiguity: Transfiguring My Experience of Colorism and Multiheritage Identity for Educational Good." An experienced dance professor, Mejia has developed some powerful pedagogical strategies "for mutual learning" and "dismantling bias" from her "visually ambiguous, multiheritage vantage point": administering an assumption index, modeling mutuality in word and deed, and fostering a classroom culture that encourages true listening and growth by normalizing "fumbling"—giving everyone in class the opportunity to "fumble forward" together.

In "Sharing Our Stories to Build Community, Highlight Bias, and Address Challenges to Authority," mathematician Sarah Mayes-Tang explores the power of personal storytelling as a tool for interrupting biases about faculty and stereotypes about what a professor "looks like." Acknowledging the complexities and vulnerabilities of personal storytelling in a pedagogical context and sharing her own experiences facing student resistance and bias as a White woman teaching math, Mayes-Tang asserts, "Our stories are valuable, and through our stories, we can build supportive networks, empower ourselves pedagogically, and empower our students to recognize bias and increase equity in the classroom."

Sociologist Celeste Atkins argues that effective pedagogy requires faculty to be able to bring their whole selves to all aspects of teaching and working in academia. In "Teaching Up: Bringing My Blackness into the Classroom," she summarizes key points from her research interviewing Black American faculty members about their professional experiences in higher education. Atkins compellingly demonstrates, using direct quotes from these interviews, the vital role that authentic expression, cultural professionalism, and personal support systems ("find your people") all play for faculty navigating systemic anti-Black racism as educators. She also strongly advocates for more just and equitable faculty evaluation methods.

Sociologist and academic consultant/coach Chavella T. Pittman also forcefully argues for better evaluation methods in "Empowered Strategies for Women Faculty of Color Navigating Teaching Inequities in Higher Ed." In this final chapter of the collection, Pittman delves into the evaluation process in more detail, offering specific, proven strategies for how women faculty of color can draw on the abundant research about teaching and learning to "craft an intentional narrative" about their own "awesome teaching." Pittman concludes with the reminder that "ally colleagues and faculty developers should work more proactively to learn and incorporate research literature about marginalized social statuses into the scholarship and practice of teaching and learning."

These authors offer a variety of strategies from a variety of perspectives. Readers' positionalities and individual teaching and institutional settings will shape the potential classroom implementation of these strategies. But the golden thread that runs through every chapter, inspiring readers in all teaching contexts, is a fiercely tenacious belief in the power of education and of educators as "change agents," in Mejia's words. It's not naive optimism or willful ignorance of the many obstacles standing in the way of justice and equity in higher education. On the contrary, every author in this volume recognizes the sexism, racism, ageism, ableism, and other systemic inequities endemic to higher education. They acknowledge and have in various ways experienced the fundamental unfairness, and the personal pain, caused by stereotypes about professors. Each author has reasons to resent those stereotypes, and many contributors face not just one but multiple intersections of biases and discrimination.

Yet as reflected in these chapters, each of these authors insists that their teaching *matters*. They *show up* for students, pouring time, energy, and creativity into building communities of learning. Again and again, they return to the classroom—in person, online, videoconferencing, or a mishmash of all these modalities. Again and again, they claim the classroom as a space uniquely suited to dismantling biases and deconstructing stereotypes. In their lived teaching practices, they affirm bell hooks's famous assertion that "the classroom remains the most radical space of possibility in the academy."[18] Again and again, they enter that "space of possibility" determined to keep finding ways to connect with students, to build trust and rapport, to foster anti-racist practices, to keep learning themselves, and to help students experience a lightbulb moment illuminating the world in a new way. They seek to facilitate nothing less than truly transformative learning.

The call for transformative learning experiences sounds particularly urgent as I write this in October 2021. The global COVID-19 pandemic has wrought enormous disruption, trauma, and upheaval on college campuses, not least in how it has changed the very definitions of teaching modalities and the role of educational technology. The emergency pivot to remote instruction and subsequent polysynchronous teaching and learning environments of the coronavirus era will have a long-term impact on many aspects of college education, including enrollment, economics, and curriculum. In light of these seismic shifts, most chapters in *Picture a Professor* include some discussion of how to adapt the recommended teaching strategies to online or hybrid classes, with the goal of making classes as resilient and flexible as possible.[19]

Additionally, there's some reason to hope that higher education may have finally reached a long-overdue moment of at least starting to reckon with entrenched inequities generally and anti-Black racism in particular. Cellphone video recording has finally made sanctioned extralegal, institutional, and police violence against Black Americans "hypervisible," as Atkins notes in her chapter, and the Black Lives Matter movement is reshaping discourse about race in many locales. All told, these events actually increase the disproportionate and inequitable burdens that fall on all BIPOC faculty but especially Black faculty, particularly in terms of unrecognized—and unpaid—service labor for the institution and emotional labor as teachers. However, these events also create the possibility of change in higher education by illuminating the undeniable need for anti-racist pedagogical practices at the same time the pandemic era has increased understanding of how students' individual circumstances impact their learning.

One of the most vital tasks for anyone teaching college today is understanding not only student positionality but also instructor positionality in higher education, including our own. In an essay about creating and sustaining more just and equitable educational systems, Sherri Spelic, an author, teacher, and leadership coach, emphasizes the need to reflect carefully on our own place in those systems:

> In our eagerness to be seen "doing the work" it seems to me that we almost never take the time to notice who we are (layers of identity), where we sit/stand in the given context (position) *and* to ask ourselves based on the first two responses, what is my contribution going to be? . . . For sustained and sustainable equity and justice work I don't see any way around taking the time to acknowledge our unique positionalities in the planning and implementation processes we adopt. . . . Positionality requires us to do more than name our layers of identity. It compels us to acknowledge that we possess varied and varying levels of influence within specific contexts.[20]

It's incumbent upon every instructor to "acknowledge our unique positionalities." Not by simply "naming our layers of identity" but rather by continually working to understand where and how we are each individually located in the institution's deep-seated systems of power, hierarchies, and historical structures of exclusion, discrimination, and marginalization.

Picture a Professor seeks to contribute to this necessary work by encouraging instructors to identify and reflect on their positionality as educators, and our intended audience is, therefore, a diverse and multifaceted one. First and foremost, these chapters aim to directly empower and speak to readers whose lived experiences encountering and responding to racialized, gendered, and other embodied stereotypes about "what a professor looks like" have not been consistently addressed in previous published advice and guidance about teaching. *Picture a Professor* attends to filling this gap by directly discussing the college teaching contexts of faculty from historically marginalized and delegitimized groups in higher education, such as women faculty of color. We hope these readers in particular will be energized as educators seeking to increase their teaching efficacy by knowing that others have had similar experiences and are now sharing some actionable insights into effective teaching and learning.

But in truth, this book is also intended for *anyone* teaching college today. The pedagogical strategies elucidated here and the "Teaching Takeaways" listed at the end of each chapter offer concrete, research-based, thought-provoking points for pedagogical reflection and class planning no matter your individual institutional context and embodied identity. Though never presuming a universally applicable approach to effective teaching, each chapter provides extensive food

for thought for all educators committed to their own pedagogical learning. Each chapter encourages and works to empower readers to think about what will help *them* facilitate
authentic student learning in their own teaching context.

Moreover, as Pittman compellingly argues at the beginning of her chapter, readers with racialized, gendered, and
other systemic privileges in higher education hierarchies
must strive to understand how those hierarchies impact
teaching:

> Don't belong to any marginalized groups? *Pay attention.*
> This is an opportunity for you to learn about teaching ineq-
> uities so you understand how embodied statuses impact
> teaching practices and how your women of color colleagues
> cannot implement teaching practices in the exact same way
> nor with the same outcomes as their White or male privi-
> leged peers.

For both practical reasons (people who serve on tenure review committees must understand how assumptions and
stereotypes can influence student biases about faculty, for
example) and ideological/moral reasons (anyone working in
higher education should be aware of how systemic racism
and sexism shape teaching and learning), the intended audience of this collection is anyone in higher education who
wants to learn about effective teaching, embodied identity,
and biases about professors' academic and intellectual authority and expertise.

As the editor of this volume, I've learned from each and
every contributor. Reading their work has increased my
teaching efficacy while deepening my understanding of my
own individual privileges in higher education as a White,
able-bodied, cisgendered, heterosexual, tenured full professor. I've also been called upon to examine my positionality

as a White woman teaching history at a small, rural state university and to explore my power as a recognized authority on pedagogy working to increase inclusivity and diversity in the SoTL. I know that reading *Picture a Professor* can fuel similar deep thinking, increase teaching skills, and encourage profound, ongoing pedagogical and personal learning for all its readers.

Learning about effective college teaching, including how we as individuals and collectively can support and enact justice, equity, diversity, and inclusion in our own classes and on our campuses, is an enduring endeavor. As Addy et al. write, "Being an inclusive instructor is an ongoing process that involves learning, mistakes, persistence, reflection, and willingness to adapt teaching practices to a diverse student population."[21] In all aspects of increasing equity and justice in higher education for everyone in higher education—students, instructors, faculty, and staff—we can't look for the finish line because there isn't one. But there are people and resources, including this book, that can inspire and energize you for the fight.

The authors in *Picture a Professor* are leading the way in exploring the connections between individual teaching strategies and the creation of more inclusive, just, and equitable higher education. The next time you picture a professor, think of these scholar-teachers and the strategies they've shared here to interrupt bias about faculty and facilitate transformative student learning. Picture yourself teaching in a world where anybody in any body can look like a professor.

....

Jessamyn Neuhaus is a professor of US history and popular culture and serves as the Center for Teaching Excellence director at State University of New York (SUNY) Platts-burgh. Recipient of the SUNY Chancellor's Award for Teaching Excellence, she is the author of *Geeky Pedagogy: A Guide for Intellectuals, Introverts, and Nerds Who Want to Be Effective Teachers* (West Virginia University Press), two historical monographs, and pedagogical, historical, and cultural studies research published in numerous anthologies and journals. Visit her website geekypedagogy.com.

Notes

1. See, for example, Nicholas Cage playing a professor in the 2015 film *Pay the Ghost*.

2. There are a few notable mainstream exceptions, such as Annalise Keating, a law professor, played by Viola Davis on ABC's *How to Get Away with Murder* (2014–20) and Dylan Reinhart, a gay psychology professor played by Alan Cummings on the CBS series *Instinct* (2018–19)—although whenever *Instinct* depicted Dr. Reinhart in the classroom, it was as a Super Professor delivering a brilliant lecture. I'd like to note here that throughout *Picture a Professor*, when authors are referring to ethnicity, "White" is capitalized (except when a direct quotation from another work does not do so). As Kristen Mack and John Palfrey of the MacArthur Foundation recently wrote, "Choosing to not capitalize White while capitalizing other racial and ethnic identifiers would implicitly affirm Whiteness as the standard and norm. Keeping White lowercase ignores the way Whiteness functions in institutions and communities." Continuing on this point, Mack and Palfrey quote the Center for the Study of Social Policy: "The detachment of 'White' as a proper noun allows White people to sit out of conversations about race and removes accountability from White people's and White institutions' involvement in racism. We intentionally capitalize 'White' in

part to invite people, and ourselves, to think deeply about the ways Whiteness survives—and is supported—both explicitly and implicitly." See "Capitalizing Black and White: Grammatical Justice and Equity," MacArthur Foundation *Perspectives*, August 2021, https://www.macfound.org/press/perspectives /capitalizing-black-and-white-grammatical-justice-and-equity.

3. Resmaa Menakem, *My Grandmother's Hands: Racialized Trauma and the Pathway to Mending Our Hearts and Bodies* (Clark County, NV: Central Recovery Press, 2017). Thanks to Michelle Cromwell for bringing this book to my attention.

4. See, for example, Susan Ambrose et al., *How Learning Works: Seven Research-Based Principles for Smart Teaching* (San Francisco: Jossey-Bass, 2010), 69; Millie Black, "Exploring Relationships Between a Teacher's Race-Ethnicity and Gender and Student Expectations," *Education Inquiry* 12, no. 2 (2021): 202–16; Angela Proviteria McGlynn, *Teaching Today's College Students: Widening the Circle of Success* (Madison, WI: Atwood Publishing, 2007), 67; Anton O. Tolman, Janine Kremlig, and Ryan Radmall, "Creating a Campus Climate to Reduce Resistance," in *Why Students Resist Learning: A Practical Model for Understanding and Helping Students*, eds. Anton O. Tolman and Janine Kremling (Sterling, VA: Stylus, 2017), 192.

5. Roxanna Harlow, " 'Race Doesn't Matter, but . . . ': The Effect of Race on Professors' Experiences of Emotion Management in the Undergraduate College Classroom," *Social Psychology Quarterly* 66, no. 4 (2003): 362.

6. Nichole Margarita Garcia, "You Don't Look Like a Professor," *Diverse Education*, June 29, 2018, https://diverseeducation.com /article/113239/.

7. Garbriella Gutiérrez y Muhs et al., eds., *Presumed Incompetent: The Intersections of Race and Class for Women in Academia* (Boulder: University of Colorado Press, 2012); Yolanda Flores Neimann, Garbriella Gutiérrez y Muhs, and Carmen G.

González, eds., *Presumed Incompetent II: Race, Class, Power and Resistance of Women in Academia* (Louisville, CO: University of Colorado Press, 2020).

8. For an introductory bibliography, visit our website: https:// pictureaprofessor.com.

9. For my bonus chapter about student evaluations of teaching strategies, visit https://pictureaprofessor.com.

10. Jessamyn Neuhaus, *Geeky Pedagogy: A Guide for Intellectuals, Introverts and Nerds Who Want to Be Effective Teachers* (Morgantown: West Virginia University Press, 2019), 23–27; Jessamyn Neuhaus, "Bodies Online," *Inside Higher Ed*, August 4, 2020, https://www.insidehighered.com/blogs/university -venus/bodies-online.

11. See, for example, Matthew Gough, "Looking after Your Pearls: The Dilemmas of Mental Health Self-Disclosure in Higher Education Teaching," *Journal of Mental Health Training, Education and Practice* 6, no. 4 (December 2011): 203–10; Katherine Hill, Macy Martischewsky, and Cynthia Erikson, "Information Type Influences Students' Perceptions of Faculty Self-Disclosures," *Teaching of Psychology* 48, no. 3 (July 2021): 215–20; Todd Jennings, "Teaching 'Out' in the University: An Investigation into the Effects of Lesbian, Bisexual, and Transgender Faculty Self-Disclosure upon Student Evaluations of Teaching Effectiveness in the U.S.A.," *International Journal of Inclusive Education* 14, no. 4 (June 2010): 325–39; Stephen Kromka and Alan K. Goodboy, "The Effects of Relevant Instructor Self-Disclosure on Student Affect and Cognitive Learning: A Live Lecture Experiment," *Communication Education* 70, no. 3 (July 2021): 266–87; Alicia Smith-Tran, "Exploring the Benefits and Drawbacks of Age Disclosure among Women Faculty of Color," *Teaching Sociology* 48, no. 1 (2020): 3–12.

12. On student resistance to learning, and to active learning in particular, see Cheryl Albers, "Teaching: From

Disappointment to Ecstasy," *Teaching Sociology* 37 (July 2009): 269–82; Stephen D. Brookfield, *The Skillful Teacher: On Technique, Trust, and Responsiveness in the Classroom*, 3rd ed. (San Francisco: Jossey-Bass, 2015), 10, 215–27; Sid Brown, *A Buddhist in the Classroom* (Albany: State University of New York Press, 2008), 25; Tolman and Kremling, *Why Students Resist Learning*; Maryellen Weimer, *Learner-Centered Teaching: Five Key Changes to Practice*, 2nd ed. (San Francisco: Jossey-Bass, 2013), 71. On student resistance and instructor identity, see, for example, Tomika Ferguson, Risha R. Berry, and Jasmine D. Collins, " 'Where Is Our Space Within This Ivory Tower?' The Teaching Experiences of Black Women Faculty in Education Programs," *Journal of Research on Leadership Education* 16, no. 2 (2021): 140–57; Chayla Haynes et al., "Existing and Resisting: The Pedagogical Realities of Black, Critical Men and Women Faculty," *Journal of Higher Education* 91, no. 5 (2020): 698–721; Kaori Katada and Christina Gay, "Double- and Triple-Minorities in the International Relations Classroom," *International Studies Perspectives* 9, no. 4 (2008): 464–68; Gary Perry et al., "Maintaining Credibility and Authority as an Instructor of Color in Diversity-Education Classrooms: A Qualitative Inquiry," *Journal of Higher Education* 80, no. 1 (January/ February 2009): 80–105.

13. I'm deeply indebted to Celeste Atkins for her extensive help in crafting a title for this book. It was her suggestion to use the phrase "interrupting bias." I'm also grateful to Donna Mejia for her input and feedback on the title and introduction.

14. Contributors to the West Virginia University Press Series Teaching and Learning in Higher Education, *Pedagogies of Care: Open Resources for Student-Centered and Adaptive Strategies in the New Higher Ed Landscape*, 2020, https://sabresmonkey .wixsite.com/pedagogiesofcare.

15. See, for example, Brookfield, *The Skillful Teacher*; Aaron S. Richmond, Guy A. Boysen, and Regan A.R. Gurung, *An Evidence-Based Guide to College and University Teaching: Developing the Model Teacher* (New York: Routledge, 2016), 60–62; Harriet Schwartz, *Connected Teaching: Relationship, Power, and Mattering in Higher Education* (Sterling, VA: Stylus Publishing, 2019); Janie H. Wilson, Rebecca G. Ryan, and James L. Push, "Professor-Student Rapport Scale Predicts Outcomes," *Teaching of Psychology* 37 (2010): 246–51.

16. Sara Rose Cavanaugh, *The Spark of Learning: Energizing the College Classroom with the Science of Emotion* (Morgantown: West Virginia University Press, 2016); Joshua Eyler, *How Humans Learn: The Science and Stories Behind Effective College Learning* (Morgantown: West Virginia University Press, 2018); Peter Felten, *Relationship-Rich Education: How Human Connections Drive Success in College* (Baltimore: Johns Hopkins University Press, 2020).

17. "Becoming an Anti-Racist Educator," Wheaton College, https:// wheatoncollege.edu/academics/special-projects-initiatives /center-for-collaborative-teaching-and-learning/anti-racist -educator/ (https://tinyurl.com/anti-racist-educator).

18. bell hooks, *Teaching to Transgress: Education as the Practice of Freedom* (New York: Routledge, 1994), 12. See also Kevin Gannon, *Radical Hope: A Teaching Manifesto* (Morgantown: West Virginia University Press, 2020).

19. Travis N. Thurston, Kacy Lundstrom, and Christopher González, *Resilient Pedagogy: Practical Strategies to Overcome Distance, Disruption, and Distraction* (Utah State University, 2021), https://www.usu.edu/empowerteaching/publications /books/resilientpedagogy/.

20. Sherri Spelic, "Who We Are, Where We Sit, and Why It Matters," *Medium*, August 7, 2021, https://medium.com

/identity-education-and-power/who-we-are-where-we-sit-and
-why-it-matters-719ef245fda7.

21. Tracie Marcella Addy, Derek Dube, Khadijah A. Mitchell, and
     Mallory E. SoRelle, *What Inclusive Instructors Do: Principles and
     Practices for Excellence in College Teaching* (Sterling, VA: Stylus,
     2021), 152.

....

THE FIRST DAY

Strategies for Starting Strong

....

CHAPTER I

HOW BLIND PROFESSORS WIN THE FIRST DAY

Setting Ourselves Up for Success

. . . .

Sheri Wells-Jensen, Emily K. Michael,
and Mona Minkara

Every human event is a story. Like a story, every college class has a setting: either the traditional room or, in the time of the pandemic, a swarm of interconnected screens and scattered study areas. The class has a narrative arc and produces a meaningful ending. The plot is the syllabus: the sequence of readings and tasks designed to catalyze learning. The characters are the students, entering the plot with their own motivations, experiences, and goals. And the storyteller is you, the instructor, vitally immersed in the story but also shepherding the characters forward—encouraging, pushing, and, sometimes, shrewdly maneuvering them onto the best path as the semester unfolds.

If you embody the stereotypical picture of a professor, the class story can emerge unquestioned from the accumulated experiences, judgments, and implicit biases of everyone present. This collective creation is still tolerable for most people most of the time. If, however, you are not the storyteller students expect, you will have to take charge of the situation immediately. If you do not, students' implicit assumptions about how you do or do not fit into the standard classroom will take the narrative away from you and change it in ways you might not expect.[1]

As blind professors, we know that the perfidy and delusion that passes for information about blindness in popular culture is a deleterious influence in our classes. Books, cartoons, and movies abound with blind fortune-tellers, monks, beggars, sorcerers, and blues musicians, with the occasional quasi-blind superhero or Starfleet engineer tossed in for dramatic effect. Popular culture has not warmed up to the blind politician, parent, or college professor. Still, remarkably, here we are, and we must pull students' attention away from these erratic, destructive stereotypes so we can build an atmosphere that makes learning happen.

The beginning of class is an exquisitely liminal moment. It's one of the rare times when people actually stop, take a breath, and ask, "What's this going to be like?" There is some real chance that those present might listen if they are given a thoughtful answer, and failure to seize that moment can make things go badly.

How badly? Here is Sheri's story of one very bad first day: As a new, enthusiastic university instructor, ink still smearable on my diploma, I insisted on my right to be "just like everyone else." I sought to remove myself from the classroom narrative, foregrounding the discipline I wanted my students to learn. I wanted student-centered and subject-centered classes. I was not there to teach about blindness or braille or how to use a white cane. I absolutely was not there to be a poster child for anything. I planned to become the friendly, generic portal through which my students would meet the field of linguistics, and I vowed that my private life would stay private. So my plan for my first day of class involved nothing beyond attending to the syllabus and course material.

This plan fell apart about thirty seconds after I entered my classroom.

Sheaf of meticulously prepared notes in one hand, white cane in the other, I stepped through the open door and paused to get a sense of where the students had situated themselves and what their general mood might be. They seemed affable enough, chatting and digging in their backpacks for supplies, and I lingered in the doorway a moment, smiling benevolently upon my assembly of fledgling linguists. I decided it would be a good class.

Apparently interpreting my moment of reflection as a cry for help, a young man scrambled up from his seat and hurried eagerly down the aisle to where I stood. He caught me by the arm holding my cane. "It's pretty crowded in here," he said eagerly, "and the teacher isn't here yet. I'll help you find a seat!" With the whole class watching, he tugged on my arm, ready to maneuver me toward some vacant desk.

What on earth was I supposed to do? My (admittedly limited) teacher training had said nothing about being mistaken for a student, and I had not prepared to be physically grabbed and tugged down the aisle like a misbehaving donkey. For a terrible moment, I considered just going with it. What if I sat down and vanished softly into the mass of students, and we all waited together for a more suitable classroom teacher to appear? But I knew there was no such rescue forthcoming. I needed to address this—embarrassing myself and probably mortifying the student in the bargain.

In what I can only describe as a spasm of primal awkwardness, I said, "No, thank you, I'm not sitting. I'm, um, going up there," gesturing vaguely toward the front of the room with my notes and dropping a few pages in the process.

History has mercifully removed the details of the next few minutes from my memory, but it was an inauspicious start to the semester. There were undoubtedly various mutual apologies and students jumping up to help retrieve notes and more ignominious moments shuffling pages back into order once I got to the front of the room. I was clearly not the picture of a professor, and everybody (including me) knew it. Nobody (also including me) knew how to fix it.

We simply cannot separate our identities from our role as teachers. The reality is that our students carry stories about how blind people are supposed to act and what jobs they are supposed to have, just as they carry cultural stories about gender, race, age, religion, and sexuality. We can either go along with those stories or consciously create our own, and we have found that creating our own not only makes the class more comfortable for us but also creates a more relaxed, active, and intellectually satisfying atmosphere for everyone, and the scholarship of teaching and learning reminds us all to start this on the very first day.[2]

Decades of research on universal design show that working with, rather than against, the reality of disability improves everything for everybody.[3] Thoughtful changes made for the nominal benefit of a disabled participant turn out to help everyone. For example, automatic door-opening devices, helpful for wheelchair users, also benefit the student with a sprained ankle, the large group walking together, and the professor with an armload of books. Teaching in a pandemic has heightened the general awareness that we are not carbon copies of each other, not mass-produced students in mass-produced classrooms with mass-produced needs. When we treat these individual needs as the foundation of our teaching, rather than as inconveniences and exceptions, everything changes.

A few of the details we have gathered in the following sections are specific to blindness, but they apply to anybody working hard to make more effective and welcoming classes. We have collected four steps for a successful first day that have worked for us. They may work for you as well.

Step #I. Grounding Ourselves

If you are a minority in a position of some social power, the conflict between what you believe about yourself and what other people believe about you is omnipresent. The rasp of accumulated miscommunications, microaggressions, and inconveniences, as well as occasional outright slights, will either exhaust you or exacerbate a cycle of outburst and recovery that will drain the joy and dedication that initially brought you to this work. You ignore this reality at your physical, emotional, professional, and spiritual peril.

To illustrate, here is a random sampling of first impressions from our own students that we have actually overheard, over the years, as our students converse among themselves: "S***. Wait. Is *that* my teacher?" "How did she even find the classroom?" "How can she grade my papers?" "How can she take attendance?" "So freaking weird! I can't wait to tell my roommate!" "I guess I'm going to be able to get away with all kinds of s*** in this class!" "I've never had to talk to a blind person before. How is that going to go?" "Will this class still count?" "Well, this is going to suck."

These reactions are not isolated examples of impropriety. They emerge naturally from a society where the online

"2020 New Teacher Challenge" recently garnered over twenty million views. In the challenge, parents pull up a picture online of someone they consider wholly unsuitable to fulfill the job of "teacher." These are sometimes pictures of models or cute, animated cats, but mostly they are photoshopped images of people with missing teeth, people who are elderly or disabled, or people with facial differences. The gleeful parents then tell their unsuspecting elementary student to "come say hi to your new teacher." The bewildered child's confusion, revulsion, fear, or barrage of giggles is rewarded by the parent as the acceptable answer, and the clip is proudly placed online for everyone's amusement. The child has done well; the parent is happy; the lesson is taught and learned. This noxious behavior, steeped in ignorance and smug superiority, only works as "fun" because "everyone understands" that some people are suitable as teachers and some are clearly not. The story that is being told is this: it is outrageous and laughable to imagine that such people could teach. Such people means us.

So, before we can introduce the syllabus, learn something about the students, or tell our regulation first-day jokes, we have to push through this tangle of cultural assumptions and misinformation that would sabotage our attempts. We are, after all, neither outrageous nor laughable.

And before we can do *that*, we have to be clear with ourselves about what is happening. We cannot deny that we are "not supposed to be" where we are, doing what we are doing.

Invest the time to sit quietly, breathe, and feel how this reality falls on you. You might find some tension in your shoulders or across your forehead, tightness in your stomach or in your throat. Greeting the physicality of your reactions may help you sort what you believe about yourself and what messages you have absorbed from the surrounding culture. There may still be things inside you that (quietly, traitorously) agree with the assessment that you do not belong where you are—despite your years of work and training. Since we all grew up soaked in the same cultural muck, it would be truly shocking if this were not the case. If you are disabled, spending some intellectual time in the wisdom generated by disability studies and some complementary time in personal reflection may accelerate this process, but nobody fully escapes the overwhelming power of cultural convention and internalized ableism that accompany disability.[4] We recommend seeking out a community of other disabled people as friends, mentors, and sounding boards because none of us can work through all of these stories on our own.

It is absolutely not necessary (or even remotely possible) that you clear all this out of your system, and there is no purity test by which the disability community sorts its members into ready and not ready. But we have found that the ongoing process of coming to peace with yourself is the best place to begin.

Step #2. Avoiding the Usual Advice

We have all received the usual advice from well-meaning colleagues and would-be allies: to be in academia as a disabled person, you must win the determination game. Your preparation must be stellar, your presentations polished, and your knowledge of the material deep, smooth, and flawless. To paraphrase: work harder than those other bums. This advice assumes that it's possible to work harder than our peers: that nondisabled academics spend the bare minimum amount of time researching and preparing classes, and most of the time, they're sitting by the pool sipping overpriced drinks and talking about their next vacation in the south of France.

Even before the pandemic, every academic we know was already working very hard indeed, with the average clocking over 53 hours a week and all these hard-working, very smart people got where they are now by beating out countless other hard-working, very smart people.[5] The admonishment that we should "do more" is ludicrous. In the days of pandemic, we have to confess that we sometimes have to repress twinges of schadenfreude as everyone around us "suddenly discovers" access barriers and extra anxiety. We are accustomed to increased levels of stress, lack of access, and abrupt changes in circumstance. We have often put in extra hours to navigate access barriers, but (and this is important) our sense of justice and self-worth requires that we acknowledge this as an occasional necessary evil rather than embrace it as a suitable life plan.

Even if we were somehow able to regularly outperform the rest of the field, it would not produce the desired effect. The barriers that thwart disabled academics rarely have anything to do with mastery of the field per se. The student reactions featured in the previous section did not target our knowledge base or our teaching chops. They were about how we as blind instructors were unexpected: out of place. Being marvelous researchers or even exceptional teachers will not eliminate this resistance. This means that we must pick apart the knots of false beliefs about disability that created their resistance to us in the first place, and that requires recasting the narrative, starting on the first day. And it requires teamwork.

Superheroes or Star Trek engineers notwithstanding, individual disabled people are not endowed with supernatural stamina or determination. We do, however, have canny intuition for working around these systemic barriers, and we have colleagues within the disabled community who are ready to help. We also have laws in place to protect us from outright discrimination, and most campuses have some office charged with setting up reasonable accommodations. Don't shy away from these valuable resources. Ask calmly (and repeatedly) for the accommodations that you require, resting comfortably in the knowledge that, while helping you to do your job, they inconvenience no one.

Step #3. Setting the Physical Stage

All three of us invest time in making sure that we can independently and reliably locate our physical classrooms. Depending on the size and complexity of the campus, this process may take a few minutes or an afternoon of strategy and practice. Once we find it, we subject the classroom to a thorough search. This is good advice for everyone. Don't dash into your new classroom and launch into teaching. Find a time to be in the space quietly beforehand, so you can *own* it when the time comes. Because the classroom is the stage where we make our initial presentation, we must own it.

For Mona and Sheri, who are fully blind, this process involves locating the front desk, the light switch, the fire extinguisher, the windows, extra exits, and the various corners, crannies, and doorknobs where we can stash a white cane when we need our hands for other tasks. Because we like to walk around the classroom while teaching, we note the default configuration of the chairs and how easily they can be moved. We might also find out if the room is painted a particular egregious color or if there is an especially pastoral or dystopian view out the window. If we are teaching a late afternoon or evening class, we might note what time the sun sets, making interior lights necessary for the students. For Emily, it means additionally ensuring the room has adjustable lighting, so she can use the vision she has, and a place to secure her dog guide.

For the three of us, it also means learning how any classroom tech works since the usual classroom tech support person called in a hurry is unlikely to know how to help us with the adaptive technology we use to access the classroom computer and whiteboard or screen. That is a much longer process and does legitimately require extra time and energy.

Such preparation does not mean that we never ask for or accept help during class. The exchange of small courtesies is normal and helps build trust within any community. But not all questions or favors are created equal. We draw a philosophical distinction between clarifying questions and requests for assistance that are incidental to classroom management and those that represent significant renegotiation of teacher-student roles. For example, there is no harm in questions such as "Is the text on the screen big enough for everyone to see?" or "Can somebody pass around these handouts?" or something pedagogically motivated such as "Will somebody read number 10?" But we avoid putting students in the uncomfortable position of assuming responsibilities that would naturally fall to the instructor.

We come to class knowing where things are, with our plans in place, and with our best academic clothes on, ready to roll. The point is not to exude authority for the sake of authority; the point is to show that we are at peace with ourselves and in control of our immediate environment and that we are comfortably in charge. We are clear that, whatever blindness-related panic might be brewing among the students, it is unfounded. Blindness is neither central to our class nor taboo.

Step #4: Setting Up the Rules and Shifting the Focus

For all teachers, there are matters of housekeeping. Will there be a midsession break? Are snacks allowed? How should the instructor be addressed? How will each class begin? What kinds of daily or weekly rituals will be employed? What are the policies about cell phones, laptops, late arrivals, and bathroom breaks? Remembering the principle of universal design and the story we are constructing, we choose classroom policies that support our needs as blind instructors and our thoughts about pedagogy. We uphold the desire to keep the teacher in charge of the class while putting students in charge of their own learning. The question is never (for example), "Should I allow laptops in class?" but rather "How do laptops affect the class environment and students' learning?" We apply this to each situation.

For example, disabled faculty sometimes request, and sometimes are urged to accept, a classroom assistant, but this option should be carefully weighed rather than automatically embraced. We recognize that when we begin to delegate tasks to any sighted person in the classroom, we need to do so thoughtfully. It is too easy for able-bodied people to talk over, past, and about disabled people. We encounter this treatment ad nauseam when, for example, we are at a restaurant and the server asks the person we are with, "What would *she* like?" Or when a delivery person asks, "Can she sign her name?"

Sheri shares this story: As a new instructor, I had a graduate student who attended class with me. It felt natural at the time that she assist in proctoring quizzes, and so she patrolled the aisles, watching students as they worked. At some point, a student had a "quick question," and the grad assistant helpfully clarified. There was a blurred word, and she easily answered this question. However, once that precedent was set, other "small questions" became her domain rather than mine. A new story began. New character roles were defined. When (slightly bored) I actually wandered out of the class during one of my own quizzes to get a drink of water, I realized that the students and I had quietly put her in charge. I needed to rethink her role.

Or take the classroom technique of calling on individual students. We refocus this as a means for encouraging students to take ownership of learning. A blind instructor is not equipped to officiate the usual (artificial) scheme for negotiating conversational turn taking in class. We all have to remind students that the silently raised hand is not a good strategy for getting our attention. Sitting slumped wearing a puzzled expression is similarly fruitless.

There are two main methods of addressing this. Emily tells students that they should speak up if they have a question, completely eradicating the raised hand. This works well and redistributes some of the teacher-centered authority in the class. Students learn to mediate their own discussion and take turns, and the professor is always there to break in or redirect as necessary. Sheri and Mona employ a slightly more formal approach. Rather than silently raising hands, students with questions say their names aloud, similar to how meetings are conducted using *Robert's Rules of Order*. The instructor then acknowledges them in turn. Students rapidly learn this routine, and it reinforces everyone's names, giving us more time to match names and voices. Since both of these methods require more initiative than the silent, half-lifted hand, the result of either method is that the students take ownership of their own class participation.

What about uncivil classroom behavior, such as using phones, eating lunch, or sleeping in class? What do we do about the rampant texting, note passing, and newspaper reading that could happen in our classes? We reframe this question, asking rather why should the professor, blind or sighted, assume the role of babysitter? We resist the automatic response that we should work harder to make our classes more intensely interesting or more fiercely rigorous than our peers. It's simply not rational to expect that every blind instructor will be absolutely spellbinding at all times, or so intimidating that students dare not stray from the stated rules. Students sometimes claim (out of a sense of integrity or injured pride) that they would *never* break rules in a blind professor's class, but we have not regularly found this to be true. Considerable time and energy have been spent worrying about how a blind instructor can ever "enforce classroom discipline," but let's admit that nobody ever controls all this behavior.

We trade the question of how to police student behavior for the question of how best to create shared responsibility. This is not a laissez-faire approach. We care about how our students behave and what they learn, but we also understand that paying attention is work that only our students can do. We remind them that if they fail to ask a question or if they miss something because they were texting or reading the paper, it's their loss. We are in charge of teaching; they are in charge of their learning.

Conclusion

During the COVID-19 pandemic, most college instructors undertook some form of online teaching. The bad news is that online teaching takes significantly more time, and if you have to deal with inaccessible technology as a blind professor, the frustration quotient can be excruciating.[6] The good news is that everything in this chapter still applies. It still helps to ground yourself, avoid the usual pitfalls, set your (virtual) stage, and decide on your ground rules.

In the case of some kinds of asynchronous classes, however, it may happen that students never actually figure out that you aren't a standard-issue professor. None of us would ever advocate burning the energy necessary to actively conceal our disability, but it's fair to say that we have all indulged a self-satisfied chuckle when we are able to avoid the emotional labor of accommodating students' automatic ableist first impressions.

Most of the questions we have heard as blind instructors over the years are about how we can manage this or that aspect of the physical classroom situation. We have answered these enough times to realize that none of this is actually what the questioners want to know. What they want to know is whether we belong in the classroom. Without positive experiences to guide them, they fall back on unsorted, untested, unrealistic memes, stories, and fears about disability. Understanding both the source of these questions and our own abilities gives us the freedom to respond skillfully, addressing their actual concerns with as much candor as we judge they can manage. Over time, we become the positive experiences they need to change the stories they have told themselves about disability. This work can be exhausting, but it is work we know how to do, and it allows us to answer their question clearly and consistently: yes, we do belong in the classroom.

Teaching Takeaways

- The first day of class is vital to crafting an effective "class narrative."
- Preparation for the first day should include grounding yourself in your own teaching context, which may also mean ignoring the usual advice.
- Before the first day, spend time getting comfortable in your classroom.
- Reframe classroom management questions as opportunities for students to assume ownership of their own learning.

SHERI WELLS-JENSEN is a linguist at Bowling Green State University. Along with aspects of TESOL (Teaching English to Speakers of Other Languages) and speech production, her research focuses on astrobiology, disability studies, and access to STEM education for disabled students. She is a fan of all things geeky, a musician, a baker of bread, and a herder of cats.

EMILY K. MICHAEL is a blind poet, musician, and writing teacher from Jacksonville, Florida. Her work centers on ecology, disability, and music. She is the poetry editor for *Wordgathering* at Syracuse University and curates the *Blind*

Academy blog. Her first book, *Neoteny: Poems*, is available from Finishing Line Press. Find more at emilykmichael.com.

MONA MINKARA earned her doctorate in chemistry at the University of Florida and is an assistant professor of bio-engineering at Northeastern University. She leads the Minkara COMBINE (Computational Modeling for BioInterface Engineering) Lab, researching pulmonary surfactant, the complex protein-lipid substance lining the alveoli in the lungs. Minkara theorizes and designs accessible tools to support disabled scientists and produces the YouTube documentary series *Planes, Trains, and Canes*.

Notes

1. Mahzarin R. Banji and Anthony G. Greenwald, *Blindspot: Hidden Biases of Good People* (New York: Random House, 2013); Emily K. Michael, "Remaking the Ideal Teacher," *NEXT*, April 30, 2019, https://howwegettonext.com/remaking-the-ideal-teacher-f65f436a6791.

2. For general first day strategies, see James M. Lang, "How to Teach a Good First Day of Class," *Chronicle of Higher Education*, January 2019, https://www.chronicle.com/interactives/advice-firstday; Marguerite Mayhall, "The Vital Importance of First-Day Activities," *Inside Higher Ed*, August 14, 2018, https://www.insidehighered.com/advice/2018/08/14/guidance-how-teach-first-day-class-opinion; Julianne Treme, "Assigned Seating with First Row Preferences: An Inclusive Teaching Strategy That Builds Classroom Community" *College Teaching* 66, no. 1 (May 2017): 6–7, https://doi.org/10.1080/87567555.2017.1320516; Maryellen Weimer, "First Day of Class Activities That Create a Climate for Learning," *The Teaching Professor*, July 2017, https://www.teachingprofessor.com/topics/

for-those-who-teach/first-day-of-class-activities-that-create
-a-climate-for-learning/. Specific to our disciplines, see Daniel
Altshuler, "Preparing for and Lecturing on the First Day of
Class," *TAPTalk* (2010), https://tap.rutgers.edu/files/taptalk
/articles/altshuler.php; Bruce Chrystal, "Beyond the Syllabus:
Using the First Day of Class in Physical Chemistry as an
Introduction to the Development of Macroscopic, Molecular-
Level, and Mathematical Models," *Journal of Chemical Education*
90, no. 9 (2013): 1180–85, https://doi.org/10.1021/ed3008
445.

3. Jordana Maisel and Edward Steinfeld, *Universal Design: Creating
    Inclusive Environments* (Hoboken: John Wiley and Sons,
    2012). See also Thomas J. Tobin and Kirsten T. Behling, *Reach
    Everyone, Teach Everyone: Universal Design for Learning in Higher
    Education* (Morgantown: West Virginia University Press, 2018).

4. Lennard Davi, *Beginning with Disability: A Primer* (New York:
    Routledge, 2017); Sally French, *Visual Impairment and Work:
    Experiences of Visually Impaired People* (New York: Routledge,
    2017); John Swain and Sally French, "Towards an Affirmational
    Model of Disability," *Disability and Society* 15, no. 4 (July 2010),
    569–82, http://dx.doi.org/10.1080/09687590050058189. On
    reflection, see Matthew Sanford, *Waking: A Memoir of Trauma
    and Transcendence* (Emmaus, PA: Rodale Books, 2008); Carrie
    Wade, "Telling Myself the Truth: 5 Strategies for Fighting
    Internalized Ableism," *Autostraddle*, September 2016, https://
    www.autostraddle.com/telling-myself-the-truth-5-strategies
    -for-fighting-internalized-ableism-350528/; Stella Young, "We're
    Not Here for Your Inspiration," *Ramp Up*, July 2012, https://
    www.abc.net.au/rampup/articles/2012/07/02/3537035.htm.

5. Ellen M. Bradburn and Emily Forrest Cataldi, "2004 National
    Study of Postsecondary Faculty: Background Characteristics,
    Work Activities, and Compensation of Instructional Faculty and
    Staff: Fall 2003," *U.S. Department of Education, National Center*

for Education Statistics, December 2005, https://nces.ed.gov /pubs2006/2006176.pdf; John Kenny and Andrew Edward Fluck, "Towards a Methodology to Determine Standard Time and Allocations for Academic Work," *Journal of Higher Education Policy and Management* 39, no. 5 (July 2017), 503–23, https:// doi.org/10.1080/1360080X.2017.1354773.

6.   Joseph Cavanaugh, "Teaching Online—A Time Comparison," *Online Journal of Distance Learning Administration* (2005), https://www.westga.edu/~distance/ojdla/spring81/cavanaugh 81.htm.

CRITICAL REFLEXIVITY AS A TOOL FOR STUDENTS LEARNING TO RECOGNIZE BIASES

A First Day of Class Conversation on What a Professor Looks Like

. . . .

Jesica Siham Fernández

Women of color in academia represent less than 20 percent of full-time female faculty in institutions of higher education across the United States.[1] A plethora of articles and publications document how women of color experience the burden of invisible work in academia, often characterized by emotional and caring labor, as well as a cultural taxation.[2] The empirical evidence attests to claims that women of color often work harder, yet are less likely to receive tenure and promotion, and commeasurable salaries, in comparison to their White and male colleagues.[3] Race and gender discrimination, along with intersecting modes of institutional marginalization, collide to shape experiences of *unbelonging* for women of color faculty in higher education, especially for Latinas in the professoriate.[4]

For Latina faculty, these conditions render us illegible, other, and suspect within academia.[5] Even when we appear to succeed at carving a space for ourselves to belong, some of us are viewed as "hot commodities, cheap labor."[6] Universities often view research and teaching that women of color faculty engage in as desirable and marketable because it demonstrates "diversity work," but such labor is often inadequately compensated, poorly ranked, and devalued in tenure and promotion. The consequences of these structural conditions cannot be understated. The transformation of institutions of higher education must include the dismantling and transformation of structural barriers that limit Latinas securing tenure and thriving in academia.

To cultivate inclusion, representation, and equity in higher education learning, the demographics of faculty must change to reflect the diversity of student experiences. The underrepresentation of women and people of color in academia forecloses opportunities for the democratization of knowledge. When institutions of higher education adequately support women of color faculty and help them thrive as scholars and educators, they are supporting the academic success, inclusion, and retention of students who may be seeing themselves for the first time in the college classroom. Students might be seeing their lived experiences reflected in the curriculum, perhaps for the first time, when they're working with a professor whose identities are similar to their own.[7] A students' experience of inclusion might come through the content of the course material, as well as by whom it is being delivered.

The experience of seeing oneself in the classroom resonates with how I began my journey into academia. In my second year of undergraduate studies, I enrolled in a social psychology course taught by the sole woman of color in the psychology department, who on the first day of class explained that she identified as a feminist Chicana. The experiences and identities she shared with our class, and how she embodied her passion for the course content, made salient the importance of having students critically reflect to recognize and work to undo their biases about who a professor is or can be. This encounter shattered my assumptions about the professoriate, and I realized that I too could one day be a professor! Telling the story of my journey into academia is beyond the scope of this chapter, but it is the basis for a classroom activity I developed, implemented, and have modified over the years to engage students in critical reflexivity.

Grounded in the understanding of the structural conditions and institutional barriers that Latinas in the professoriate experience, and the importance of critical reflexivity for facilitating inclusive learning communities in the college classroom, in this chapter, I describe the "What Comes to Your Mind?" activity as a tool to help students recognize and work to transform their problematic biases about who a professor is. I offer this activity as a pedagogical tool for educators to use during the first day of class.[8] Critical reflexivity can help facilitate students' understanding of how their perceptions of who a professor is, or what a professor looks like, undermine opportunities for meaningful learning and the cultivating of positive student-educator relationships.

I'll begin by briefly sharing who I am and the experiences that shaped my identities and pedagogy. Next, I describe the "What Comes to Your Mind?" activity and explain how I've implemented it in the classroom. Then, I offer some reflections on student responses in the context of the activity. Student responses demonstrate their process of engaging in critical reflexivity by identifying and naming their biases about what a professor is supposed to look like and do, and how that is juxtaposed by the professor they see before them. Together, we unpack how these biases impact learning, especially when the identities of a professor are counter to students' expectations. Beyond this intervention, the activity also offers strategies to cultivate positive student-professor relationships that can aid student learning and participation.[9] I conclude with implications for engaging critical reflexivity as a pedagogical tool toward equity and racial justice.

Who Am I? Some Brief Reflections

When members of my college community see me they often wonder: Am I really a professor? Did I really complete my PhD? Do I really know [fill in the blank]? Students, staff, and even other faculty often question my credentials and knowledge: What did you earn your PhD in? And what do you teach?[10] Thereafter, I get a rather ubiquitous question many people of color with an accent and non-English-sounding surname frequently hear: Where are you from? When this question is asked, it resurfaces the renewal of suspicion about whether I belong. Specifically, whether I belong in the United States, academia, and the university.[11] These lines of inquiry, which may often emerge out of genuine curiosity, underscore for me a constant lingering feeling: I do not "look like" a professor. Indeed, I recognize that for many students and colleagues, I very well do not look like one because what a professor "looks like" reflects a very limited stereotype. What I look like and who I am challenge the schemas of what a professor should look like. Most of all, they contest how a professor embodies themselves in relation to their pedagogy, students, and the classroom environment. As a Mexican American, first-generation immigrant, cisgender woman in her mid-thirties and a first-generation college student and PhD, I am a professor. As of this writing, I am an assistant professor at a private Jesuit institution in Silicon Valley.

Critical Reflexivity as a Pedagogical Tool

Critical reflexivity is characterized as an intentional introspective practice of discerning, engaging, and working through thought processes that surface when people focus on their feelings, emotions, and thoughts and how these relate to an experience, perspective, or belief. Kenneth Gergen defines critical reflectivity as an "attempt to place one's premises into question, to suspend the 'obvious,' to listen to alternative framings of reality and to grapple with the comparative outcomes of multiple standpoints. . . . If we are to build together toward a more viable future then we must be prepared to doubt what we have accepted as real."[12] A critically reflexive practice embraces subjective understandings of reality as a basis for intentional and deep critical thinking about the impact of particular assumptions, perspectives, and actions toward others.

The "What Comes to Your Mind?" activity engages critical reflexivity as a tool to aid students in identifying, recognizing, and working to transform their biases, the schemas of who they view as a professor, and the assumptions associated with this perception. As an iterative practice, critical reflexivity requires consistent introspection about feelings, emotions, and thoughts, and how these shape behaviors.[13] Critical reflexivity can help students understand how they constitute their assumptions and actions through their biases. Once they are aware of their biases, and the challenges these might present for their capacities to connect with the course content and the professor, they can begin the work of recognizing and transforming their biases. The intention is to help cultivate student learning and the development of more authentic student-professor interactions that reinforce student academic engagement.

The "What Comes to Your Mind?" Activity

The "What Comes to Your Mind?" activity builds on the pedagogical practices of Gloria E. Anzaldúa's critical decolonial feminist scholarship and evidence-based teaching informed by critical race theory.[14] The objectives are to help students engage in critical reflexivity in order to facilitate their process of becoming aware of their biases and learn how to challenge and transform these. The goal is to help students become more cognizant about their associations and beliefs about what a professor embodies—or looks like—and to strive to undo these. Otherwise, these can limit their capacity for learning, academic engagement, and relationship building with the professor. Students are tasked with identifying and thinking through the sources of these associations and biases and how these may be juxtaposed, challenged, or nuanced by the presence of a professor who is unlike who they imagined.

» INTRODUCING THE ACTIVITY

The activity engages students in a practice of critical reflexivity that involves a process of thinking about their thinking, or introspecting, in relation to a series of prompts and questions about who and what a professor embodies. Students are asked to identify, or visually imagine, a professor. Before implementing the activity, however, I share with students a brief autobiography of who I am: "I was born in Mexico and immigrated as an undocumented child to the United States. I grew up in a migrant farmworking community. And I am the first in my family to attend and graduate from college." I do this so they know who I am, and how the content we will engage with cannot be devoid of my identities. Because the courses are personal and connected to my scholarship, I cannot fragment these from my role as an educator. In sharing these experiences in relation to my pedagogy, I highlight for students that who I am as a professor cannot be devoid of who I am as a person. I cannot tease apart nor compartmentalize my experiences apart from the classroom space; such a binary cannot be drawn. When I engage with students, I strive to be fully present in expressing and embodying my most authentic self.

Next, I ground the activity in the course content. I explain how social constructions of race and gender in the United States are shaped by hegemonic discourses and unconscious beliefs that can shape individual biases and behaviors. I demonstrate with empirical examples the problematic consequences of unconscious biases and how these reproduce inequities, discrimination, and stereotyping. I describe the activity in relation to my pedagogy, which strives to cultivate learning communities of critical compassion.[15] Specifically, learning communities where we challenge our biases with compassion as we engage in critical reflexivity. Having set up the "why" to the activity, I invite students to participate with an openness of mind and feelings, emphasizing that they will not be judged for what they "see" as they are asked to imagine, reflect, and respond to the activity.

» **CLASSROOM IMPLEMENTATION**

The following is a script I use to facilitate the activity. Some of these questions can also be adapted to synchronously or asynchronously online or remote learning. For example, via an online discussion forum, invite students to post a photo or image of what a professor looks like and then respond to a series of reflexive questions:

If you are comfortable and willing to participate, please close your eyes. I will ask you to engage your imagination in response to the following questions. After I read each prompt, I will pause before reading the next question. You do not need to share thoughts out loud; this is the silent critically reflexive portion of the activity. Please know that you can withdraw your participation at any time; however, I encourage you to join us.

- What comes to your mind when you think of education? What do you associate with education? Who do you associate with education?
- When you think of education, specifically in a classroom setting, who comes to your mind? Who is that person?
- Envision the college classroom. Who is the educator/ professor?
- What does that person look like? What is their race, ethnicity, gender age, or other identities?
- Now open your eyes please and write three to five characteristics about the professor. Next, pair up with a classmate to reflect on and dialogue about what you

envisioned. Consider reflecting on why you noted such characteristics or how these relate to your experiences with a professor.

Once students are provided with an opportunity to reflect and share with each other, we transition to a class dialogue. The characteristics students write, and the pair-share activity, are meant to help scaffold student engagement toward an encompassing class dialogue. I begin the class dialogue by asking students to raise their hand if they imagined any of the following characteristics associated with a professor: White, male, and old. These three characteristics are the most common that students associate with a professor. I then open up the dialogue to the class and ask them to freely share what they imagined and whether this was consistent or different from what I named. Several students will name or describe a professor they had before and with whom they really enjoyed learning. Some will name the class and how the professor engaged with students. Occasionally some students will even describe how the professor behaved, their demeanor, and appearance, including how they dressed.

The quotidian image of the professor most students will describe, however, is someone who is a White male in their late fifties, who wears glasses and tweed suits. The professor is also someone with an impersonal, straightforward attitude. Some students will go further by describing the teaching style: long and boring lectures, out of touch with technology. Clearly, several of these responses are based on stereotypes reinforced by how the media often portrays professors. Yet experience and research indicate that these traits are not inherently true. Sure, there might be some professors who are a bit outdated in their knowledge of technology, or they might express varied levels of care toward students, but most who enter the professoriate do so because they have a passion for teaching and sharing their knowledge with students. I know this to be true among my colleagues, and I know this is certainly my case.

» RECOGNIZING AND TRANSFORMING STUDENT BIASES

Upon having students reflect on, share, and dialogue as a class about the characteristics they associated with a professor, I list these on the board. Then, I ask students to name the associated or legible characteristics they have ascribed to me based on how they see me. Although a few students have had me as a professor before, it is often the case that many students are meeting me for the first time. Consistent with our process for reflecting on who they imagined as a professor, we generate a list of identities and traits they have ascribed to me. Some of these may include the following: Latina, woman, young, petite, with an accent, and passionate (which even comes through on the first day of class and underscores the importance of enthusiasm for effective teaching).[16] We compare and contrast the traits we listed for a professor and those associated with me. The purpose of this comparative exercise is to facilitate students' critical reflexivity about how their unconscious biases surfaced, often without them noticing, and how these may have rendered my position as a professor other or illegible. My intention is to have students work to transform their biases of who a professor is against the embodiment of the professor standing before them: me.

Almost always, I am not whom they envisioned as a professor. With this realization, we begin our work of addressing race, ethnicity, gender, age, and biases within the classroom. We proceed on to identifying and discerning the sources for our knowledge (Why did I imagine an old White male?) and how these sources in turn shape how we come to see others (Why did Professor Fernández not come to my mind?). Engaging students in critical reflexivity by prompting them with a simple question—What comes to your mind?—helps us recognize, address, and transform our biases, especially the placement of people in particular roles. In the college classroom, where and how we fit (or not) as professors has implications for our capacity to teach and build meaningful relationships with students that can support their learning. The activity invites students, and educators, to create a classroom space where we can challenge our biases in order to acknowledge our full being. At my institution, we describe this as *cura personalis* (care for the person).

» **IMPLICATIONS OF THE ACTIVITY**

Because I openly acknowledge, without judgment, that I am not whom most students expect to see as a professor, students are more likely to reciprocate openness and humility to learn and engage in a practice of critical reflexivity.[17] I emphasize for students that by virtue of my identities, what and how I teach will be different than what they might have experienced or expect of a professor who is White, male, and old, as I am not any one of these identities. The lack of diversity in the professoriate is empirically evident, as well as part of the biases that circulate among students. Further, the underrepresentation of women of color in academia, specifically in tenure-track and tenured positions, has implications for the discourses and cognitive schemas that students implicitly, or explicitly, generate about who they will be interacting with and learning from in higher education. The fact that students encounter these inequitable conditions and a lack of diversity should be a cause of concern for all educators, regardless of their identities. For those of us who are not White, male, or old, these conditions challenge our presumed qualifications, credibility, and righteous place in the academy as educators and scholars. Leaving such discourses and biases unquestioned grants some students the permission or authority to dismiss us as educators and discredit and devalue what and how we teach, and who we are.

Conclusion

A critically reflexive dialogue of what a professor looks like opens up opportunities for students and educators alike to cultivate a classroom space of critically compassionate learning that allows us to confront our deepest biases. Acknowledging that some of these biases are implicit is the first step in interrogating and working to challenge them. Once we begin this process of working on unlearning them, new insights and knowledge are gained that align with humanizing values of integrity, dignity, and respect for others. Failing to do so, however, can constrain or challenge student-professor relationships, which can further the racially biased, sexist beliefs some students and faculty alike might hold about who is and can be a professor. In other words, who is deserving of respect, dignity, and equitable inclusion and representation in the academe is shaped by how we as a society come to socially construct what a professor embodies. As educators, we must strive to recognize, challenge, and transform students' biases about who a professor is and what a professor looks like. We must seek to unearth where these assumptions came from and what these might or could mean for building a thriving critically compassionate learning community.

....

Teaching Takeaways

....

- Recognizing, challenging, addressing, and transforming problematic student biases about professors, starting the first day, can help students and professors establish a mutual openness to engage in difficult dialogues that are rooted in critically compassionate pedagogies.[18]

- Society conditions us to feel a sense of unease among those whom we see as different from ourselves or unlike us. Therefore, we must engage, reflect, and work to recognize and challenge problematic biases, especially in light of recent demands for racial justice and support for the Black Lives Matter movement.[19]

Through critical reflexivity, students, as well as professors, can begin to forge opportunities to build relationships toward meaningful learning across what we might perceive as differences. The biased perception of difference and othering limits our capacities for connecting and learning. Critical reflexivity can help set the foundation for a learning community environment in the college classroom.

Jesica Siham Fernández is assistant professor in the ethnic studies department at Santa Clara University. Fernández completed her PhD in social psychology and Latin American and Latino studies at the University of California, Santa Cruz. Grounded in a decolonial feminist praxis, she engages a participatory action research paradigm to support communities, youth, and students in efforts to create systemic change. Interconnected with her activist-scholarship, her pedagogy aims to cultivate transformative justice, well-being, and liberation.

....

Notes

....

1. Harriet Curtis-Boles, Diane M. Adams, and Valata E. Jenkins-Monroe, *Making Our Voices Heard: Women of Color in Academia* (Hauppauge, NY: Nova Science Publishers, 2012), 35–46.

2. On emotional labor, see Karen M. Cardozo, "Academic Labor: Who Cares?," *Critical Sociology* 43, no. 3 (2017): 405–28; Gabriella Gutiérrez y Muhs et al., eds., *Presumed Incompetent: The Intersections of Race and Class for Women in Academia* (Boulder: University Press of Colorado, 2013). On cultural taxation, see Alyssa Garcia, "Latina Faculty Narratives and the Challenges of Tenure: Identifying Strategies, Institutionalizing Accountability," in *Mentoring Faculty of Color: Essays on Professional Development and Advancement in Colleges and Universities,* eds., Dwayne Mack and Michelle M. Camacho (Jefferson, NC: McFarland, 2012), 69–87; Amado M. Padilla, "Research News and Comment: Ethnic Minority Scholars; Research, and Mentoring: Current and Future Issues," *Educational Researcher* 23, no. 4 (1994): 24–27.

3. Social Sciences Feminist Network Research Interest Group, "The Burden of Invisible Work in Academia: Social Inequalities and

Time Use in Five University Departments," *Humboldt Journal of Social Relations* 39 (2017): 228–45.

4. "The Condition of Education 2019 (NCES 2019–144), Characteristics of Postsecondary Faculty," US Department of Education, National Center for Education Statistics, 2019, https://nces.ed.gov/programs/coe/indicator_csc.asp.

5. Mike Lopez, "The Majority in the Minority: Expanding the Representation of Latina/o Faculty, Administrators and Students in Higher Education," *Journal of College Student Development* 45, no. 2 (2004): 253–55; Matilde Sanchez-Peña et al., "The Factors Affecting the Persistence of Latina Faculty: A Literature Review Using the Intersectionality of Race, Gender, and Class," 2016 IEEE Frontiers in Education Conference (FIE) (2016), 1–9; Raquel Sapeg, "Underrepresentation of Latina Faculty in Academia," in *Accessibility and Diversity in the 21st Century University*, eds., Gary A. Berg and Linda Venis (Hershey, PA: IGI Global, 2020), 115–39.

6. Patti Duncan, "Hot Commodities, Cheap Labor: Women of Color in the Academy," *Frontiers: A Journal of Women Studies* 35 (2014): 39–63.

7. Margaret Cantú-Sánchez, Candece de Leon-Zepeda, and Norma E. Cantu, *Teaching Gloria E. Anzaldúa: Pedagogy and Practice for Our Classrooms and Communities* (Tucson, AZ: University of Arizona Press, 2020), 1–20.

8. On the importance of the first day of class, see, for example, James M. Lang, "How to Teach a Good First Day of Class," *Chronicle of Higher Education*, January 4, 2019, https://www.chronicle.com/interactives/advice-firstday.

9. Harriet Schwartz, *Connected Teaching: Relationship, Power, and Mattering in Higher Education* (Sterling, VA: Stylus Publishing, 2019).

10. In the words of the groundbreaking anthology, I'm "presumed incompetent." Gutiérrez y Muhs et al., *Presumed Incompetent*;

Yolanda Flores Niemann, Gabriella Gutiérrez y Muhs, and Carmen G. González, eds., *Presumed Incompetent II: Race, Class, Power, and Resistance of Women in Academia* (Salt Lake City: Utah State University Press, 2020).

11. Brian Armenta et al., "Where Are You From? A Validation of the Foreigner Objectification Scale and the Psychological Correlates of Foreigner Objectification among Asian Americans and Latinos," *Cultural Diversity and Ethnic Minority Psychology* 19, no. 2 (2013): 131–42; Nichole M. Garcia, "You Don't Look Like a Professor," *Diverse Education*, 2018. https://diverseeducation .com/article/113239/.

12. Kenneth J. Gergen, *An Invitation to Social Constructionism* (Thousand Oaks, CA: SAGE Publications, 1999), 50.

13. Stephen D. Brookfield, "Using the Lenses of Critically Reflective Teaching in the Community College Classroom," *New Directions for Community Colleges* 2002, no. 118 (2002): 31–38; Jesica S. Fernández and Alejandra Magaña Gamero, "Latinx/Chicanx Students on the Path to *Conocimiento*: Critical Reflexivity Journals as Tools for Healing and Resistance in the Trump Era," *Association of Mexican American Educators Journal* 12, no. 3 (2018), 13–32.

14. Gloria Ladson-Billings and William F. Tate, "Toward a Critical Race Theory of Education," *Teachers College Record* 97 (1995): 47–68; Cantú-Sánchez et al., *Teaching Gloria E. Anzaldúa*, 166.

15. Julio Cammarota and Augustine Romero, "A Critically Compassionate Intellectualism for Latina/o Students: Raising Voices above the Silencing in Our Schools," *Multicultural Education* 14, no. 2 (2006): 16–31; bell hooks, *Teaching to Transgress: Education as the Practice of Freedom* (New York: Routledge, 1994).

16. Jessamyn Neuhaus, *Geeky Pedagogy: A Guide for Intellectuals, Introverts, and Nerds Who Want to Be Effective Teachers* (Morgantown: West Virginia University Press, 2019), 57–59.

17. Fernández, "Latinx/Chicanx Students on the Path to *Conocimiento*," 15.

18. hooks, *Teaching to Transgress*, 35.

19. Jennifer L. Ferguson and Michael Musheno, "Teaching with Stories: Engaging Students in Critical Self-Reflection about Policing and In/justice," *Journal of Criminal Justice Education* 11, no. 1 (2000): 149–65.

....

CHAPTER 3

COMMONALITIES AND RESEARCH

A One-Two Punch to Combat STEM Fears and Biases on the First Day of Class

....

Kelly E. Theisen

When students walk into my class on the first day, they are often thinking something like "I'm not good at science classes; I don't belong here," or "Biochemistry is so hard; I'm not going to do well in this class." My self-appointed mission is to show them, in seventy-five minutes, first that they belong, and second, that they can succeed in my course. This part of my mission isn't a secret, but the part that I don't mention is that my third goal is to convince them that *I* belong here as their professor: to demonstrate that I know the content and I know how to teach it so they can learn and succeed in our class. In this chapter, I will outline the activities I use during the first day and explain how to implement them. Additionally, I describe both my face-to-face class as well as my Zoom-based class, showing how these teaching methods may be used in both formats for the all-important first class meeting.[1]

I begin class by sharing some things I have in common with my students. Similar to about 54 percent of the students at my university, I am a first-generation college student, meaning neither of my parents went to college. I also happen to be dyslexic, and therefore very much understand the purpose and importance of academic accommodations, and I build some directly into my course. About 10 percent of the class usually works with our Student Support Services office because of a learning difference or disability, and several students also have English as their second language. As part of this discussion, I inform them that I record my lectures and post them on Moodle in addition to sharing the slides. Previously, I would carry around a digital recorder and post the audio file, but when my class went on Zoom due to COVID-19, I was able to easily record a video lecture on that platform.

Often, some student will ask to have the slides posted ahead of class, and I explain that I don't do that because we use several active elements and critical thinking questions during the lecture, explained more in this chapter, and having the slides would negate the good effects of these practices. I also use fonts and colors that are dyslexia friendly; otherwise, I couldn't read them well either! In addition, I explain that my dyslexia is why I use slides instead of writing all the notes out on the board. It's difficult for me to write quickly and accurately on my own, much more so with an audience, and in the past, I've found it stressful for myself and confusing for students when I made lots of mistakes using this teaching method. I do frequently write student responses on the board, as it can improve student confidence to see something they said up on the board,[2] or I will draw quick diagrams as needed, and this works well in combination with the slides.

To show them another commonality, I ask how many of them have been told that they are not good at STEM or that they didn't belong in STEM for whatever reason. I don't usually see a lot of hands. I expect many don't want to disclose this information, but the point of asking is that I can tell them how often this happened to me. So many times over my career! Teachers told me that I "wasn't good at computers" because I couldn't type accurately in high school, before I knew I was dyslexic. Today, I'm a computational biochemist who works with Linux and several programming languages. By the time I was in graduate school, I was used to hearing comments such as "You shouldn't be a scientist," and "You don't belong in this class." Although the majority of my professors were supportive, when I asked for assistance, some instructors questioned my choice to pursue a graduate degree.[3]

Often, discussing growth mindset with students leads to a better understanding of how to overcome others' fixed opinions of you and focus on what you're capable of learning (i.e., anything you want!). This also helps remove some possible student biases against me as a cisgendered woman with blond hair who is younger than some other STEM faculty they've had. (It should be noted that any bias due to having a youthful appearance can't and shouldn't be equated with systemic racism and other types of embodied discrimination.) By showing them how biases against them are wrong, it also opens their eyes—at least somewhat—to their own possible biases about what faculty "should" be and look like.

One new commonality we all shared in fall 2020 was

anxiety about how the semester would go in the midst of the pandemic and other major world and national events. This is why I introduced a new first-day activity called "First-Day Fears." In the Zoom breakout rooms, students worked with their groups to add anything they were anxious about to a collaborative shared Google Doc. This accomplished several things. First, they could see that they were not alone in being anxious. Lots of groups had similar concerns about online learning, time management, and online labs. Second, they were able to share those concerns with me and know that I actually cared about addressing them. I read through some of them immediately after the activity and explained how I had or would take them into account in planning the course. And finally, I told them what *I* was anxious about as well, that teaching online was new for me, and that I worried I wouldn't know when someone was confused on Zoom if everyone's cameras were off. Many faculty will avoid admitting, at all costs, that something is new to them in the classroom; they believe they'll look foolish if they mess something up in front of the class. Keeping in mind the ways that my White privilege is a factor, I've found that sharing when something is new invites students to work *with* me to help the class go well, and it helps them adjust their expectations of the course and of me. I believe it can help instructors demonstrate a personal pedagogical growth mindset, which helps students develop their own.[4]

We next talk about what a growth mindset is, including the evidence-based research about the ways it can help people effectively navigate new and challenging situations.[5] In the fall of 2020, I went a step further and explained how to reframe academic anxieties with a growth mindset, starting with mine specifically: I described how I spent the summer learning about teaching online, informed them that I would need their feedback on how the course was going, and explained how they could help me during Zoom lectures by telling me when they were confused and by asking questions. When technical problems caused the breakout rooms to fail during the first two class sessions (in two different ways no less), I modeled growth mindset for them by not getting angry or giving up on them but just moving on to Plan E or F until I found a method that worked (shout out to my awesome teaching assistant who ended up assigning them manually every class while I was talking). I assigned students a "Growth Mindset Group" to work with during our Zoom sessions to provide some additional support. I also did periodic check-ins on growth mindset, including a question worth a few points on the first exam and a learning reflection afterward.

Having a growth mindset helps students persist and succeed in challenging classes. This is what I want for all of my students, and I repeatedly remind my students that with effort, practice, and by learning from their mistakes and improving, they can succeed in biochemistry and, really, any subject. So far, this has been borne out by the results because not one student failed my class from the beginning of my tenure-track career in fall 2018 through spring 2020. Can you tell I'm pretty proud of this? Because I am. A few students started off failing after the first exam, but with the grading system I use that weights in-class work and homework equal to the exams, and with the exam retakes offered when I was doing face-to-face exams, they've all turned it around and passed. No easy task for a 300-level STEM course. Unfortunately, this streak did not continue through the 2020 pandemic because of the pressure of forces outside our control (and outside our students' control), a result of multiple global and national health, social, and political crises.

In the fall of 2020, I also tied growth mindset into a discussion of academic dishonesty and told them that if they felt they would fail an exam or the class unless they resorted to cheating that they should tell me so that I could help them. Basically, I work to counteract academic dishonesty by making every assignment and assessment transparent and "do-able" for students so that they don't feel the *need* to cheat. Which is not much different than previous semesters, except that I wouldn't be watching them take the exam this time. My new exam format—a take-home exam— in addition to some basic exercises, requires them to apply their class knowledge to explain a big course concept by creating an original representation of it that covers the key ideas. Three students wrote protein folding poems for the first exam, and they were an amazing, creative demonstration of authentic learning!

The exams also have the students read a peer-reviewed research paper and summarize the experiment and results as they relate to the course content. In the lead-up to the exam, the students need to find an appropriate research paper and have it approved. This approval allows me to make sure the paper has the information they need to complete the exam questions. They also gain practice in searching for relevant research papers with specific information. For one exam, I ask students to find an enzyme kinetics paper with the same type of data we've looked at in class. Most students submit papers that simply have the word "kinetics" in them for the first round, without checking that the paper is about an enzyme or that the type of data is correct. This shows that they are not used to doing this type of literature searching, so the approval process provides necessary practice. As an added bonus, this process allows me to ensure that each student has a unique research paper, so they effectively can't cheat on this portion of the exam.

Another change in 2020 was how I explained my teaching methods to students during our first class meeting. Previously, this happened organically as part of the "Classroom Graffiti" activity in which I asked the students to respond to several questions posted around the room, including "I learn best in classes where the instructor . . . " and "I am most likely to participate in class when . . . " This gives me the chance to talk about how I'm always okay with them asking questions during the lectures, how I present information in multiple ways—lecture, using active elements, and posting videos online—and with the textbook as an optional resource as well. Because they see me three times a week (two times for lecture plus one lab), we get to know each other relatively quickly. Without the weekly in-person lab times during the fall of 2020 and with lectures on Zoom, I knew this wouldn't happen nearly as quickly. So I decided to share a slide on the first day, titled "How I Teach." The slide says, "I will try to tell you how doing something will help your learning, but you can also ask if I forget (I'm a huge nerd; I love talking about the science of teaching and learning!)." As well as being transparent about my teaching, this approach reinforces my own individual expertise as a scholar and a teacher, demonstrating that I use teaching methods backed by research.

Part of the same slide was the phrase "I show I care about my students by . . ." I wanted to be as transparent as possible, in the hope that it would reassure them and help them manage their expectations for me and the class. I'm not a very touchy-feely person, as is often expected of women, and as an introvert, I can sometimes come off as reserved or "too private." So I explained that I show I care about them by using evidence-based teaching practices, setting clear expectations with learning objectives, asking for their feedback, and implementing it when possible; by responding to emails and questions quickly; and by posting grades on our learning management system as I finish them so they always know where they stand in the course. Showing students that you care, in your own way, is key; in my experience, students will forgive pretty readily if they truly believe that you care about them and their learning.[6]

As illustrated in the earlier discussion, active learning is another method I use to ensure that the first day of class and all subsequent classes are accommodating and inclusive. Each "lecture" is actually two or three shorter lectures where I ask the students questions frequently, and they are broken up with active elements.[7] We start this on day one, with a "Critical Thinking in the News" activity or with the "First-Day Fears" activity. The students, therefore, get used to the idea of working and participating in class from day one. There is not much resistance later, in part because this is how the class "always goes." I explain the research behind active learning and its benefits, and that it might not "feel" better while they're doing it compared to passively listening to a lecture, but it *is* helping them learn better. I even say things like "This technique is called desirable difficulty, so you're trying the problem before I explain it on purpose so that you'll remember it better when I do explain it. So don't Google the answer!" Based on the number of well-thought-out but incorrect answers, they followed my directions, even on a Zoom lecture with the internet freely available to them.

Using a growth mindset and active learning, as evidenced by high rates of student success, I believe my class begins on day one helping students succeed. As someone who struggled in college because of sexism and undiagnosed dyslexia, inclusion and success for everyone are vitally important to me. There is some evidence that I'm off to a good start here as well. Several students who required accommodations have told me that the active learning helped them to keep up with the class and that they felt "it was the first class that was set up so that I could succeed." Best. Course. Feedback. Ever!

Teaching Takeaways

- Set the tone for your class and the rhythm for how things will go on the first day. Students will get into the "groove" of your class faster if the format (lecture, active element, followed by more lecture, for example) is consistent from day one.

- In ways that are authentic and comfortable for you, share something about yourself that you have in common with your students; it will help your students see your success as their possible success with the material.

- Discuss growth mindset with your students and how research shows it can help them persist with difficult

> subject matter and in challenging courses/majors.
> Remind them that they are in charge of their learning.
> • Don't be afraid to tell students exactly what teaching
>   methods you use and the evidence available for how/
>   why they work. They will appreciate this transparency
>   because it shows you care about their learning.

....

KELLY E. THEISEN earned her doctorate in chemistry at the University of Cincinnati and is an assistant professor of biochemistry at SUNY Plattsburgh. She teaches general biochemistry, physical biochemistry, and computational biochemistry. Her research areas include using computer simulations to study bacterial cytoskeletal proteins, and the development and use of hands-on models to teach biochemistry concepts. When not working, she enjoys reading and spending time with her husband and their pet rabbit Bigwig.

Notes

1. Pre-COVID-19, my in-person first day of class activities included an introduction (About Me); discussion of growth mindset; review of syllabus, office hours, and other course information; "Classroom Graffiti" activity; "Critical Thinking in the News" activity; some review content, and "Cellular Components Classification" activity. During COVID, my first-day class activities via Zoom included an introduction (About Me); overview of how I teach and demonstrate care for students; a "First-Day Fears" activity; discussion about

reframing anxiety with growth mindset; information about syllabus, work sessions, and other course information; "Course Netiquette and Group Dynamics" activity; and discussion about academic honesty and scientific ethics.

2. Thanks to Becky Kasper for this insight.

3. These types of sentiments are an example of (conscious or unconscious) bias and gatekeeping. See Bayer Corporation, "Bayer Facts of Science Education XIV: Female and Minority Chemists and Chemical Engineers Speak about Diversity and Underrepresentation in STEM," March 2010, https://www .bayer.com/sites/default/files/2010_fose_xiv_0.pdf.

4. Katherine Muenks, Elizabeth A. Canning, Jennifer LaCosse, Dorianne J. Green, Sabrina Zirkel, Julie A. Garcia, and Mary C. Murphy, "Does My professor Think My Ability Can Change? Students' Perceptions of Their STEM Professors' Mindset Beliefs Predict Their Psychological Vulnerability, Engagement, and Performance in Class," *Journal of Experimental Psychology: General* 149, no. 11 (2020): 2119–44; Elizabeth A. Canning, Katherine Muenks, Dorainne J. Green, Mary C. Murphy, "STEM Faculty Who Believe Ability Is Fixed Have Larger Racial Achievement Gaps and Inspire Less Student Motivation in Their Classes," *Science Advances* 5, no. 2 (2019): 1–7.

5. Carol Dweck, *Mindset: The New Psychology of Success* (New York: Ballantine Books, 2008), is the foundational text on this topic. For additional research on growth mindset and college student achievement generally, see, for example, Anindito Aditomo, "Students' Response to Academic Setback: 'Growth Mindset' as a Buffer against Demotivation," *International Journal of Educational Psychology* 4, no. 2 (June 2015): 198–222; Nicholas Bowman and Anat Levtov, "Understanding and Using Growth Mindset to Foster College Student Learning and Achievement," *New Directions for Teaching and Learning* 164 (2020): 75–83;

Aaron Hochanadel and Dora Finamore, "Fixed and Growth
Mindset in Education and How Grit Helps Students Persist
in the Face of Adversity," *Journal of International Education
Research* 11, no. 1 (2015): 47–50; Jennifer McCabe, Sam Kane-
Gerard, and Dara G. Friedman-Wheeler, "Examining the Utility
of Growth-Mindset Interventions in Undergraduates:
A Longitudinal Study of Retention and Academic Success
in a First-Year Cohort," *Translational Issues in Psychological
Science* 6, no. 2 (June 2020): 132–46; Janice Wiersema et.
al., "Mindset about Intelligence and Meaningful and Mindful
Effort: It's Not My Hardest Class Any More!" *Learning
Communities: Research and Practice* 3, no. 2 (2015): Article 3,
http://washingtoncenter.evergreen.edu/lcrpjournal/vol3
/iss2/3; David S. Yeager et al., "A National Experiment Reveals
Where a Growth Mindset Improves Achievement," *Nature* 573,
no. 7774 (September 2019): 364–69; Hui Zhao et al., "Growth
Mindset and College Students' Learning Engagement during
the COVID-19 Pandemic: A Serial Mediation Model," *Frontiers
in Psychology* (February 2021), http://dx.doi.org/10.3389
/fpsyg.2021.621094. On STEM education specifically,
see, for example, Gokhan Hacisalihoglu et al., "Enhancing
Undergraduate Student Success in STEM Fields through
Growth Mindset and Grit," *Education Sciences* 10, no. 1 (October
2020), https://doi.org/10.3390/educsci10100279; Lisa Limeri
et al., "Growing a Growth Mindset: Characterizing How and
Why Undergraduate Students' Mindsets Change," *International
Journal of STEM Education* 7, no. 1 (July 2020): 1–19; Jennifer
LaCoose et al., "The Role of STEM Professors' Mindset Beliefs
on Students' Anticipated Psychological Experiences and Course
Interest," *Journal of Educational Psychology* (September 2020),
https://doi.apa.org/doi/10.1037/edu0000620.

6. Jessamyn Neuhaus, *Geeky Pedagogy: A Guide for Intellectuals,*

Introverts, and Nerds Who Want to Be Effective Teachers
(Morgantown: West Virginia University Press, 2019), 53–54.

7.   Gail Taylor Rice, *Hitting Pause: 65 Lecture Breaks to Refresh and
Reinforce Learning* (Sterling, VA: Stylus Publishing, 2018). On
effective lecturing in general, see Christine Harrington and
Todd Zakrajsek, *Dynamic Lecturing: Research-Based Strategies
to Enhance Lecture Effectiveness* (Sterling, VA: Stylus Publishing
2017). With the increase of recorded lectures during the
COVID-19 pandemic, online teaching and learning scholars
recommended "chunking" video lectures as well. See, for
example, Kelly Lovell and Gracia Ostendorf, "Record Lectures
That Make an Impact with Chunking," March 27, 2020, Miami
University E-Campus Faculty and Staff, https://miamioh.edu
/regionals/eccoe/news/2020/03/chunking-video-lectures.html.

. . . .

CHAPTER 4

WHERE'S THE PROFESSOR?

First-Day Active Learning for Navigating Students' Perceptions of Young Professors

. . . .

Reba Wissner

Without fail, every semester since I taught my first college class in fall 2006, when I have students who don't know me, those students ask other students in front of me, "Where's the professor?" The looks on their faces when I say, "Hi, I'm Dr. Wissner!" are priceless. I've taught college classes for over a decade, but I look younger than I am, and I have an inner ankle tattoo of a treble clef, which makes me simultaneously the cool music history professor and the one who students assume may not know what she's doing—enthusiasm about the course material, while important, can only go so far in building credibility with the students.[1] This is equally true for the traditionally college-aged students as for my older, nontraditionally aged students, both undergraduate and graduate, who are skeptical about the ability of someone who looks like they could be their daughter to teach and fairly evaluate them.

As a woman, the issue of looking too young (or otherwise) to be a professor is compounded since women are often treated suspiciously regarding their expertise in the classroom.[2] It is important to consider that ageism is real, and appearing young all too often contributes to student bias, but it is also important to note that this should not be equated with systemic racism and other types of discrimination, such as gender discrimination. Young-looking, female-identifying professors of color often have an even more challenging time in getting their students to consider them competent, skillful, and credible, frequently facing microaggressions throughout their careers.[3] One study using computer-animated lecturers demonstrated that students who listened to the same lecture delivered by a White male professor versus an African American professor or a male professor versus a female professor scored higher on a postlecture quiz on the material. It is the same lecture, but students simply paid more attention to the White male professor as a more credible, more normative, source of knowledge.[4] Black, Indigenous, and People of Color (BIPOC) professors who teach at predominantly White institutions have all of these issues amplified, even if those students are also the same race as the professor.[5] But it's not only young women—young men also face skepticism, as Kevin Gannon (a heavily tattooed White male who does not immediately appear to fit the professor stereotype) has recounted of his early teaching career, "To compensate for what I imagined were dubious stares and doubts about how well I, a young white dude, could teach them, a racially diverse class of older students, I resolved to be prepared for any eventuality and to dazzle them with my command of the material."[6] So, how can we simultaneously dispel doubts and dazzle students with our knowledge?

Not surprisingly, students' first impressions of a professor can bring forth preconceptions about them simply because of their gender, age, or how they look, all of which can affect how the class runs for the rest of the semester and students' perceptions of their professor's ability as a teacher.[7] One study demonstrated that in comparing White and Hispanic instructors, students ranked the White professors as having a greater sense of immediacy, caring, and competence than the Hispanic instructors.[8] Immediacy and caring, as we know, are crucial for creating trust and rapport in the classroom. So we must address these preconceptions on the first day to avoid them clouding the course and the students' ability to take you seriously. While some of these preconceptions can be eliminated through one's dress (which is problematic), organized and clear syllabi, and demeanor, the more effective solution is to do so through the classroom activities on the first day.[9] One instructional strategy we can use on the first day to help dispel students' skepticism is active learning activities. Using active learning activities in the first class helps the professor to demonstrate their expertise by getting students right into "doing" the discipline and the course. This approach allows faculty to confidently create an energizing learner-centered classroom from day one.

Active Learning on the First Day to Build Instructor Credibility

Active learning means having students perform activities that help them to learn without passively listening to a lecture. This might mean group work, or work with tangible objects, or both. Active learning is an effective pedagogical technique, proven to aid students' development of critical thinking skills.[10] It also empowers students, is learner-centered, and stimulates engagement.[11] The more students are actively learning, the more information they will be able to retain and transfer to other contexts.[12] If one's discipline facilitates it, active learning with physical or material objects aids students in critical analysis and evaluation skills.[13] It also helps students to make the course topic seem relevant and interesting rather than a nebulous or irrelevant thing they're required to take a course on to graduate.

The first day of class occurs in a preconstructed learning space, but "how it invites students in or discourages them from entering, can decisively shape our everyday pedagogical practices."[14] This invitation to learning includes how students perceive us and our courses. It is crucial that the first day of class cover some aspects of the course content; this can help faculty gain credibility.[15] James M. Lang identifies four basic principles that help faculty construct a good first day of class: curiosity, community, learning, and expectations. These four principles can also be used to dispel students' preconceived notions about their new professor. Essentially, you want to create a spark of interest in the course material, create a sense of community and humanize yourself, encouraging students to engage with the course material and shaping the future of the course for students.[16] This can help set expectations for students about what they should take away from the course. Marguerite Mayhall suggests that these first-day activities must connect to the course material and allow the students to discuss and consider these topics and their interconnected issues.[17]

Maryellen Weimer notes the importance of faculty

sharing their commitment to student learning and success on the first day as a way to build classroom community.[18] We often underestimate the power of faculty enthusiasm when teaching, but doing so, and demonstrating one's commitment to student learning, has powerful implications for whether or not the students perceive the professor as credible as early as the first class meeting.[19] The instructor's enthusiasm can be contagious and help students gain more interest in the course, but enthusiasm cannot replace students' confidence in their professor's knowledge and ability to teach the content.[20]

Setting course expectations doesn't end on the first day. This also extends to the first week of classes, when students (hopefully) continue to be enticed by the course.[21] The very beginning of the semester is when we leave a lasting impression on our students, for better or worse.[22] These first impressions are not easily dispelled after the first day—or even the first moments—especially if we do things that reinforce them. We must, therefore, give the students confidence in us and our skills if we want to eliminate any questions about our right to be in the front of the classroom.[23] But there is a more practical reason to be sure students are confident in our ability to teach: student perceptions about instructors' credibility are shown to correlate with learning gains over the course of a single semester.[24] After all, as Jessamyn Neuhaus writes, "Student perception often becomes teaching reality."[25] We don't want to jinx ourselves, do we?

Ultimately, we must consider that students scrutinize everything we say and do from the moment we walk into the classroom. This includes not only being our true selves but also personable and—dare I say it—human.[26] By the end of the first class, successful teachers introduce themselves, demonstrate accessibility and immediacy toward students, and model their instructional methods, all of which create perceptions of us and our courses.[27] Regardless of whether we fit into the traditional professor mold, if students believe we are competent, then they are more likely to view us as competent.[28] The idea that what a professor looks like and what to expect from her is called implicit professor theory (IPT), and these IPTs shape what our students think of us as early as the first time they meet us.[29] The experiences that we provide for our students and what they think about us on the first day correlate with higher motivation throughout the course—and even higher grades.[30] As faculty, we need to not only entice and engage our students but also consider our expectations of our students and our students' expectations of us.

While we want to entice our students (with good reason), we also want to set expectations for how the course will be run and the material that it will cover—what Gannon calls "peeking under the hood."[31] We can do this by presenting some of the most unusual or intriguing aspects of the course to keep students wanting more. We do not have an opportunity for a second first impression, neither for us nor our course, so we must be very careful how we present both.[32] Even if you are someone who lectures regularly, active learning can be a way for students to become more involved in the course from the beginning. First-day active learning activities can include bringing in material objects relevant to the course that the students likely have never seen, allowing them to encounter firsthand what the course is about and experience the course material.

But, despite its increased use and proven success in college classrooms, some faculty remain hesitant to incorporate active learning into their courses. One common fear among faculty considering using active learning in their courses is that students may feel that the professor is incompetent or doesn't know the material; the perception is that these activities will force the students to teach themselves rather than be taught. Students must not only be taught to trust their professors, but they also must understand that they are not doing more work than their professors.[33] Because of appearance and identity, women-identifying and BIPOC instructors will face additional obstacles in terms of student preconceptions and stereotypes and therefore experience more resistance to nontraditional learning formats than their White male counterparts. We must acknowledge the roles that the professor's identity and appearance play in student perceptions of them and therefore how they play into the way active learning activities are received.

As if these fears were not enough, faculty also fear that as a result of this perception, the use of active learning in classes will negatively impact their student evaluations of teaching (SET). One recent study showed that this fear is unwarranted: 48 percent of physics faculty members at one university who incorporated active learning in their introductory courses believed that using this technique increased their SET rankings, and 32 percent felt that it had no effect on their SETs.[34] Therefore, there is good reason to try active learning, especially on the first day of class when the students are building their impressions of your competence as a teacher and your knowledge of the course material.

My First-Day Activity: The Object Petting Zoo

In facilitating active learning activities on the first day, you are cultivating trust among your students and creating rapport, making for a learning environment conducive to learning.[35] Part of creating expectations is to run the class on the first day how you plan to all semester. For classes like mine that are heavily interactive, I don't want the students to think for a moment that I'm not lecturing because I don't know the content; after all, students consider a professor credible if they can show they know more than the text-book and provide real-world examples of course material.[36] So, having students participate in an interactive activity with objects related to the course not only sets the stage for how I will run the class all semester, showing them around "under the hood," but also grounds the course in a real-world context with the unusual and interesting things we'll cover. I love to have students interact with material objects, es-pecially since so many of the things that students will en-counter in my course are those they may never have heard of or seen in real life (or even virtually). While this use of material objects may not be possible in every discipline, it is beneficial for orienting students to the course, building positive views of the professor and her qualifications, and cultivating student interest from day one.

On the first day of my music history classes, I hold a "material objects petting zoo," depending on the course topic. I place students in teams—students tend to be less resistant to group work when you don't actually call them groups—to circulate and examine objects. When I teach early music, for example, I bring in various music books, vellum chant manuscript fragments, and other relevant objects and have the teams tell me what they think the object is, what year they think it's from, and what it can tell us about music history. They use worksheets from the National Archives to guide their answers, using the written document analysis sheets for everything but those related to instruments (instruments or gut strings) or the vellum chant fragments; for those, students use the artifact or object analysis sheets.[37]

During each activity, I circulate, and the students always ask me, "Is all of this yours?" or "Did you buy these with your own money? The university didn't pay for any of this?" (For the record, the answer is yes, these are mine and no, the university did not pay for any of this). My answers help to dispel the notion that I'm a novice. After the activity, we reconvene and discuss their findings. That's when I reveal a lot of information about the objects, often not covered in the textbook (as they soon find out when they start their reading) and that helps them to continue to alter their perceptions about my content knowledge. These objects, often unfamiliar, allow us to spend some time on intercultural competency and lead to a discussion on assumptions and stereotypes. Inadvertently, we're drawing attention to exactly what the students may be doing with us!

I refer to the items used in these activities throughout the semester, so this sets the stage on the first day for the semester's material. For example, when talking about music printing, I can say, "Remember the partbooks you looked at the first day?" I've had students who take subsequent courses with me—sometimes a year or so later—refer to those objects in the context of that class. If planned correctly, these kinds of activities can also serve as icebreakers (though students don't know that—this is good since many students hate typical "icebreakers") that can create a sense of community not only between the students but also with you.

These material object activities achieve all four of Lang's criteria for teaching a good first day of class, as well as Gannon's and Mayhall's suggestions. By putting the students in teams, they are building a sense of community through learning. They are learning about the course material by handling the objects that they will be discussing throughout the semester. This kind of active learning is like hiding the broccoli in a kid's dinner so that they eat their vegetables; students are learning to analyze materials and objects, teaching them to become visually and culturally literate, but they just don't know it! In both cases—the broccoli and the learning—it's good for them!

In the first day of class context, hiding the broccoli is especially crucial since one recent study showed that students disliked delving into course material during the first class session, but if they have to, they feel it should be accessibly presented.[38] In doing this kind of activity, I accessibly set expectations for active learning and the use of material objects in the course. Regardless of the objects chosen, these activities can allow students to directly engage with historical and cultural objects that promote the synthesis of knowledge through analysis.[39] Therefore, they don't notice (or don't notice right away) that they're learning about the course and its material. This conveys to students that you care about them, their preferences, and the course material and helps to dispel any skepticism about your qualifications while you demonstrate the course format.

With a little planning, these activities can be incorporated into online and remote classrooms. Using photos, videos, and audio files from existing sources like YouTube helps provide a similar experience and demonstrate how the items work. You can make a video demonstrating these objects yourself. Having digital analogues for these items helps you be more inclusive, even if it is in the face-to-face environment. For example, having a digital version of a handwritten letter posted on the learning management system allows a student who may have a vision impairment to enlarge the text or adjust the playback speed of video or audio.

Even if you teach in a discipline where using material objects is not an option, active learning activities are useful for providing the students with course context and making them confident in you. So how, if you are in this kind of a discipline, can you use active learning to increase students' confidence in you and decrease the chance that their preconceptions of your ability become reinforced? Find something that is part of the course topic that might seem interesting or unusual to students. This should be something that may seem esoteric (what I think of as knowledge that seems useless to the ordinary person but still cool) that will pull students in and that is not part of any of the course readings or materials. By showing students how much you know while giving them little-known material to grapple with, you are telling them that you know your stuff, despite looking young (or otherwise not like the "typical" professor).

Conclusion

Despite what people may assume, we *can* influence what our students think of us. One study showed that race and gender combined with teaching style influenced the way students perceived certain professors.[40] How we teach from the beginning of the course can also help with student perceptions. With careful planning, we can dispel any skepticism about our abilities as teachers from the very first class meeting that will last far beyond the end of the semester. This will likely increase the number of students who will return for more of your courses and giggle when new students ask, "Where's the professor?"

Teaching Takeaways

- Students are more likely to be engaged from the first day of class when active learning activities are employed immediately in the course.
- These active learning activities help the professor build rapport and trust with the students, who will soon realize that any preconceived notions about their professor that surfaced from their appearance or identity are unwarranted.
- Using primary sources and material objects as part of a hands-on active learning activity helps to foster inclusive and diverse teaching practices.

REBA WISSNER is assistant professor of musicology at Columbus State University. She is the author of *A Dimension of Sound: Music in The Twilight Zone* (Pendragon Press, 2013), *We Will Control All That You Hear: The Outer Limits and the Aural Imagination* (Pendragon Press, 2016), and *Music and the Atomic Bomb on American Television, 1950–1969* (Peter Lang, 2020). As a faculty developer, her interests are in universal design for learning, adjunct support, and active learning.

Notes

1. On instructor enthusiasm, see Sarah Rose Cavanagh, *The Spark of Learning: Energizing the College Classroom with the Science of Emotion* (Morgantown: West Virginia University Press, 2016) and Joshua R. Eyler, *How Humans Learn: The Science and Stories behind Effective College Teaching* (Morgantown: West Virginia University Press, 2018).

2. Judith K. Lang Hilgartner, "My Response to 'You Look Too Young to Be A Professor,'" *Medium*, November 23, 2018, https:// medium.com/the-ascent/my-response-to-you-look-too-young -to-be-a-professor-9a5fadd8e0fc/.

3. See Tammy Boyd, Rosa Cintrón, and Mia Alexander-Snow, "The Experience of Being A Junior Minority Female Faculty Member," *Forum of Public Policy Online*, 2010, no. 2 (2010): 1–23, and Tracey Owens Patton, "Ethnicity and Gender: An Examination of Its Impact on Instructor Credibility in the University Classroom," *Howard Journal of Communications* 10, no. 2 (1999): 123–44.

4. Susan A. Basow, Stephanie Codos, and Julie L. Martin, "The Effects of Professors' Race and Gender on Student Evaluations and Performance," *College Student Journal* 47, no. 2 (2013): 361.

5. See Frank Tuitt, "Black Like Me: Graduate Students' Perceptions of Their Pedagogical Experiences in Classes Taught by Black Faculty in a Predominantly White Institution," *Journal of Black Studies* 43, no. 2 (2012): 186–206.

6. Kevin Gannon, *Radical Hope: A Teaching Manifesto* (Morgantown: West Virginia University Press, 2020), 134.

7. Cavanagh, *The Spark of Learning*, 79.

8. Jack Glascock and Thomas E. Ruggiero, "The Relationship of Ethnicity and Sex to Professor Credibility at a Culturally Diverse University," *Communication Education* 55, no. 2 (2006): 203–4.

9.   Mara S. Aruguete, Joshua Slater, and Sekela R. Mwaikinda,
     "The Effects of Professors' Race and Clothing Style on Student
     Evaluations," *Journal of Negro Education* 86, no. 4 (2017):
     494–502; Paige Reynolds, "Confessions of A 'Formerly Young'
     Professor," *Chronicle of Higher Education,* September 18, 2016,
     https://www.chronicle.com/article/Confessions-of-a-Formerly
     /237810.

10. Larry P. Nelson and Mary L. Crow, "Do Active-Learning
     Strategies Improve Students' Critical Thinking?" *Higher
     Education Studies* 4, no. 2 (2014): 77–90. However, the type
     of classroom environment, including size and layout of your
     classroom, will dictate whether an active learning activity is
     appropriate.

11. Anastasia Misseyanni et al., "Introduction," in *Active Learning
     Strategies in Higher Education: Teaching for Leadership,
     Innovation, and Creativity*, eds. Anastasia Misseyanni et al.
     (Bingley, UK: Emerald Publishing, 2018), 161.

12. John Biggs and Catherine Tang, *Teaching for Quality Learning
     at University*, 4th ed. (Berkshire, England: Society for Research
     Into Higher Education/Open University Press/McGraw Hill,
     2011), 125.

13. Marcus C. Robyns, "The Archivist as Educator: Integrating
     Critical Thinking Skills into Historical Research Methods
     Instruction," *American Archivist* 64 (2001): 372.

14. Gannon, *Radical Hope*, 32.

15. Marguerite Mayhall, "The Vital Importance of First-Day
     Activities," *Inside Higher Ed,* August 14, 2018, https://www
     .insidehighered.com/advice/2018/08/14/guidance-how-teach
     -first-day-class-opinion/.

16. James M. Lang, "How to Teach A Good First Day of Class,"
     Chronicle of Higher Education, August 21, 2018, https://www
     .chronicle.com/interactives/advice-firstday.

17. Mayhall, "The Vital Importance."

18. Maryellen Weimer, "The First Day of Class: A Once-a-Semester Opportunity," *The Teaching Professor,* August 19, 2015, https://www.teachingprofessor.com/for-those-who-teach/the-first-day-of-class-a-once-a-semester-opportunity/.

19. Linda B. Nilson, *Teaching at Its Best: A Research-Based Resource for College Instructors Third Edition* (San Francisco: Jossey-Bass, 2010), 79.

20. Cavanagh, *The Spark of Learning,* 50.

21. David Gooblar, "Reeling Them in Early," *Chronicle Vitae,* August 23, 2017, https://chroniclevitae.com/news/1886-reeling-them-in-early/.

22. Gooblar, "Reeling Them In Early."

23. Jennifer Garrett and Mary Clement, "Advice for the First Day of Class: Today We Will," *Faculty Focus,* August 23, 2018, https://www.facultyfocus.com/articles/effective-classroom-management/advice-for-the-first-day-of-class-today-we-will/.

24. Patton, "Ethnicity and Gender," 123.

25. Jessamyn Neuhaus, *Geeky Pedagogy: A Guide for Intellectuals, Introverts, and Nerds Who Want to Be Effective Teachers* (Morgantown: West Virginia University Press, 2019), 8.

26. Maryellen Weimer, "Five Things to Do on the First Day of Class," *The Teaching Professor,* August 21, 2013, https://www.teachingprofessor.com/for-those-who-teach/five-things-to-do-on-the-first-day-of-class/.

27. Barbara A. Iannarelli, Mary Ellen Bardsley, and Chandra J. Foote, "Here's Your Syllabus, See You Next Week: A Review of the First Day Practices of Outstanding Professors," *Journal of Effective Teaching* 10, no. 2 (2010): 35.

28. David J. Schneider, *The Psychology of Stereotyping* (New York: Guilford Press, 2005), 56.

29. See Julie Yermack and Donelson R. Forsyth, "Students' Implicit

Theories of University Professors," *Scholarship of Teaching and Learning in Psychology* 2, no. 3 (2016): 169–78.

30. Janie H. Wilson and Shauna B. Wilson, "The First Day of Class Affects Student Motivation: an Experimental Study," *Teaching of Psychology* 34, no. 4 (2007): 226.

31. Kevin Gannon, "The Absolute Worst Way to Start the Semester," *Chronicle Vitae*, August 3, 2016, https://chroniclevitae.com /news/1498-the-absolute-worst-way-to-start-the-semester/.

32. Gannon, "The Absolute Worst Way."

33. Richard Bale, *Teaching with Confidence in Higher Education: Applying Strategies from the Performing Arts* (London and New York: Routledge, 2020), 127–28.

34. Charles Henderson, Raquib Khan, and Melissa Dancy, "Will My Student Evaluations Decrease If I Adopt an Active Learning Strategy?" *American Journal of Physics* 86, no. 12 (2018): 934–42.

35. Zaretta Hammond, *Culturally Responsive Teaching and the Brain: Promoting Authentic Engagement and Rigor Among Culturally and Linguistically Diverse Students* (Thousand Oaks, CA: Corwin, 2015), 75–76.

36. Scott A. Myers and Leah E. Bryant, "College Students' Perceptions of How Instructors Convey Credibility," *Qualitative Research Reports in Communication* 5 (2004): 22.

37. The National Archives, Educator Resources, Teaching with Documents, Document Analysis Worksheets, last reviewed August 2, 2021, https://www.archives.gov/education/lessons /worksheets/.

38. Katherine E. Eskine and Elizabeth Yost Hammer, "Students' Perspectives on the First Day of Class: A Replication," *International Journal for the Scholarship of Teaching and Learning* 11, no. 1 (2017): 1–4; Baron Perlman and Lee I. McCann, "Student Perspectives on the First Day of Class," *Teaching of Psychology* 26 (1999): 277–9.

39. Ellen E. Jarosz and Stephen Kutay, "Guided Resource Inquiries: Integrating Archives into Course Learning and Information Literacy Objectives," *Communications in Information Literacy* 11, no. 1 (2017): 204–20.

40. Kristin J. Anderson and Gabriel Smith, "Students' Preconceptions of Professors: Benefits and Barriers According to Ethnicity and Gender," *Hispanic Journal of Behavioral Sciences* 27, no. 2 (2005): 184.

139. Ebert, Dieter, and Stephan Kaiser. "Muscle Relaxation..."
...

63. ...

....

PART TWO

MAKING CONNECTIONS

Strategies for Building Trust and Rapport with Students

....

....

USING EXPERIENTIAL LEARNING TO HUMANIZE COURSE CONTENT AND CONNECT WITH STUDENTS

....

Breanna Boppre

"Wow, you don't look like a professor!" remarked the stylist at a local makeup store who helped me pick out new red lipstick. Most people are surprised when I tell them I am a professor. I'm in my early thirties. Sometimes my hair is blonde, or more recently purple, and I have a full-color tattooed sleeve and half sleeve. I also wear vintage-style dresses and wing-tipped liner with bright lipstick and big funky glasses. According to students, my style has been equated to a mix of Ms. Frizzle from *The Magic School Bus* and Jessica Day from *New Girl*.

I have always felt something of an outsider in academia as a former first-generation college student and because of my age, gender, and style. Criminal justice, in particular, is a male-dominated field, particularly in positions of prestige and power.[1] As I prepared to teach my first classes as a doctoral student, tenured faculty advised me to act more masculine (e.g., lower my voice, wear full pantsuits) to "gain the respect and perceived legitimacy" among students. It is no secret that women faculty face gender bias in course evaluations, which impact tenure and promotion decisions, and the implications of this are multiplicative for faculty of color and other marginalized groups.[2]

Through this chapter, I outline pedagogical strategies that have been fundamental and transformative in my own teaching, specifically how experiential learning allows me to form deep and authentic connections with students. Such techniques can be used by any instructor to connect students with real-world experiences and those with lived experience.

Experiential Learning Approaches

Experiential learning helps students bridge their understanding of course material through real-world experience or exposure. Students learn by doing, through hands-on immersive activities focused on applied contexts. The experiential learning theory model is composed of four stages: (1) the experience itself, (2) observation and reflection, (3) assimilation of the experience into abstract concepts and knowledge, and (4) conceptualization to guide future experiences.[3]

Higher education is an opportunity to challenge existing worldviews students bring into the classroom. White privilege shapes how students view the instructor and the course material. Incorporating experiential learning into the classroom connects students with marginalized populations they may never have interacted with or been exposed to before. Depending on where students grew up, they may have never been taught by Black, Indigenous, and People of Color (BIPOC) or other marginalized individuals before higher education (as was the case for me growing up in rural Nevada). Opening the classroom to diverse experiences and perspectives challenges students' existing biases to improve their cultural awareness. Such activities are crucial in any discipline but especially in criminal justice courses.[4]

A major component of experiential learning is reflection occurring in pre- or postactivities. Reflection assignments encourage students to think critically about their own lived experiences in relation to the activity. Students also apply course concepts to their experiences and reflect on how the activities facilitated their learning. The reflection assignments allow instructors to clearly identify student reactions and achievement of learning objectives.

Experiential learning has the potential to benefit all instructors but especially those who have been historically and systemically marginalized. First, students often prefer experiential learning.[5] Students indicate more favorable perceptions of courses with experiential learning in comparison to those with a traditional lecture style.[6] Second, experiential learning helps build students' empathy.[7] The humanizing and immersive nature of experiential learning forces students to self-reflect and consider the perspectives of those with lived experience that may differ vastly from their own. Reflections on privilege and marginalization build students' self-awareness and understanding of others' positionality, including their instructors. Finally, experiential learning reflects inclusive pedagogy. Experiential learning aligns with culturally responsive teaching through caring, empathy, and communication.[8] First-generation and Hispanic students are better able to learn and connect in courses with experiential learning components in comparison to traditional lecture-style courses.[9] Thus, experiential learning can help foster authentic relationships between faculty and students while countering potential biases in evaluations.

Nonetheless, instructors may feel apprehensive about incorporating experiential learning. A recent study examined a national sample of faculty members' perceptions of experiential learning.[10] Less than 25 percent of faculty surveyed used experiential learning approaches, and the majority (91 percent) used a traditional lecture. Although 97 percent of faculty indicated they felt experiential learning enhances students' life skills (e.g., critical thinking, problem-solving), more than half indicated barriers to implementation, including lack of time and resources. Such constraints may be particularly salient among BIPOC, women, and other marginalized educators who too often bear the brunt of service work and mentorship.[11] Marginalized faculty may also feel increased pressure to discuss information from a position of authority and control to counteract biased perceptions of incompetency.[12] Accordingly, departments and institutions need to effectively support faculty who are interested in adopting experiential learning into their classrooms.

Instructors can incorporate experiential learning through a variety of activities. In my courses, students interact with guest speakers, attend facility tours, engage in service-learning, and reflect on documentaries. Content warnings, expectations, and alternatives should be provided to students in advance, as the immersive material may be emotionally triggering.[13]

Guest Speakers

Guest speakers facilitate student engagement when paired with active learning and reflection prompts. Students construct knowledge by listening and interacting with an expert who has lived experience, which students usually would not have access to on a daily basis.[14] Guest speakers can provide insight into how systems and processes work.

Several guest speakers come to my class virtually or in person each semester, including practitioners and individuals who are/were system involved. Students interact and ask direct questions. Many note that they've never talked to a person who was incarcerated until my course. The experience humanizes those in the system. As one student wrote:

> The guest speaker gave me a chance to see the other side of corrections from the lens of a person who experienced [incarceration]. [It helped to be] able to hear about reality [in relation to] what is taught [in class]. . . . Most of us [have] never been through the correctional system, so there could be a disconnect between what is being taught and what really happens or what really works [to rehabilitate]. Having someone who [was incarcerated] gave us the chance to ask questions and [determine] what is true.[15]

Exposing students to new or different perspectives encourages their attitudes and views to shift, allowing for a transformative learning experience. Transformative learning "occurs when learners change their frames of reference by critically reflecting on their assumptions, beliefs, and understanding of the world."[16] Experiential learning helps challenge students' self-awareness of power and privilege by interacting with marginalized populations in real time.

During my first year teaching, I had an older White male student in my class who seemed resistant most of the term. After my father came in as a guest speaker to discuss his experiences with incarceration and substance use, the student told me that up until that day in class, he had a hard time connecting with me because I was young and seemed like I had a lot of "textbook" learning but not any real-world experience. He appreciated being able to interact with my father, who did have lived experience. This moment became central to my teaching approach. From that point forward, I decided to be honest and open about my own experiences or lack thereof. I wanted to connect students with the best resources possible: diverse individuals with lived experience and expertise.

Tours and Field Trips

Well-organized field trips allow for increased comprehension and interest in the course material, enhanced observational skills, and connections to the local community.[17] Tours of facilities related to one's field can help students understand the day-to-day operations, staff perspectives of practices in the field, the subculture, and organizational structure firsthand. Staff members provide their own commentary, and students are encouraged to ask questions. Being able to see, hear, and feel what a facility is like has a lasting impression on student learning. The experience also helps prepare students' expectations for potential careers. The tours also grant students access to staff and recruiters for future employment.

When I taught Corrections, the facility tours of jails, prisons, and work release centers were key to addressing students' preconceptions or myths about the correctional system. Many students enter my class with preconceptions of what prison is like from movies or television shows that sensationalize violence and disrespect. Such an experience is far more immersive than what can be provided in a textbook. One student in my course noted:

> The tour really helped me visualize and enhance my learning of the concepts we have studied in class over the course of the semester. Throughout the semester we have talked so much about inmates, incarceration, and programs for incarcerated inmates. Seeing inmates with my own eyes and being inside of a [correctional facility] was a very eye-opening experience.[18]

Implementing field trips can be challenging, as doing so requires building relationships with local agencies. There can also be anxiety related to giving up control of the classroom. Attending tours in advance helps establish trust and set expectations. There are also warranted ethical concerns surrounding facility tours. Depending on the facility, the populations served may be present or in view. Instructors should make efforts to engage with the populations served, if possible. The tours themselves can be time-consuming: facilitating background checks, arranging transportation, travel to and from the site, and at least one hour to two hours at the facilities. For some students, it may not be feasible for them to attend the tours because of transportation, work schedules, or disabilities. An instructor can offer tours to local students remotely or help students set up tours within their own communities for increased accessibility. For example, the instructor could walk through the facility and film it for students to watch later.[19] The facilities themselves may also have videos for educational use.

Regardless of the challenges, I use tours because students consistently discuss the impact tours had on them beyond the end of the semester. While I myself have limited direct experience besides interning as a graduate student and having family members incarcerated, tours allow students to connect with individuals with more lived experience than me. Connecting students with others who have lived experience helps counter biases about how a professor should look or act. Instead of a stoic person standing at the front of the classroom lecturing, we learn together outside our physical classroom. This approach puts less focus on me and more emphasis on the class as a collaborative learning space.

Service-Learning

Service-learning seeks to address human and community needs through structured educational techniques involving active participation and reflection.[20] It builds students' civic engagement and utilitarianism through service work connected to the learning objectives. Service-learning provides an opportunity for a transformational learning experience.[21] The immersion into the environment can help students understand the experiences of both staff and populations served. The hands-on volunteer work also provides desirable skills for potential employers in the field.[22] The core elements of service-learning are education, action, and reflection.[23] Similar to experiential learning, an integral component of service-learning is reflection.

I partnered with various community agencies, ranging from domestic violence shelters to campus organizations. In the past, I assigned students volunteer work at the agency physically. However, the COVID-19 pandemic quickly led me to rethink remote options for students, including writing grant applications, making homemade donation bags out of T-shirts, translating documents, and creating social media campaigns with relevant statistics and information. Indeed, there are plenty of opportunities for students to engage in service-learning remotely.[24]

Beyond traditional volunteer work, service-learning emerges in the form of research partnerships aimed at improving community outcomes.[25] I partnered with local agencies to develop survey instruments. One particularly successful partnership for research methods was with a local drug court. The program manager came to our class to describe the program and desired goals of the surveys. As a class, we developed the survey items together. Students also attended drug court to conduct observations for qualitative research practice, which helped inform the survey creation. Giving students hands-on skills with local agencies helps them understand the value and importance of research.

Similarly, my students and I created campus surveys on topics ranging from perceptions of safety and victimization, inclusivity on campus, and instruction formats during the pandemic to inform and benefit our campus community. With my guidance, students created the survey questions and analyzed the results by creating graphs and interpretations. This service-learning research component can be a more local or accessible option for instructors (with institutional review and approval) than connecting with a community organization.

Research on experiential learning and project-based learning indicates students are more motivated to learn in such settings.[26] The approach can improve students' satisfaction in the course, which is usually measured through instructor evaluations.[27] I noticed this firsthand in my courses by comparing student evaluations across courses with and without service-learning components. Student evaluations were noticeably higher in the service-learning courses than others (i.e., 4.4–4.5 versus 4.7–4.9 out of 5). Thus, using effective high-impact teaching can counteract and confront the biases marginalized faculty face in student evaluations.

Documentaries

Lastly, film and media can be used as experiential learning. Documentaries, which can be watched in person in a classroom or remotely, are particularly useful to facilitate understanding abstract concepts when it's impossible to facilitate other experiential learning activities.[28] Students are able to live unfamiliar experiences vicariously, humanizing the course material. Additionally, documentaries hold the potential to promote critical thinking skills among students by challenging stereotypes and myths through more realistic visual representations.[29] A student in my corrections course discussed the impact of a documentary called *Toe Tag Parole: To Live and Die on Yard A* about incarcerated men serving life without parole sentences: "The video helped me to understand what it's like to be incarcerated and the emotional trauma it can have and why it would lead people to contemplate suicide when serving life without the possibility of parole."[30]

Just as traditional lectures may encourage student passivity and discourage active engagement with course content, if presented without careful planning and purposeful assignments, documentaries can have the same effect.[31] When I show documentaries in person, I stop the films at important points and ask students discussion questions.

This can also be accomplished remotely with a guide and stop points for students to watch and engage on their own. Instructors can schedule and facilitate virtual watch parties or discussions to help students feel connected to the instructor, the material, and each other. Also, reflection questions with prompts related to various content throughout the documentary can help students watch the film with the purpose of connecting with larger course concepts. These active learning appraisals are especially important to provide in increasingly remote settings, such as during the COVID-19 pandemic.

With instructor guidance, documentaries push students to reflect on how gender, race, social class, and other categories of difference shape individuals' experiences. Such activities help encourage students to view the world through an intersectional lens.[32] When used effectively, such appraisals can lead to lasting inclusive outcomes, including increased awareness, openness, and empathy among students.[33] Outcomes in individual courses may translate to the culture of the institution as a whole and student interactions with faculty as well.

Conclusion

Experiential learning is an impactful pedagogical tool to link course material with real-world experiences. When students have a personal and emotional connection to the material, they are more likely to remember and engage beyond the semester.[34] Ultimately, opening the classroom to those with lived experiences provides a more engaging, collaborative, and inclusive, learning environment for me and my students. I now view my students as allies rather than adversaries.[35]

Each guest speaker, tour, documentary, or service-learning experience is unique to the individual course, and we experience them *together*.

Experiential learning has empowered me to become more authentic and personable with my students. Humanity is a key component to my teaching at every level, not just to humanize the course content but also to humanize us in the classroom together. When I am comfortable being myself (i.e., showing my tattoos, discussing my experiences with the carceral system, showing photos of my dogs, talking about pop culture or recent events), students feel more comfortable being themselves as well. As discussed by Michelle Pacansky-Brock and her colleagues, "instructor-student relationships lie at the heart of humanizing, serving as the connective tissue between students, engagement, and rigor." [36] When we remove the misconceptions of what "professionalism" or professor-student relationships should look like, which traditionally have been biased by Western, White, male-based, heteronormative, and classist standards, we are able to form more authentic connections to the material and to each other.

Undoubtedly, my position as a White cisgender woman is distinct from other marginalized groups. A nontraditional appearance (tattoos and clothing choices) can be a source for student bias but should not be equated with systemic racism and other types of discrimination. I do believe experiential learning has the potential to break down unfair biases and empower marginalized faculty by humanizing the classroom. The immersive activities help build students' self-awareness and cultural awareness of others, pushing them to confront privilege, marginalization, and discrimination in their everyday lives. Further, high-impact teaching techniques, such as experiential learning, encourage students to have more holistic perceptions of the classroom setting, which can help counter potential biases about individual instructors.

Teaching Takeaways

- Experiential learning is a high-impact learning technique that can enhance the classroom setting by encouraging students to reflect on their own positionalities, confront preconceptions and biases, and build empathy.
- Experiential learning connects students to real-world experiences and contexts but must be coupled with reflection assignments that connect to the course material.
- Experiential learning activities come in a variety of forms, both in person and remote, including guest speakers, tours, documentaries, and civic engagement.

....

BREANNA BOPPRE is an assistant professor in the department of victim studies at Sam Houston State University. She earned her PhD in criminology and criminal justice from the University of Nevada, Las Vegas, in 2018. Her research examines the carceral system and the impacts of incarceration on families. She has been recognized internationally for her teaching methods as the American Society of Criminology Division of Victimology Faculty Teacher of the Year in 2021 and the Academy of Criminal Justice Sciences Innovations in Teaching Awardee.

Notes

....

I would like to thank Sarah Daly for her insight and feedback on this chapter.

1. Meda Chesney-Lind and Nicholas Chagnon, "Criminology, Gender, and Race: A Case Study of Privilege in the Academy," *Feminist Criminology* 11, no. 4 (2016): 311–33.

2. Colleen Flaherty, "Teaching Evaluations: Bias and Tenure," *Inside Higher Education*, May 20, 2019, https://www.inside highered.com/news/2019/05/20/fighting-gender-bias-student -evaluations-teaching-and-tenures-effect-instruction.

3. David A. Kolb, *Experience as the Source of Learning and Development* (Upper Saddle River, NJ: Prentice Hall, 1984), 3–4.

4. Sarah E. Daley and London Smith, "Legitimacy at Stake: Learning about Race and the Criminal Justice System," in *A Closer Look at Criminal Justice*, eds. Jonathan A. Cooper and Kayla G. Jachimowski (Hauppauge, NY: NOVA Science Publishers, 2019), 3–26.

5. Laura Helle et al., " 'Ain't Nothin' Like the Real Thing': Motivation and Study Processes on a Work-based Project Course in Information Systems Design," *British Journal of Educational Psychology* 77, no. 2 (2007): 397–411.

6. Karen E. Pugsley and Laura H. Clayton, "Traditional Lecture or Experiential Learning: Changing Student Attitudes," *Journal of Nursing Education* 42, no. 11 (2003): 520–23.

7. Linsey Belisle et al., "Bringing Course Material to Life Through Experiential Learning: Impacts on Students' Learning and Perceptions in a Corrections Course," *Journal of Criminal Justice Education* 31, no. 2 (2020): 161–86.

8. Geneva Gay, *Culturally Responsive Teaching: Theory, Research and Practice* (New York: Teachers College Press, 2018).

9. Christy S. Teranishi, "Impact of Experiential Learning on Latino

College Students' Identity, Relationships, and Connectedness to Community," *Journal of Hispanic Higher Education* 6, no. 1 (2007): 52–72; Devon Thacker Thomas, Berna M. Torr, and Eileen T. Walsh, "Experiential Learning: Benefits for Hispanic and First-Generation College Students," *International Journal of Learning, Teaching and Educational Research* 16, no. 5 (2017): 102–17.

10. Scott Wurdinger and Pete Allison, "Faculty Perceptions and Use of Experiential Learning in Higher Education," *Journal of e-learning and Knowledge Society* 13, no. 1 (2017): 15–26.

11. Cassandra M. Guarino and Victor MH Borden, "Faculty Service Loads and Gender: Are Women Taking Care of the Academic Family?" *Research in Higher Education* 58, no. 6 (2017): 672–94; Zawadi Rucks-Ahidiana, "The Inequities of the Tenure-Track System," *Inside Higher Ed*, June 7, 2019, https://www.insidehighered.com/advice/2019/06/07/nonwhite-faculty-face-significant-disadvantages-tenure-track-opinion.

12. Buffy Smith, "Forming Classroom Communities to Help Students Embrace Discomfort," in Stephen D. Brookfield (Ed.), *Teaching Race: How to Help Students Unmask and Challenge Racism* (New York: John Wiley and Sons, 2018), 171–89.

13. Kevin M. Gannon, *Radical Hope: A Teaching Manifesto* (Morgantown: West Virginia University Press, 2020).

14. Barbara A. Rockell, "Challenging What They All Know: Integrating the Real/Reel World into Criminal Justice Pedagogy," *Journal of Criminal Justice Education* 20, no. 1 (2009): 75–92.

15. Belisle et al., "Bringing Course Material to Life," 11.

16. Peter Felten and Patti H. Clayton, "Service-Learning," *New Directions for Teaching and Learning* no. 128 (2011): 82.

17. Molly George et al., "Learning by Doing: Experiential Learning in Criminal Justice," *Journal of Criminal Justice Education* 26, no. 4 (2015): 471–92.

18. Belisle et al., "Bringing Course Material to Life," 11.

19. Karen Costa, *99 Tips for Creating Simple and Sustainable Educational Videos: A Guide for Online Teachers and Flipped Classes* (Sterling, VA: Stylus Publishing, 2020).

20. Jaya Davis, "Engaging Criminal Justice Students through Service Learning," *Journal of Criminal Justice Education* 26, no. 3 (2015): 253–72; Barbara Jacoby, *Service-Learning in Higher Education: Concepts and Practices. The Jossey-Bass Higher and Adult Education Series* (San Francisco: Jossey-Bass Publishers, 1996), 3–25.

21. Ricky S. Gutierrez, Debra Reeves-Gutierrez, and Ronald Helms, "Service Learning and Criminal Justice Students: An Assessment of the Effects of Co-curricular Pedagogy on Graduate Rates," *Journal of Criminal Justice Education* 23, no. 3 (2012): 356–80; Sharon Redhawk Love, "Keeping It Real: Connecting Feminist Criminology and Activism through Service Learning," *Feminist Criminology* 3, no. 4 (2008): 303–18; Brian Chad Starks, Lana Harrison, and Kathy Denhardt, "Outside the Comfort Zone of the Classroom," *Journal of Criminal Justice Education* 22, no. 2 (2011): 203–25.

22. Alison S. Burke and Michael D. Bush, "Service Learning and Criminal Justice: An Exploratory Study of Student Perceptions," *Educational Review* 65, no. 1 (2013): 56–69.

23. Everette B. Penn, "Service-Learning: A Tool to Enhance Criminal Justice," *Journal of Criminal Justice Education* 14, no. 2 (2003): 371–83.

24. Andrew Furco, *EService-Learning: Creating Experiential Learning and Civic Engagement through Online and Hybrid Courses* (Sterling, VA: Stylus, 2015).

25. Sharyn J. Potter, Elizabeth M. Caffrey, and Elizabethe G. Plante, "Integrating Service Learning into the Research Methods Course," *Teaching Sociology* (2003): 38–48.

26. Helle et al., " 'Ain't Nothin' Like the Real Thing,' " 400–9.

27. Ali El. Hanandeh, "Can Experiential Learning Help Students' Learning Improve Course Satisfaction?" *27th Annual Conference of the Australasian Association for Engineering Education: AAEE 2016* (Lismore, Australia: Southern Cross University, 2016), 243.

28. Greg L. Pugh, "The Experiential Learning Cycle in Undergraduate Diversity and Social Justice Education," *Journal of Teaching in Social Work* 34, no. 3 (2014): 302–15.

29. Angela M. Nickoli et al., "Pop Culture, Crime and Pedagogy," *Journal of Criminal Justice Education* 14, no. 1 (2003): 149–62.

30. Belisle et al., "Bringing Course Material to Life," 13.

31. Shelly Celvenger and Jordana Navarro, *Teaching Criminological Theory* (San Diego: Cognella, 2018), 80–81.

32. Rebecca M. Hayes, Kate Luther, and Susan Caringella, eds., *Teaching Criminology at the Intersection: A How-to Guide for Teaching about Gender, Race, Class and Sexuality* (New York: Routledge, 2014).

33. Mitchell J. Chang, "The Impact of an Undergraduate Diversity Course Requirement on Students' Racial Views and Attitudes," *Journal of General Education* (2002): 21–42.

34. Ken Bain, *What the Best College Teachers Do* (Cambridge: Harvard University Press, 2004), 31, 110; Sarah Rose Cavanagh, *The Spark of Learning: Energizing the College Classroom with the Science of Emotion* (Morgantown: West Virginia University Press, 2016), 33–57.

35. Gannon, *Radical Hope*, 31.

36. Michelle Pacansky-Brock, Michael Smedshammer, and Kim Vincent-Layton, "Humanizing Online Teaching to Equitize Higher Education," *Current Issues in Education* 21, no. 2 (2020), 2.

....

CHAPTER 6

COLLABORATIVE RUBRIC CREATION AS A QUEER, TRANSGENDER PROFESSOR'S TACTIC FOR BUILDING TRUST IN THE CLASSROOM

....

Fen Kennedy

Transgender and non-binary professors are a rarity in the American university system. Like other rarities, we've been hunted almost to extinction. A recent Supreme Court decision extending Title VII employment protections to lesbian, gay, and transgender people may provide future safety. But this legislative precedent does not protect us from accusations of "unprofessionalism" or substantively higher workloads/standards than our cisgendered colleagues or from retribution if we do not successfully navigate the boundary between pro forma "diversity" and diversity that actually confronts institutional discrimination. I am an assistant professor of dance in a large southern university, and as a non-binary, transgender instructor who also experiences marginalizations of being a first-generation student and immigrant, I don't know if my position will ever feel stable. But I can use the wisdom of my identities to create a pedagogical environment that elevates the lives and learning of my students and, hopefully, make the world a safer place for myself and other marginalized faculty.

The topic of this chapter—collaborative rubric creation—gives students the opportunity to design how their learning will be assessed and draws on theories of queer pedagogy to cultivate trust in the classroom. I align with Stacy Waite to assert that queer pedagogy goes beyond queer subjects, students, or professors. Rather, queer theories and experiences can be the basis for "sets of theorized practices that any student or teacher might engage," moving toward a validation of liminal, fluid, and multipositional approaches to teaching and learning.[1] By co-creating a shared set of metrics for course goals for assessing progress toward those goals, students gain space to articulate their own priorities as learners and emergent professionals. In this chapter, I argue that a clear and transparent rubric increases student engagement, encourages meaningful student learning and success, and, for a marginalized professor, combats systemic queerphobia and other student biases that frequently manifest as distrust.

Queering Academia, Navigating Trust

Due to a lack of formal study, the direct marginalizations of non-binary and transgender faculty members are difficult to elucidate beyond anecdotal experience, but the broader effects of marginalization within higher education are well documented. Andreana Clay summarizes such experiences

for queer faculty of color: "We face being thought of as specialized hires (sometimes too specialized) who don't really
represent or understand the discipline they are hired into."
Clay also describes how queer professors must routinely
contend with student hostility: "We regularly meet to discuss anonymous student evaluations that call my out gay
colleagues 'faggots,' chastise my white lesbian colleagues
for being 'intimidating,' or any of us for 'favoring queer
students in the classroom.'"[2] As Clay points out, students
routinely weaponize student evaluations of instruction (SEI)
to demean and attack marginalized instructors, a significant issue since most colleges and universities use SEI as a
factor in the granting or denial of tenure.[3] Although numerous studies demonstrate student biases regarding instructor
race, academic field, and perceived "sexiness," others claim
that student evaluations are "relatively unaffected by a variety of variables hypothesized as potential biases."[4] Whether
or not we can measure biases empirically, the overwhelming
perception of evaluations as biased places a much higher burden on marginalized professors to make themselves palat-
able to their students in an attempt to avoid being "trashed"
in their evaluations.[5]

While no major statistical studies of student evaluations
of queer, transgender, or non-binary faculty members currently exist, anecdotal evidence suggests that student prejudices and preconceptions negatively impact our SEI. For
example, Cary Costello, an intersex, transgender professor
at a large midwestern university describes the institutional,
systemic discrimination he encountered when the university prohibited him from openly discussing his transition,
resulting in colleagues, computer systems, and internal
email lists regularly misgendering and deadnaming him.[6]
Moreover, Costello also repeatedly faced negative student

reactions. Much of the literature on LGBTQIA+ faculty focuses on "coming out" and "disclosure," but transgender and non-binary instructors often have no choice about being identified.[7] As Costello writes:

> My very androgynous body made students anxious, and they stood much farther away from me when speaking to me after class than students had in prior years. Every time my voice cracked, a little ripple or shudder moved across the lecture hall. I often caught students inappropriately staring at my chest or my groin, and both they and I would flush when I caught them.[8]

Costello's previously positive student ratings declined as students' perceptions of his gender became central in their reactions to his teaching, describing him as "pushing an agenda" or "forcing [his] issue down other people's throats." One student lashed out at Costello by submitting a paper arguing that all children with intersex conditions should be aborted. Those who earned poor grades on assignments about gender claimed that Costello shouldn't be teaching on the subject because of his bias.

Like Costello, students can visually perceive my transgender identity. I'm transparent about my non-binary gender and use the pronouns they/them (although I don't correct students for not using them or for misgendering me). I make it explicit to every class, in writing, that they are not graded on their political alignment, and every semester, my SEI are largely positive, even exceptional. However, they also always include at least one or two comments accusing me of bias/political agenda or even saying that my courses are a waste of time. Although these comments trouble me, I'd like to offer empathy toward transphobic students by reframing their reticence as distrust rather than malice. Taking this more generative approach to the issue enables me to create effective tactics to address transphobia in my classrooms.

When I enter a professional setting, people see a diminutive, energetic figure. They often assume that I'm an undergraduate student until I identify myself as "doctor." Then I announce that "I take they/them pronouns." As much as I sometimes enjoy the shock that this process engenders in others, I also understand that this repeated resetting of perceptions leaves a lasting impression of wariness: Who am I? What else have people assumed wrong about me? I occupy a place on the political spectrum that may be new and alien, even taboo, to students, and I hold power over their grading and academic well-being. I audition them for our programs, and I have a say in casting them for major performances. Not knowing how to act around me, or how I might abuse that power if they offend me, understandably creates trepidation, sometimes translating into retaliation.

I've developed a variety of pedagogical responses, including co-creating assessment rubrics, to cultivate trust with my students. I approach pedagogy from a generous place rather than a protective one. Co-created rubrics foster students' power and agency that my identity might seem to take away. If students know that they have collectively agreed on how I will be assessing their learning based on the values we hold as a class community, they have a concrete document affirming the integrity of the assessment process. The rubric that we agreed upon together becomes a structure for meaningful, authentic learning, helping them explore and grow their own artistic and scholarly identities rather than an imposition of my own "political" desires.

Rubrics for Assessing Artistry

Co-created rubrics are also a pedagogically effective strategy for assessing dance. Choreography is a notoriously difficult subject to teach and to grade because there are very few standardized criteria for its teaching and assessment. In a university environment where students are working in ballet, jazz, and contemporary techniques, establishing choreographic "norms" for a dance work can be seen as a personal choice by the instructor, favoring some students while damaging the aspirations of others. Choreography classes frequently impose aesthetic standards that maintain and promote Euro-American creative practices. As Larry Lavender, scholar of choreography pedagogy, observes, "The use of results-based criticism as a primary mode of instruction in choreography locks students into prescriptive formalist codes both of movement and of dance structure." He describes the negative impact this has on student learning:

> The very idea, in students' minds as they create, that rule-based teacher/peer criticism waits in the wings to perform a regulatory function over their work fosters a "what does the teacher want?" anxiety in students and channels them into a subservient role within a vertical-domain, "expert/critic" gate keeping orientation to teaching and learning.[9]

While Lavender offers several strategies for adapting the feedback process within the classroom in order to promote creative engagement, he does not address the fact that most professors must assign a letter grade to each student at the end of the semester.

If a choreography class should be focused on process, not the application of formalist methods, how should the results be graded? How can students receive tangible feedback? In developing my own grading process, I was inspired by dance professor Jessica Zeller's work on "ungrading"— the idea that by allowing students to submit their own grades, and by writing narrative reports of why that grade is justified, students have "some space to try new things, fail miserably, laugh at yourself, and try again, without pressure. We'll do the work of the course for its own sake— for the sake of learning something new."[10] Working toward authentic learning, I use a co-created rubric that combines holistic and analytical practices to address the issues of grading creative practices in a choreography class.[11]

Holistic rubrics describe a series of criteria for a whole piece of work or a total semester experience, with descriptive passages offering an indication of the overall sense of an A, B, C, and so on. Analytical rubrics subdivide the overall grade into several criteria for assessing work and assign each criterion a number of potential points to be earned. Each rubric type has its pros and cons. Language professor Lucy Spence points out that an analytical rubric can disadvantage students if it doesn't take into account individual engagement, process, and growth, and can be disadvantageous to marginalized students who may not be fluent with the codified norms of academic writing.[12] Holistic rubrics offer flexibility but are also more ambiguous and thus leave instructors open to accusations of unfair grading. A holistic rubric must contain enough tangible descriptors, or quantitative assessment metrics, for students to understand and buy in to the grading process. A holistic grade should be accompanied by written or oral feedback that explains the specific strengths and weaknesses of a piece of work and offers actionable suggestions for improvement, as well as documenting improvement over time. An analytical rubric must make room for diverse modes of expression, including the demonstration of non-European cultural literacies, so students from all backgrounds can feel that their work is valued.[13]

In my own teaching, I use both analytical and holistic rubrics.[14] For example, a "Choreographic Skill" rubric I co-created with students included the following criteria defining an A-level "exceptional choreographer":

- Has a strong sense of their own choreographic identity
- Can be versatile, using a range of choreographic tools to support their identity
- Can clearly articulate their choreographic concepts, including answering questions and explaining to people outside the dance community
- Deliberately invites multiple perspectives into their creation process
- Runs rehearsals that are prepared, engaging, and productive and creates partnerships with collaborators

This rubric, one of the three I used in the class to assess choreographic skill, self-education, and citizenship, offers clear evaluative criteria fostering a classroom culture of trust and creative freedom. We created similar criteria for B and C grades, defined as "a competent choreographer" and "a learning choreographer," respectively. At the end of the semester, students used evidence from the semester to pitch their own grades.

The criteria provided tangible, actionable suggestions for "getting the grade" while leaving the process of implementation open to each student. For example, a student must use "a range of choreographic tools to support their identity" but can make a free selection from tools discovered inside or outside the classroom. Students created research processes through freewriting, score-making, historical research, analysis of visual art, ethnographic observations—developing a process around their own practice rather than following one prescribed research journey and hoping to get a variety of results. One unexpected result of this open framework was that it introduced me to new modes of engagement. For example, one requirement under "Self-Education" is for students to "draw on a wide range of different mediums" as a resource for learning. A number of students told me that they had engaged with this prompt by following artists on Instagram or TikTok, and as a result, they could fluently discuss and practice their working methods and physical styles.

The rubrics for this class offered analytical criteria for assessment within a holistic framework. For students who struggle to align their work with an assessment rubric, I also provided a series of prompt questions on each rubric to help students self-assess their own progress:

- What is my artistic heritage?
- What are my favorite choreographic tools?
- When was the last time I tried something new?
- Do my rehearsals feel like a positive community?
- Why am I doing what I'm doing?
- What would I do if [blank] happened? How would it change the work?
- What is my work about? How am I realizing that?

These questions helped students check in throughout the semester and demonstrate how they were meeting assessment criteria. Transparency around our shared value of "trying something new" was a powerful motivator for students to experiment outside of their existing practice— for example, by creating dance films, working within a new movement genre, and seating the audience around or even in the middle of the performance. Students felt like they could experiment and make mistakes because the rubrics we had created showed them that it was valuable to do so.

An additional benefit to these rubric criteria was that students assumed responsibility for documenting their processes and articulating their choreographic processes. Within the professional sphere, choreographers need to write grant applications, speak about their work, educate others, work flexibly, and otherwise demonstrate their value beyond the dances they make. The rubrics devised for this class took into account the professional practice of choreography, not just its classroom requirements.

Clearly, this rubric is not applicable to every class or even to every choreography class. But by showing its benefits, I hope to advocate for teaching practices that build trust and facilitate authentic learning. As Harriet L. Schwartz suggests, feedback to students is most productive as part of a relational process that establishes shared languages and humanities.[15] I did not write this rubric, and I did not come up with its criteria and impose them on students. Students asked to be assessed according to these criteria because of a deep understanding of what they meant and why they were valuable. During the COVID-19 pandemic, this approach to grading proved even more crucial. As Zeller explains, "Ungrading allowed me to preserve trust with students during a pedagogic transition that might've exploded even the most collaborative student-teacher relationships."[16]

Collaborative Rubric Design Processes: In Person and Online

Collaborative rubric creation begins with members of a class articulating their values and their professional aims. In the articulation of community values, students work in three small "teams" to create their own manifesto for exceptional choreographic skill, exceptional citizenship, and exceptional self-education. I offer them prompts such as "An exceptional citizen can . . . " or "When I think of a skilled choreographer, I think of . . ." They brainstorm ideas on large sheets of paper to then use as prompts for discussion and identifying our learning community's key values. Articulation of professional aims is vital for upper-level students who hope to graduate and get jobs in the dance industry but have a wide variety of ideas about their own niche in the field. We start the process with every student getting a stack of Post-it sticky notes and creating a wall of ideas about what skills and activities they want the class to include, sorting repeated ideas into groups. This process gives the whole class a clearer picture of what is important to *everyone* in the room and how the class can accommodate a broad range of professional goals. Only after the class has a clear picture of what they want as a community do I pose the question, "What do you want to be assessed on?" A key question for upper-level classes is about technical standards (i.e., should a student going to graduate school for exercise science or nutrition be held to the same standard as someone who already has a professional performing contract for when they graduate?). Solving problems like this as a class, and using our solutions to articulate a rubric together, gave students confidence in the assessment process.

Some components of these activities are essential to the process of collaborative rubric creation. First, the process starts with a lot of thinking time so that students can move past their initial ideas and get to what they really want. Giving time to the initial exploratory phase also means that students less inclined to speak up on the first pass had the opportunity to contribute meaningfully to the process. Second, initial expressions of values create deeper understanding and clarity. Pushing students to think about not only *what* values they hold but also *why* they hold them and *how* those values might be expressed helped get us all on the same page with language and helped overcome disagreement. Third, when I translate the values articulated into a written rubric, I use as many of the students' own words as possible from notes taken during our discussion. I also give students a week to read the rubrics and make corrections before adopting them as final.

These strategies have helped me adapt the collaborative rubric creation process to online teaching during the 2020 pandemic. While we do not have the materiality of pens and paper and sticky notes, I've used Google Forms and Docs to generate the prompts for a discussion on grading and assessment. I recommend using breakout rooms to facilitate small-group private discussions *before* asking students to formalize what they want a rubric to look like. I also found that the discussion got easier when I shared hypothetical examples of where we *could* go: "Do you think a participation grade is useful in an online class, or should we scrap it?" While faculty teaching large-scale classes might have to get creative about how they receive feedback on these questions, digital classrooms can facilitate the collaborative process, as students can see the documents being generated in real time in response to their needs.

Conclusion

....

Today, we must facilitate student learning during possibly the most politically charged moment of students' lives to date. Students in my classes hold different beliefs about who should be president, about the Black Lives Matter movement, and about how to cope with COVID-19. Remote schooling highlights the inequities of time, space, and technological access in our classrooms. Moreover, as the political landscape in the United States becomes more and more polarized, a professor like me whose embodied identity places them firmly on the left is a target of automatic suspicion, queerphobia, and professorial mistrust by some. At the same time, I and others like me have a unique opportunity as educators because as Susie Nam powerfully argues, marginalized professors share ways in which our students are exploited and oppressed, and we continue to do our work in conditions of oppression not because we have "been there" but because we are *still* there and may be for the foreseeable future.[17] Using a collaboratively created rubric is one of the ways I hope to cultivate more trust, facilitate authentic learning, and create a class environment where all students feel able to come and learn safely regardless of their personal circumstances.

....

Teaching Takeaways

....

- Students may experience fear and distrust interacting with marginalized faculty. Everyone benefits when our teaching practices mitigate that fear by building class community and trust.

- Co-created assessment rubrics make grading practices more transparent, increase student buy-in for the assessment process, and help facilitate authentic learning.
- Collaborative rubric creation gives students power and agency and, when guided by deep and honest discussion, makes the classroom a more equitable space for everyone.

．．．．．．．．．．．．．．．．．．．．．．．

FEN KENNEDY holds a doctorate in dance studies from Ohio State University and is assistant professor of dance at the University of Alabama. Their research, practical and theoretical, explores how dance articulates the norms and values of our society and how those norms can be challenged and changed. Their work can be seen in *Dance Chronicle* and the *Journal of Dance Education,* as well as in performance with Alabama Repertory Dance Theatre and VINEGAR Projects.

Notes

1. Stacy Waite, *Teaching Queer: Radical Possibilities for Writing and Knowing* (Pittsburgh: University of Pittsburgh Press, 2017), 5.
2. Andreana Clay, " 'Colored' Is the New Queer: Queer Faculty of Color in the Academy," in *Written/Unwritten: Diversity and the Hidden Truths of Tenure*, ed. Patricia A. Matthew (Chapel Hill: University of North Carolina Press, 2016), 110–11.
3. Suzanne M. Hobson and Donna M. Talbot, "Understanding Student Evaluations: What All Faculty Should Know," *College Teaching* 49, no. 1 (Winter 2001): 26–31.

4.   William E. Cashin, "Students Do Rate Different Academic Fields
      Differently," *New Directions for Teaching and Learning* 43 (Fall
      1990): 113–21; James Felton and John B. Mitchell, "Web-Based
      Student Evaluations of Professors: The Relations between
      Perceived Quality, Easiness and Sexiness," *Assessment and
      Evaluation in Higher Education* 29, no. 1 (June 2003): 91–108;
      Herbert W. Marsh, "Students' Evaluations of University
      Teaching: Dimensionality, Reliability, Validity, Potential Biases
      and Usefulness" in *The Scholarship of Teaching and Learning in
      Higher Education: An Evidence-Based Perspective,* eds. Raymond P.
      Perry and John C. Smart (Dordrecht, The Netherlands:
      Springer), 319–83; Bettye P. Smith and Billy Hawkins,
      "Examining Student Evaluations of Black College Faculty: Does
      Race Matter?" *Journal of Negro Education* 80, no. 2 (Spring
      2011): 149–62.

5.   Sylvia R. Lazos, "Are Student Teaching Evaluations Holding
      Back Women and Minorities?: The Perils of 'Doing' Gender
      and Race in the Classroom," in *Presumed Incompetent: The
      Intersections of Race and Class for Women in Academia*, eds.
      Gabriella Gutiérrez y Muhs et al. (Louisville, CO: University
      Press of Colorado, 2012), 164–85.

6.   Carey Costello, "On Teaching (Trans) Gender," *TransFusion*,
      July 24, 2013, https://trans-fusion.blogspot.com/2013/07
      /on-teaching-trans-gender.html. Deadnaming is used by the
      trans to describe others using a name they were given at birth
      or known by before transition. Deadnaming can lead to outing
      a trans person and does significant psychological harm as an
      indicator that the trans person's birth name, and therefore their
      gender assigned at birth, overrides their real name and gender
      identity. Use of a transgender person's real name is associated
      with a 29 percent decrease in suicidal ideation and a 56 percent
      decrease in suicidal behavior. See Maggie O'Neill, "What Does
      It Mean to 'Deadname' Someone? Here's How It Affects the

Transgender Community," *Healthline*, July 28, 2020, https://www.health.com/mind-body/deadname.

7. Manning Madison, "Redefining Controversy and Outness: Honest Queer Art Education in the South," *Visual Arts Research* 46, no. 1 (Summer 2020): 61–65; Mary Elliott, "Coming Out in the Classroom: A Return to the Hard Place," *College English* 56, no. 6 (October 1996): 693–708; Jeffrey Ringer, ed., *Queer Words, Queer Images: Communication and the Construction of Homosexuality* (New York: NYU Press, 1994); and others.

8. Costello, "On Teaching (Trans) Gender."

9. Larry Lavender, "Dialogical Practices in Teaching Choreography," *Dance Chronicle* 32, no. 3, (2009): 385. See also Jo Butterworth and Liesbeth Wildschut, "Processes of Making," in *Contemporary Choreography: A Critical Reader*, eds. Jo Butterworth and Liesbeth Wildschut (New York: Routledge, 2010), 85–88.

10. Jessica Zeller, "Pedagogy for the End Times: Ungrading and the Importance of Arson," *Jessica Zeller* (blog), August 16, 2020, https://www.jessicazeller.net/blog/pedagogy-for-end-times. See also Susan D. Blum, ed., *Ungrading: Why Rating Students Undermines Learning (and What to Do Instead)* (Morgantown: West Virginia University Press, 2020).

11. Julie Luft, "Design Your Own Rubric," *Science Scope* 20, no. 5 (February 1997): 25–27.

12. Lucy K. Spence, "Discerning Writing Assessment: Insights into an Analytical Rubric," *Language Arts* 87, no. 5 (May 2010): 337–52.

13. Spence, "Discerning Writing Assessment," 346.

14. Charles Ciorba and Neal Smith argue that students are best served by a combination of feedback types. "Measurement of Instrumental and Vocal Undergraduate Performance Juries Using a Multidimensional Assessment Rubric," *Journal of Research in Music Education* 57, no. 1 (April 2009): 5–15.

15. Harriet L. Schwartz, *Connected Teaching: Relationship, Power and Mattering in Higher Education* (Sterling, VA: Stylus, 2019), 62–63.

16. Zeller, "Pedagogy for the End Times."

17. Susie Nam, "Making Visible the Dead Bodies in the Room: Women of Color/QPOC in Academia," in *Presumed Incompetent II: Race, Class, Power, and Resistance of Women in Academia*, eds. Yolanda Flores Niemann, Gabriella Gutiérrez y Muhs, and Carmen G. Gonzáles (Louisville, CO: University of Colorado Press, 2020), 173.

. . . .

CHAPTER 7

REFLECT TO DEFLECT

Using Metacognitive Activities to Address Student Perceptions of Instructor Competence and Caring

. . . .

Melissa Eblen-Zayas

Starting a tenure-track position as a White woman in my late twenties, my mentors warned me that some students would doubt my competence as a physics professor because of my gender and age. The reality was driven home in my second year when I was teaching a required electricity and magnetism course and a student stopped by my office to ask a question about a topic we were covering in class that week. I happily engaged in a discussion with the student, and he left my office seemingly satisfied. But then I overheard the same student who had just left my office asking my senior male colleague next door the exact question he had just asked me. Thankfully, my senior colleague made an excellent move, and rather than responding to the student's question, he said, "You should really ask Professor Eblen-Zayas since she's the professor for your course." That moment cemented for me all the abstract warnings I had heard about the ways my authority, expertise, and competence would be doubted as someone who didn't "look like" a physicist.

That was not the first time students questioned my competency. After not doing as well as they had hoped on an exam, a few students grumbled that they would be getting better grades if they had a physics teacher who knew what she was doing. My internal reaction to those comments was empathy rather than frustration. College-level courses can be challenging, and many students struggle to find their academic footing. I thought about how I might address the two intertwined issues of student presumptions of my incompetence and student disappointment with how their approaches to the course were not leading to their desired success.

Research shows faculty who do not fit White male norms are held to different standards by students. Students judge Black faculty as less credible and less competent than White faculty, and challenge their intellectual authority.[1] Latinx and all women faculty also must navigate students' stereotyped expectations.[2] Younger-looking women faculty members, regardless of race, encounter challenges from students as a persistent problem and are more likely to face challenges when teaching topics considered to be male domains.[3] Gendered expectations around caring and kindness can also influence student perceptions of women faculty.[4]

When I was a struggling junior faculty member, the only research I was aware of was the work of Madeline Heilman and her colleagues showing that women in traditionally male-dominated fields suffer a double bind in terms of expectations.[5] If women working in a male-dominated field exhibit ambiguous performance, they are rated as likable as, but less competent than, men. If a woman's performance suggests clear competence, she is rated as less likable than her male counterparts. In a follow-up study, Heilman and Okimoto found that successful women in male-dominated fields could mitigate some negative reactions if they exhibited nurturing and communal traits.[6] This echoes research showing that students rated women professors more highly if they were friendly, but friendliness did not impact student ratings of male professors.[7]

I am naturally reserved, so I worried if I didn't adopt a warm and friendly affect to an extent that felt unnatural for me, students would view me as unlikable, incompetent, or both. Carbado and Gulati describe how women and Black, Indigenous, and People of Color (BIPOC) who are faculty members must "perform identity" to counteract stereotypes; identity performance, which involves a negotiation between one's own sense of self and the work environment, consumes time and effort.[8] As a new faculty member, I occasionally got advice encouraging me to focus on being friendly and outgoing. As an introvert, I simply could not sustainably perform the role of nurturing caregiver or energetic cheerleader to garner positive responses from students. What could I do that would demonstrate my deep caring for students and their success while also reinforcing my competence?

Metacognition in the Classroom

Rather than relying on perceptions of kindness based on performing identity, I choose to use pedagogical approaches that convey my care for students and their success while also reinforcing my competence as a physics educator. Metacognitive activities allow me to demonstrate that my

expertise extends beyond physics to the domains of teaching
and learning, and simultaneously signal that I care about
students. The strategies I use help students reflect on their
approaches to learning and deflect misplaced attributions
that their difficulties are due to having a professor who looks
less authoritative or competent.

The past two decades have seen a growing interest
in helping students develop metacognitive knowledge.[9]
Metacognitive knowledge relevant for teaching and learning takes three forms: strategic knowledge, knowledge of
cognitive tasks, and self-knowledge.[10] Strategic knowledge
consists of strategies for learning and problem-solving that
are relevant across domains. Cognitive task knowledge includes an understanding that different tasks may require
different strategies or cognitive tools and that some tasks
will be more difficult than others. Finally, self-knowledge is
having an accurate awareness of one's strengths and weaknesses; it also includes one's ability to effectively set goals
for completing a task and being aware of how to manage
one's motivation. Exploring undergraduates' approaches
to academic challenges and failures in STEM, Henry et
al. found students' goal orientations and "fear of failure"
dispositions shape students' attributions for academic challenges.[11] Some students cope with challenges by looking for
external attributions for their difficulties. One maladaptive
coping strategy is opposition, where students external-
ize their negative emotions around academic challenges
through behaviors directed toward others.[12]

Although metacognition is often framed in terms of
student success, incorporating metacognitive activities in
my classroom has benefited me as an instructor by reducing student opposition. Encouraging students to reflect
on their approaches to studying and engaging with course

material leads students to take responsibility as partners in the teaching and learning endeavor and challenges the presumption that the instructor is solely responsible for how well students learn. When I started adding metacognitive activities to my instructional tool kit, I worried about how students would respond. By intentionally talking with students about the reasons for choosing these activities, including providing references to the primary literature and discussing the benefits for students, I have not faced significant pushback, and students express appreciation for these activities. The positive student response is consistent with research on active learning that shows using thoughtful explanation and facilitation strategies can reduce student resistance.[13]

Introductory physics is where students most often question my competence. Many first-year students enrolling in introductory physics do so because they are considering a physics major. For some of these students, their interest in physics is built, at least in part, on the success that they experienced in high school physics, and they are frustrated when they cannot breeze through their first college physics course. To help students develop strategies to become reflective and successful physics practitioners, I aim to create a classroom environment that encourages the development of all three metacognitive knowledge domains.

In-Class and Homework Activities to Support Metacognition

I use class time to foster strategic and cognitive task knowledge by emphasizing the process and documentation of approaches to solving problems and how to make choices about when to use various approaches. To do this, I either ask students to come to class with drafts of an attempted problem-solving effort or provide time during class for small-group, problem-solving efforts; then I provide opportunities for students to talk with each other and explain the principles that guided their choices in their problem-solving. Such self-explanation helps learners connect general principles with specific examples, monitor comprehension, and modify their understanding.[14] Comparing different approaches to solving the same problem launches a discussion about why particular strategies work more effectively in some contexts than others. Rather than starting discussions by asking students to compare answers, I foreground the various approaches to working toward an answer.

My efforts to reduce student focus on answers are not always successful; therefore, I also work to create a positive error climate in my classroom. Steuer, Rosentritt-Brunn, and Dresel define a favorable error climate as one in which errors are perceived and used as integral to the learning process within the social context of the classroom.[15] Self-explanation and discussion of problem-solving approaches support the analysis of errors and using errors to initiate learning, two factors that contribute to a positive error climate.[16] One benefit of creating a positive classroom error climate is that it reduces the frequency of students searching for "gotcha" moments to highlight my mistakes. Thus, I feel less pressure to avoid making errors. I should note that BIPOC faculty who face additional scrutiny from students may not experience the same benefit.

Within the strategic knowledge domain, I introduce students to retrieval practice: the concept that actively trying to retrieve knowledge or perform a skill from memory is a more effective way to learn and retain information than passively reviewing examples.[17] I suggest that students make a first attempt at homework problems without using or referencing outside resources, including the textbook, their notes, or websites. Encouraging students to try to apply new skills without consulting examples from class or before searching the internet for a similar problem helps students develop the ability to identify and use relevant concepts. In addition to promoting retrieval, this approach provides students with a way to monitor their understanding. Helping students cultivate study strategies that are relevant to the course context is important because STEM students often use low-impact study strategies.[18]

To promote self-knowledge, I use homework wrappers, which include several reflective questions that students must respond to and submit when they submit their homework. Tanner provides an extensive list of questions that instructors can include as part of assignments or exams to foster student metacognition.[19] My homework wrappers include questions such as "How much time did you spend on the problem set, and what was the environment in which you worked? How did you start approaching the problems? When you got stuck, who or what did you turn to for help? Which problems did you find easy and which did you find challenging?"

Although the questions are designed to foster student self-knowledge, I also appreciate the insights that the responses provide me as an instructor. For example, the first question allows me to learn which students work alone, which students collaborate, and whether students work in front of a computer in their dorm room, in an academic study space with peer support nearby, or elsewhere.

The wrapper responses can become the basis for in-class discussions about how long various students spent on homework and what resources they used for help, as well as providing some suggestions about studying and working practice problems. By asking for individual submissions, but responding via a collective conversation, I save myself time by not needing to respond to each students' submission. However, I can invite individuals to my office if I see responses that merit additional conversation.

Quiz and Exam Activities That Support Metacognition

As a junior faculty member, I regularly found myself on the defensive after quizzes and exams. A few students were always ready to argue about the grades they had earned or make pointed comments about my instructional incompetence after a disappointing result. Exam wrappers helped me reduce the frequency of these problematic responses by encouraging student reflection and providing some distance between receiving their results and talking with me.[20]

My quiz/exam wrappers ask students to do three things: identify how they prepared, revisit problems on which they did not receive full credit and try to make sense of what happened (a flaw in their conceptual understanding, failure to adequately detail their problem-solving approach, a mathematical error, a shortage of time), and determine what they will maintain and what they will change when studying for the next quiz or exam. After students have completed the wrapper, I welcome students to come talk with me. Before we review problems where the student struggled, we discuss when they started studying, whether they focused on rereading notes/texts or attempting problems, and the environment in which they studied. Exam wrappers change the conversation from adversarial to collaborative by allowing me to establish that teaching and learning are a partnership. I am prepared to support students, but they also have a role in planning their engagement.

While exam wrappers and individual follow-up conversations are effective at my small institution, this strategy has limited transferability to large courses. Louisiana State University's Saundra McGuire has developed successful in-class interventions for large introductory courses to help students develop metacognitive learning strategies.[21] After students have information about the demands of the course and have gotten back their first exam, she suggests devoting an entire class period to administering a learning strategies survey and introducing metacognition and the study cycle. Then throughout the course, students are consistently reminded to monitor their learning strategies. These interventions improve student performance on subsequent exams, and student comments suggest that they recognize that the strategies introduced have helped them become more effective learners.

Offering students the opportunity to make quiz corrections is another way to foster metacognition and diffuse tension. I employ quiz corrections on an as-needed basis, but BIPOC faculty, or others who face persistent challenges from students, may want to formally build assessment corrections into their courses. As Henderson and Harper argue, assessment corrections reinforce the formative nature of assessment and provide an opportunity for students to get feedback and respond to it, helping students develop metacognitive skills and also provide this added benefit:

Many instructors have doubtlessly experienced the "mob" mentality that can take over a class when an exam on which they performed poorly is returned. We find that these types of incidents are almost completely eliminated when assessment corrections are implemented, making the testing experience less stressful for both the students and instructors![22]

Combining quiz corrections with retrieval practice, by only allowing students to use notes and textbooks but not providing solutions to students, leads students to struggle more on the quiz corrections, but they are more likely to be successful on equivalent problems later.[23]

Metacognition in Online Classes

In the primarily asynchronous online courses I have taught, incorporating metacognitive activities helped me identify student progress, or lack thereof, and support them appropriately. The same principles that guide my choices in my face-to-face courses guide my choice of online activities, although the extent to which they need to be redesigned for the online environment varies. For example, engaging in discussions about problem-solving strategies can be challenging via videoconference because sketches, graphs, and equations are hard to communicate in real time without the appropriate online collaboration tools. Rather than focusing on synchronous engagement, I invite students to record a video where they show a photo of the problem that they have tried to solve and talk through the approach. Then I can ask students to compare the approaches of two or three other students and write a summary comparing strengths, weaknesses, and ease of understanding various approaches. Although different from what happens in the physical classroom, it achieves many of the same goals.

Homework and exam wrappers are actually easier to employ in online courses than in face-to-face courses because the conditional release of content in the learning management system allows me to require completion of the wrapper before students can see solutions to homework or quizzes. Another way to improve students' metacognitive self-knowledge in online environments is to ask students to predict their performance on an online homework or quiz activity before they start, and then to provide students with immediate feedback about how accurate their prediction was after they have completed the activity. If this exercise is regularly included (e.g., on a weekly basis), students in the bottom quartile of the class become less likely to dramatically overpredict their performance.[24]

But not everything translates well into an online learning environment. Encouraging retrieval practice is difficult when students are not in a classroom and have easy access to online resources. I have focused on encouraging students to practice self-regulation, and I explicitly talk with students about developing the ability to monitor their work environment and remove digital distractions, for example, by turning off wireless connections or going to the library without one's devices.[25]

Conclusion

When I started incorporating metacognitive activities into my courses, I did so with some trepidation. After all, I'm a physicist. Shouldn't I focus my time and effort on the physics content? But organizing course activities to increase students' knowledge about learning itself benefits both the students and me. Students are better able to regulate their studying approaches and monitor their learning, and thus they become more successful in my courses. The metacognitive activities also allow me to demonstrate to students that my expertise is not limited to physics; I also have expertise in the domains of learning and teaching. Additionally, incorporating metacognitive activities in my courses helps me navigate the double bind that women in traditionally male-dominated fields face—namely, that one cannot be both competent and likable unless one specifically demonstrates a nurturing demeanor. These activities allow me to show my caring for and commitment to student success without having to perform identity in a manner that feels unnatural to me.

Teaching Takeaways

- Instructors who because of their embodied identities must navigate the double bind that they can either be viewed as competent or caring, but not both, may want to incorporate metacognitive activities as one approach to demonstrate caring for student success while reinforcing their expertise in the domain of teaching and learning.
- Including self-explanation and discussion of problem-solving as a primary activity within the classroom provides opportunities to analyze errors and identify what students can learn from approaches that

do not lead to correct answers. This increases student metacognitive knowledge and contributes to a positive error climate in the classroom.

- Homework wrappers, exam wrappers, and assessment corrections can help students develop metacognitive skills and diffuse oppositional responses to instructors.

....

MELISSA EBLEN-ZAYAS is a professor of physics at Carleton College in Northfield, Minnesota, and she previously served as director of the Perlman Center for Learning and Teaching at Carleton. She is an experimental condensed matter physicist who studies correlated electron materials. Additionally, she is engaged in the scholarship of teaching and learning around advanced laboratory instruction and technology-enhanced teaching, with a focus on making STEM classrooms more welcoming for students from diverse backgrounds.

Notes

1. Katherine Grace Hendrix, "Student Perceptions of the Influence of Race on Professor Credibility," *Journal of Black Studies* 28, no. 6 (1998): 738–63; Arnold K. Ho, Lotte Thomsen, and Jim Sidanius, "Perceived Academic Competence and Overall Job Evaluations: Students' Evaluations of African American and European American Professors," *Journal of Applied Social Psychology* 39, no. 2 (2009): 389–406; Roxanna Harlow, " 'Race doesn't matter, but . . .': The Effect of Race on Professors' Experiences and Emotion Management in the Undergraduate College Classroom, *Social Psychology Quarterly* 66, no. 4 (2003): 348–63.

2.	Kristin J. Anderson and Gabriel Smith, "Students' Preconceptions of Professors: Benefits and Barriers according to Ethnicity and Gender," *Hispanic Journal of Behavioral Sciences* 27, no. 2 (2005): 184–201; Kristin J. Anderson, "Students' Stereotypes of Professors: An Exploration of the Double Violations of Ethnicity and Gender," *Social Psychology of Education* 13, no. 4 (2010): 459–72; Jack Glascock and Thomas E. Ruggiero, "The Relationship of Ethnicity and Sex to Professor Credibility at a Culturally Diverse University," *Communication Education* 55, no. 2 (2006): 197–207.

3.	Valerie Ann Moore, "Inappropriate Challenges to Professorial Authority," *Teaching Sociology* 24, no. 2 (1996): 202–6.

4.	Christine M. Bachen, Moira M. McLoughlin, and Sara S. Garcia, "Assessing the Role of Gender in College Students' Evaluations of Gender," *Communication Education* 48, no. 3 (1999): 193–210; Alison Burke, B. A. Whitney Head-Burgess, and Mark Siders, "He's Smart and She's Nice: Student Perceptions of Male and Female Faculty," *International Journal of Gender and Women's Studies* 5, no. 1 (2017): 1–6.

5.	Madeline E. Heilman et al., "Penalties for Success: Reactions to Women Who Succeed at Male Gender-Typed Tasks," *Journal of Applied Psychology* 89, no. 3 (2004): 416–27.

6.	Madeline E. Heilman and Tyler G. Okimoto, "Why Are Women Penalized for Success at Male Tasks? The Implied Communality Deficit," *Journal of Applied Psychology* 92, no. 1 (2007): 81–92.

7.	Diane Kierstead, Patti D'Agostino, and Heidi Dill, "Sex Role Stereotyping of College Professors: Bias in Students' Ratings of Instructors," *Journal of Educational Psychology* 80, no. 3 (1988): 342–44.

8.	Devon W. Carbado and Mitu Gulati, "Working Identity," *Cornell Law Review* 85 (2000): 1264–65, 1279.

9.	David R. Krathwohl, "A Revision of Bloom's Taxonomy: An Overview," *Theory into Practice* 41, no. 4 (2002): 212–18; Paul R.

Pintrich, "The Role of Metacognitive Knowledge in Learning, Teaching, and Assessing," *Theory into Practice* 41, no. 4 (2002): 219–25; Gregory Schraw, Kent J. Crippen, and Kendall Hartley, "Promoting Self-Regulation in Science Education: Metacognition as Part of a Broader Perspective on Learning," *Research in Science Education* 36, no. 1 (2006): 111–39; Kimberly Tanner, "Promoting Student Metacognition," *CBE—Life Sciences Education* 11, no. 2 (2010): 113–20.

10. Pintrich, "The Role of Metacognitive Knowledge," 220.

11. Meredith A. Henry et al., "FAIL Is Not a Four-Letter Word: A Theoretical Framework for Exploring Undergraduate Students' Approaches to Academic Challenges and Responses to Failure in STEM Learning Environments," *CBE—Life Sciences Education* 18, no 1 (2019): 11.

12. Henry, "FAIL Is Not a Four-Letter Word," 10.

13. Cynthia J. Finelli et al., "Reducing Student Resistance to Active Learning: Strategies for Instructors," *Journal of College Science Teaching* 47, no. 5 (2018): 80–91.

14. James M. Lang, *Small Teaching: Everyday Lessons from the Science of Learning*, 1st ed. (San Francisco: John Wiley and Sons, 2016), 137–59.

15. Gabriele Steuer, Gisela Rosentritt-Brunn, and Markus Dresel, "Dealing with Errors in Mathematics Classrooms: Structure and Relevance of Perceived Error Climate," *Contemporary Educational Psychology* 38, no. 3 (2013): 198.

16. Gabriele Steuer and Markus Dresel, "A Constructive Error Climate as an Element of Effective Learning Environments," *Psychological Test and Assessment Modeling* 57, no. 2 (2015): 262–75.

17. Jeffrey D. Karpicke, Andrew C. Butler, and Henry L. Roediger III, "Metacognitive Strategies in Student Learning: Do Students Practise Retrieval When They Study on Their Own?" *Memory* 17, no. 4 (2009): 471–79; Lang, *Small Teaching*, 19–40; Tianlong Zu,

Jeremy Munsell, and N. Sanjay Rebello, "Comparing Retrieval-Based Practice and Peer Instruction in Physics Learning," *Physical Review Physics Education Research* 15, no. 1 (2019): 010105.

18. Matthew T. Hora and Amanda K. Oleson, "Examining Study Habits in Undergraduate STEM Courses from a Situative Perspective," *International Journal of STEM Education* 4, no. 1 (2017): 1–19.

19. Tanner, "Promoting Student Metacognition," 115.

20. Marsha C. Lovett, "Make Exams Worth More Than the Grade: Using Exam Wrappers to Promote Metacognition," in *Using Reflection and Metacognition to Improve Student Learning: Across the Disciplines, Across the Academy*, ed. Mathew Kaplan et al. (Sterling, VA: Stylus, 2013), 18–52.

21. Saundra Yancy McGuire, *Teach Students How to Learn: Strategies You Can Incorporate into Any Course to Improve Student Metacognition, Study Skills, and Motivation* (Sterling, VA: Stylus, 2015); Ningfeng Zhao, "Metacognition: An Effective Tool to Promote Success in College Science Learning," *Journal of College Science Teaching* 43, no. 4 (2014): 48–54.

22. Charles Henderson and Kathleen A. Harper, "Quiz Corrections: Improving Learning by Encouraging Students to Reflect on Their Mistakes," *Physics Teacher* 47, no. 9 (2009): 585.

23. Andrew Mason et al., "Learning from Mistakes: The Effect of Students' Written Self-Diagnosis on Subsequent Problem Solving," *Physics Teacher* 54, no. 2 (2016): 87–90.

24. Brock L. Casselman and Charles H. Atwood. "Improving General Chemistry Course Performance through Online Homework-Based Metacognitive Training," *Journal of Chemical Education* 94, no. 12 (2017): 1811–21.

25. Hora and Oleson, "Examining Study Habits in Undergraduate STEM Courses from a Situative Perspective," 16.

. . . .

CHAPTER 8

FROM ABSENTMINDED PROFESSOR TO EPISTEMIC COLLABORATOR

Reframing Academic Expertise through Vulnerability and Metacognition

. . . .

Rebecca Scott

One way to frame the problems faced by faculty whose identities do not cohere with the stereotype of what a professor is "supposed" to look like is through the lens of what philosophers call epistemic injustice. In this chapter, I consider the challenge of "not looking like a professor" through this lens and argue that to address epistemic injustice in the classroom, it is not enough to diversify the professoriate. Instead, we need strategies that aim to more radically restructure our very conception of academic expertise so that we can better recognize how knowledge is constructed and maintained in community. That is, rather than viewing academic experts as individual possessors and creators of knowledge, I argue that we need to think of academic expertise as grounded in collaboration and community. This shift in our understanding of academic expertise results in a transformation in how we create community and embody authority in the classroom. To concretize this change, I end the chapter by offering two strategies for accomplishing this goal: first, we can acknowledge and model epistemic vulnerability ourselves, and second, we can encourage students to engage in metacognitive reflection on the epistemic dynamics of the classroom community.

Epistemic Injustice and the Social Imaginary

Epistemic injustice, as defined by philosophers, is a particular form of injustice involving our relationships with one another as *knowers*, as people who construct, revise, and share knowledge. Epistemic injustice occurs when these epistemic relations are constituted such that certain people are systematically mistreated or disadvantaged with regard to their participation in the construction and sharing of knowledge. One prominent form of epistemic injustice is testimonial injustice—when someone is given too little or too much credibility in a testimonial exchange.[1] In the context of the classroom, marginalized faculty often face this form of injustice. They may not be trusted as experts in their field by students, colleagues, and coworkers, while others who are recognized as fitting the cultural norm are trusted too much. These credibility gaps can lead to a number of concrete problems for faculty. They may end up spending time and mental/emotional bandwidth trying to *prove* that they really are experts in their fields in ways that are not always helpful for students or for their own well-being. Students may also perceive that they are learning less, which may end up becoming a self-fulfilling prophecy as students disengage from the learning experience. Marginalized faculty may also understandably double down on rules and procedures to shore up their credibility, leading to oppositional relationships that can be harmful to the learning environment.

In his work on epistemic injustice, the philosopher José Medina traces many of the problems of testimonial injustice to our social imagination. He argues that credibility excesses and deficits arise out of who we imagine when we think of who is and is not credible.[2] Medina's framework suggests that to address credibility gaps some professors face, we need a transformation in our imagining of who and what a "professor" is or can be.

This transformation, it seems to me, can take at least two forms, one of which is more radical and, ultimately, more helpful, than the other. The first is to transform our image of a "professor" so that the concept of "professor" is more diverse. That is, we could expand our social imagination in such a way that we keep the idea of a "professor" relatively intact but increase the different kinds of bodies and social identities that we associate with professors. This approach would involve focusing primarily on representation. It would involve helping students to see that all different kinds of people can be "professors" in the way that we currently understand professors to be.

But another approach would be to change our very idea of what a "professor" is or should be. The problem, in my view, is not only that we imagine a "professor" to be a White, cisgender, able-bodied, older man but also that these social markers are intertwined with a problematic kind of epistemic authority, one in which knowledge is produced, held, and maintained by individuals. To fully address the problem of not "looking like a professor," we, therefore, need to change what being a "professor" means in the first place.

This transformation cannot take place overnight or in a single classroom. Nevertheless, I believe that we can make progress in our own classrooms by modeling and encouraging a different kind of epistemic authority. Rather than shoring up our authority by attempting to present ourselves in the mold of the traditional professor who is an invulnerable, individual possessor of knowledge, I argue instead for a pedagogy in which we acknowledge and embrace our vulnerability and encourage and support our students in doing the same.

The "Professor" in the Social Imaginary

While not a perfect proxy for our social imagination, a Google image search can provide a clue into our collective cultural imagination. A search for the word "professor" reveals a cadre of mostly male-presenting, mostly White people, almost all standing in front of a chalkboard often filled with obscure equations. The professor, in short, *professes*. He is the possessor of complex and difficult-to-understand knowledge that he offers to students who passively absorb his wisdom. If we think about the archetype of the professor in the media, we see that the "professor" is also often seen as quirky and absentminded due to his all-consuming focus on his research. Furthermore, his genius often appears incompatible with social and emotional expertise, and so his inability to relate to or understand other people is seen as a mark of his eminence.

This image of the "brilliant," absentminded professor

reveals assumptions we collectively hold about how knowledge is shared, constructed, and maintained. On this stereotypical account of epistemic expertise, it is the absentminded genius who advances our knowledge through a single-minded focus on his research. And this research is *his*. He is considered solely responsible for and largely maintains ownership over the knowledge his work produces. While we know that, particularly in STEM fields, people often work collaboratively, our image of the genius working in isolation stubbornly persists.

When we think of knowledge in this way as a kind of private property earned by the hard work of the individual thinker, the sharing of knowledge is conceived of as unidirectional, with the researcher-professor generously sharing his hard-won insights with the rest of us. Similarly, in the classroom, the professor may share his knowledge with students, but the work of knowledge *production* is thought to take place outside of and separate from the learning environment. Within the classroom, the professor's role is not to be a co-learner but to be the dispenser of knowledge that has already been produced, while students are the mostly passive recipients of this generosity.[3]

Some might argue that the previously described caricature of the professor persists in our collective imagination, but this is an outdated portrait that no longer describes the reality of how most students engage in the classroom. The traditional "banking model" of education as Paolo Freire termed it, wherein knowledge is simply transferred from teacher to student, has long been criticized by scholars of teaching and learning.[4] And faculty are increasingly adopting active and collaborative learning in their classrooms. But while these more constructivist approaches to learning may be more effective for achieving certain outcomes, they do not *necessarily* challenge our traditional assumptions about academic expertise.

Even in collaborative learning, the focus on the individual as the site of knowledge does not entirely disappear. Students may help one another to learn, but the dominant models of teaching and learning continue to focus on *individual* student learning outcomes. Students, at the end of the day, are assessed at the individual level, and in the classic backward design model of learning, the goal of teaching is for *each* student to be able to do or know particular things. Learning outcomes and assessments, as they are typically construed, rarely or never focus on what *we* as an epistemic community will be able to do or know or what professors might learn from their students. For example, in Fink's taxonomy of significant learning outcomes, outlined in his influential work on integrated course design, the outcomes are defined in terms of individual accomplishments. The category of the "human dimension" involves learning about oneself and about others, and his account of "caring" involves developing new feelings, interests, and values. But all of these experiences involve outcomes that refer to the individual, not to the community of learners as a whole.[5]

In their work, *Teaching Crowds*, Dron and Anderson helpfully describe how this focus on the individual is maintained in constructivism:

> In cognitivist-constructivist approaches, learning is seen as a process of construction, building models, and connecting old knowledge with new. Every individual constructs a view of the world for him- or herself. . . . [T]hough epistemologically more advanced, the emphasis of such approaches is very much on the learner as an autonomous agent, learning

alone. Although the learner may learn from others, learning itself is seen as something internal to the individual.[6]

While they may do otherwise, there is a danger that even active and collaborative learning models could simply reinscribe the idea that knowledge is produced and possessed by individual efforts.

To truly address the problem that some faculty are thought to not "look like" professors, I, therefore, propose that we need, as Paulo Freire argues, a more radical transformation of our understanding of what knowledge is and how it is produced and maintained, "a pedagogy . . . forged *with,* not *for.*"[7] Both in the dominant social imaginary in which the professor is a (White, male, cisgendered) genius researcher and in many of the countercurrents that push against that traditional model, the same epistemic presuppositions persist. That is, the roles of students as learners and professors as teachers remain relatively fixed, and knowledge is seen as being produced and possessed by individuals.

Reimagining Expertise as Vulnerability: Concrete Strategies for the Classroom

In rethinking epistemic expertise, we need not eliminate entirely the role that professors have as experts. Professors and students play different roles in the classroom, and these differences are important. But our current imagined conception of the "professor" is harmful to the epistemic community of a classroom. When the "professor" is the one who *has* all the knowledge and skills and students are the ones who *lack* this knowledge and these skills, the professor's role in the epistemic community is one in which any transformation that occurs happens *within* and *to* students. Professors can remain at a distance from the learning that happens in the classroom, remaining unchanged by the learning process.

As an alternative, I suggest we conceive of professors not as the ones who create change in *others* without themselves being transformed but instead as epistemic agents within the learning communities of which they are a part. If we understand professorial expertise in this way, professors are not quirky, self-made geniuses but expert *collaborators* and *organizers* who have developed capacities for pursuing, interpreting, and building knowledge with others to create vibrant and just epistemic communities. Such an epistemic community is one in which the members of the community support one another in taking responsibility for individual and collective knowledge and ways of knowing. The goal is not for individuals to gain as much knowledge as possible but for all members of the community to help improve the conditions that allow us to produce and maintain a just epistemic community. The role of the professor in this account is not merely to provide knowledge to others who lack it but also to help create the conditions for this community—of which the professor is a part—to develop and thrive.[8] Of course, the professor also has disciplinary expertise, but if we transform how we conceive of the professor's role from one who only or primarily is someone who knows a lot into someone who has developed capacities that help to foster and maintain positive epistemic communities, we can work toward creating more just and responsible epistemic communities.

So what might this look like in practice? First, we can model epistemic vulnerability by being more transparent about our own and others' learning processes.[9] For example,

Stephen Bloch-Schulman, a professor of philosophy at Elon University with whom I have co-taught and co-facilitated many classes and workshops, often has students take time to read and discuss the acknowledgments section of the works that he assigns. This assignment helps students see that everyone requires feedback and support from others. Another strategy is to share with students drafts of our own work to show how many revisions our writing undergoes before arriving at a final product. Or we might talk with students about our own experience with getting feedback, perhaps even from the dreaded "Reviewer 2." In my own classes, I often share with students a story about how I had to start over on my dissertation proposal after receiving devastating feedback from my advisor. I talk to them about how difficult this experience was for me and how I recognize that getting critical feedback can be challenging.

Second, we can encourage metacognition about epistemic responsibility in the classroom.[10] We can do this, for example, by creating assignments that invite students to reflect on how and why they have changed their minds or their thinking about a topic. And to show that this work happens in community, we can invite students to reflect on how others in the class have helped them to come to know and understand something new or given them a new perspective. For example, Bloch-Schulman often has students write letters to each other in which they acknowledge and express gratitude for specific ways that their classmates have helped them to learn.

Another way that I have encouraged this kind of metacognition in my own classes is by framing contributions to class discussions in terms of conversation "moves."[11] Students work together to generate a list of the different kinds of "moves" that we make in academic conversations.

For example, someone might agree or disagree and give a reason, propose a hypothetical scenario, connect a reading to their own experience, ask someone for more evidence for a claim, try to restate what someone else has said, and so on. This list can continue to grow throughout a term as new moves are made in class discussions or encountered in texts. A number of activities can be designed around this list. For instance, we can ask students to try to make particular moves or to identify the moves made by others. And we can discuss what kinds of moves are most or least helpful, which tend to occur more or less often, and so on. The moves provide a framework to think about class discussions in a new way that encourages students to think about how their ideas develop within the epistemic community of the classroom, a community that is dynamic and that requires our explicit attention.

Alison Bailey describes a similar strategy in her work on combating privilege-preserving discourse in her classes that focus on race and gender.[12] Bailey suggests that we ask students to list possible responses to a text and evaluate them in terms of their discursive functions. Students ask not whether a response is right or wrong but rather what it *does* to the conversation. Does the response help us to see a problem in a new way? Or does it distract? Or does it allow certain people to distance themselves from the problem, thereby preserving their privilege? Students practice recognizing the ways in which epistemic forces shape the conversations that take place in the classroom.

Matt Whitt, in his work on student distancing strategies in conversations about race, similarly argues for metacognitive strategies in which students are encouraged to take greater responsibility for their knowledge and the ways they come to know.[13] For example, Whitt suggests that we engage in metadialogues in our classes focused on increasing epistemic self-awareness and responsibility. We might, for example, ask students to reflect on *why* they made a particular contribution to a discussion. Or, to help students reflect on their own epistemic practices, he suggests we might ask students *how* they came to know what they know about a particular topic. In these ways, we can shift the focus from knowledge as something possessed to knowledge as something that we all have a responsibility to construct and maintain together.

There are many ways one might approach this problem, but the core strategies that I am advocating for here are aimed at transforming our understanding of expertise by explicitly attending to the ways in which knowledge is produced and maintained in community with others. These strategies are not limited to the face-to-face classroom but could be implemented in any community of learners.[14] The key is to ameliorate epistemic injustice in the classroom by helping students see the value and importance of epistemic vulnerability and metacognitive reflection on the dynamics of epistemic communities. In this way, we can all come to take greater responsibility for the epistemic communities of which we are a part both in and outside the classroom.

Conclusion

To address the problem that marginalized faculty are given too little credibility in the classroom, I have suggested that we should take what may be a counterintuitive approach. Rather than focusing on showing that marginalized faculty members also deserve credibility in the traditional sense, I have argued here that we should work to transform our conception of credibility itself. This strategy is not without risk in that it asks that we not avoid being vulnerable but instead double down on our own vulnerability. But, in fact, to be human is to be vulnerable, and in reality, as Judith Butler notes, we do not have a choice about whether to be vulnerable. We only have a choice about how we deal with our inevitable vulnerability.[15] Acknowledging and encouraging vulnerability and attending more specifically and deliberately to the epistemic dynamics in our classes can allow for a more radical restructuring of how we understand knowledge to be produced, shared, and maintained that goes beyond increasing the *kinds* of people we imagine to be professors.

It is important to note that the solution I have proposed is not in itself sufficient to solve the short-term problem of epistemic and testimonial injustice in the classroom. That is, these strategies may not end with the complete elimination of the credibility gap. But we also have to acknowledge that we do not have the power to end racism, sexism, ableism, and transphobia on our own. These systems and forces will inevitably show up in our classes because our classes are part of the world. And believing that we can fix these problems as teachers is in itself indicative of the very idea that tough problems are solved by individuals with ingenious solutions. Or in other words, to think that we can, on our own, "fix" the problem by employing the right pedagogical strategies might even serve to perpetuate the problem and increase the burden marginalized faculty may feel. Therefore, it is necessary to recognize that the problem marginalized faculty face is not a problem solved all at once by individuals. It is a collective and systemic problem that requires collective and systemic solutions. Yet we must act as individuals. By focusing on the epistemic communities of our classrooms, perhaps we can begin to chip away at the socially imagined "professor" and begin the work of constructing an alternative vision of expertise and of what it means to live together in a responsible and just epistemic community.

Teaching Takeaways

- Knowledge is constructed and maintained in communities not by individuals.
- Modeling epistemic vulnerability can offer students a new way of understanding knowledge and expertise as co-constructed.
- Encouraging metacognition about the relational dynamics of the classroom community can foster greater epistemic responsibility and more just epistemic communities.

REBECCA SCOTT is an assistant professor of philosophy at Harper College. She received her PhD from Loyola University Chicago with a dissertation on the concept of teaching in the work of French phenomenologist Emmanuel Levinas. Her current research focuses on inclusive pedagogies and the use of play and creativity in the classroom.

Notes

1. The literature on epistemic and testimonial injustice is vast. See, for example, José Medina, *The Epistemology of Resistance: Gender and Racial Oppression, Epistemic Injustice, and the Social*

Imagination (United Kingdom: Oxford University Press, 2013); Miranda Fricker, *Epistemic Injustice: Power and the Ethics of Knowing* (United Kingdom: Oxford University Press, 2007); Kristie Dotson, "Tracking Epistemic Violence, Tracking Practices of Silencing," *Hypatia* 26, no. 2 (2011): 236–57; Jeremy Wanderer, "Varieties of Testimonial Injustice," in *The Routledge Handbook of Epistemic Injustice*, eds. Ian James Kidd, José Medina, and Gayle Pohlhaus (London: Routledge, 2017), 13–26.

2. See Medina's analysis of Miranda Fricker's analysis of *To Kill a Mockingbird* in *The Epistemology of Resistance*, 57–70.

3. Despite the popularity of active learning models, lecture remains the predominant mode of instruction in many classrooms. For evidence of this trend in STEM classes, see Marilyne Stains et al., "Anatomy of STEM Teaching in North American Universities," *Science* 359, no. 6383 (2018): 1468–70.

4. Paulo Friere, *Pedagogy of the Oppressed*, trans. Myra Bergman Ramos (New York: Continuum, 1970), 71–86.

5. Dee L. Fink, *Creating Significant Learning Experiences: An Integrated Approach to Designing College Courses* (New York: John Wiley and Sons, 2013), 35.

6. John Dron and Terry Anderson, *Teaching Crowds: Learning and Social Media* (Edmonton, Canada: Athabasca University Press, 2014), 39.

7. Freire, *Pedagogy of the Oppressed*, 48.

8. For more on the role of community in learning, see Albert Bandura's influential work, *Social Learning Theory* (New York: Prentice-Hall, 1977). For more recent scholarship, see Joshua R. Eyler, *How Humans Learn: The Science and Stories behind Effective College Teaching* (Morgantown: West Virginia University Press, 2018).

9. The literature on effective feedback bears out the importance of focusing on process over product. See, for example, Ronald

Lunsford, "When Less Is More: Principles for Responding in the Disciplines," *New Directions for Teaching and Learning* 69 (March 1997): 91–104; David J. Nicol and Debra Macfarlane-Dick, "Formative Assessment and Self-Regulated Learning: A Model and Seven Principles of Good Feedback Practice," *Studies in Higher Education* 31, no. 2 (April 2006): 199–218; D. Royce Sadler, "Formative Assessment and the Design of Instructional Systems," *Instructional Science* 18, no. 2 (June 1989): 19–144.

10. John Perry, David Lundie, and Gill Golder, "Metacognition in Schools: What Does the Literature Suggest about the Effectiveness of Teaching Metacognition in Schools?" *Educational Review* 71, no. 4 (July 2019): 483–500. See also John D. Bransford, Ann L. Brown, and Rodney R. Cocking, *How People Learn* (Washington, DC: National Academy Press, 2000).

11. I am indebted to Ann Cahill who originally developed the idea of creating discussion move cards for students to "play" in class discussions. In addition, Claire Lockard, Ann Cahill, and I worked together to further develop this idea for the American Philosophical Association, Teaching Hub Poster Session at the 2020 Central Division Meeting, "Using Metacognition to Improve Classroom Discussions."

12. Alison Bailey, "Tracking Privilege-Preserving Epistemic Pushback in Feminist and Critical Race Philosophy Classes," *Hypatia* 4 (Fall 2017): 876–92.

13. Matt Whitt, "Other People's Problems: Student Distancing, Epistemic Responsibility, and Injustice," *Studies in Philosophy and Education* 35 (2016): 427–44.

14. For example, the metacognitive exercises described here could easily work as reflections on discussion forums. And modeling vulnerability as an instructor may be even more important in an online setting in which establishing presence and humanity as an instructor is crucial for establishing relationships with students.

15. Judith Butler, "Violence, Mourning, Politics," *Studies in Gender and Sexuality* 4, no. 1 (2003): 9–37. For more on vulnerability in the classroom, see Jeanine Weekes Schroer, "Fighting Imperviousness with Vulnerability: Teaching in a Climate of Conservatism," *Teaching Philosophy* 30, no. 2 (2007): 185–200.

. . . .

CHAPTER 9

BLACK MAN IN A STRANGE LAND

Using Principles of Psychology and Behavior Science to Thrive in the Classroom

. . . .

Erik Simmons

My grandparents grew up poor in a segregated United States of America. Raised by teenage parents in New York and Philadelphia in the 1960s and 1970s, as Black Americans, my mother and father had to climb a mountain with one hand tied behind their backs. But they defied a narrative of systemic oppression that stymies upward mobility to this day. They were the first in their families to earn college degrees. They rebelled against what they were told they could be and instead reached for something greater through education. My grandparents, who never finished high school, were speechless when I earned a doctorate degree—the first in our family. They are thrilled that I teach at a prestigious institution in Australia. Institutions that they always believed were out of reach for people like us. This is my legacy as a Black American man. It makes the act of teaching a precious experience. It fuels my passion for connecting with students and facilitating learning, shaping my pedagogical approach.

In this chapter, I discuss that approach, focusing on how positive humanistic psychology provides a lens to appreciate student circumstances and tools for building psychologically safe spaces. I show how teachers can embody tenets of social identity leadership to create an atmosphere of inclusion and collective growth in the classroom, and I provide practical teaching strategies informed by evidence and derived from behavioral science literature. These strategies encourage desirable behaviors to enable us to connect with students and to help instructors, as well as students, thrive.

A Humanistic Approach

Growing up Black in America is far different from growing up White in Australia, so every semester, I stand in front of a classroom of young adults who look different than I do. I sound different. I often feel the need to speak slower. The references I use and stories I tell to make a point often miss the mark. The foods we grew up eating, places we find familiar, the shows we watched as kids, our musical tastes all serve as constant reminders to my students and me that we are different. However, being able to connect with students is crucial for student experience and learning outcomes.[1] This issue plagued me during my first year of teaching as I repeatedly met blank stares when I referenced Wu-Tang Clan lyrics and stories about the college experience in the United States. I watched as other teachers around me appeared to effortlessly weave narratives sparking "aha!" moments in students, building a dispositional kinship from day one.

Then my student evaluations came in: "He's a great teacher. I feel I learned more because he cares about us and treats us as equals." There it was. Finally some clarity. The essence of my excellent teaching was a humanity-first approach. I see students holistically, as people with a multitude of features, talents, virtues, and values. Sometimes rapport starts with likeness—being able to see yourself in the model present. However, there are many paths to effective teaching that do not rely on shared qualities: Humanity comes first. People are at the center of the learning experience.

Abraham Maslow, a positive psychologist and pioneer of humanistic psychology, described teachers as horticulturists and students as flowers.[2] In this metaphor, each flower is different. Roses are different from tulips; tulips are different from lilies. As a horticulturist, you cannot treat all flowers the same way. Different flowers require different nurturance. Your job is not to turn all roses into lilies or guarantee all flowers can be managed with identical techniques. Your job is to ensure that a rose becomes the best rose it can possibly be and to ensure every tulip becomes the best tulip it can be.

Students bring a multitude of individual stories and a constellation of differences, traits, habits, and ambitions to the classroom. To help them realize the truest and best version of themselves is supporting a process known in humanistic psychology as self-actualization: reaching their own unique highest potentials.[3] As educators, it is our duty to support this process of self-discovery and self-realization in our students.[4] To do so, we must avoid the fundamental attribution error trap and create psychologically safe environments.

Avoiding the Fundamental Attribution Error Trap

A mentor once told me that teachers should be grateful to see a student sleeping in their classroom. Why? If students opted to take a snooze, wouldn't that imply these students did not take their education seriously? Or worse, they found us—the teachers who try so hard—boring. My mentor encouraged me to cognitively reframe my perception of a student sleeping. Perhaps this is the only place that student feels safe enough to get some rest; they find your classroom soothing and peaceful. Perhaps the student is working an unimaginable number of hours to pay bills. Either way, the act of sleeping in class may be reframed from our view to not be an act of classroom treason but rather a function of the student's circumstances.

This lesson transformed my approach to teaching. It allowed me to appreciate the complexities of my students. Circumstance often directs behavior. It is easy to believe every student who behaves poorly or performs inadequately is just a bad student. It is hard to be graceful and forgiving. Interestingly, the COVID-19 pandemic has made the lives of students more visible for many instructors, showing more clearly how the fundamental attribution error can distort our perceptions and how our psychology can help us better appreciate each student as a human being first and a student second.

The fundamental attribution error in social psychology is the tendency people have to attribute undesirable behavior to the character of a person instead of circumstances surrounding them, such as attributing sleeping behavior to a lack of motivation to learn rather than a less than ideal home life that prohibits a healthy sleep schedule.[5]

Avoiding the fundamental attribution error is critical for a humanistic approach to teaching. It is the acceptance of a student inside the classroom, with the knowledge that an ocean of factors outside the classroom affects their actions. Conversely, avoiding the fundamental attribution is equally important for students when viewing their teachers, especially when those teachers do not conform to stereotypes for college professors. For example, if I were to show up late to a class, I would hope that students would not determine this was a function of my Blackness. Avoiding the fundamental attribution error is a conduit to more understanding classrooms, classrooms that detour past snap judgments based on heuristic thinking and cognitive biases.

Avoiding the fundamental attribution error trap can be tricky. It is our default setting to blame the person before blaming the circumstance. Nevertheless, there is a simple set of questions I use to stop my mind from jumping to assumptive conclusions: Is there a reasonable explanation for this behavior that could be attributed to an environmental factor? If the roles were reversed, how would I expect to be treated? Is this an action that occurs habitually, and if so, have I inquired why it might be happening? The answers to these questions may be irrelevant, but by asking them, I can slow myself down just enough to dodge the insidious fundamental attribution error trap.

Psychological Safety

Years ago, Google embarked on an endeavor to understand what factors contributed to high-performing teams. After reviewing the evidence, conducting experiments, and examining high-performing units, they came to an emphatic conclusion. High-functioning teams don't necessarily need to be made up of superstars, but they do possess psychological safety—that is, the shared belief that individuals can take risks and be vulnerable around their peers.[6] Additional research regarding psychological safety suggests that psychological safety strength leads to better performance, higher adaptability, better communication and knowledge sharing, and more positive attitudes.[7]

Creating a psychologically safe classroom is crucial in today's learning environment. The world is constantly changing. We ask more of students today than potentially any other time in human history. Students, and underrepresented educators, are bombarded by controversial and confounding global events. Without psychological safety, there is no room to be vulnerable. There is no forum for honest discussion. To create psychologically safe environments, we as educators can aspire to view material that is conflict-provoking as a basis for collaboration by approaching complex and seemingly intractable issues as teammates rather than adversaries. Instead of blaming individuals for their viewpoints, we must explore the reasons for how such viewpoints became established. We need good faith discussions about evidence, perspectives, and ways forward in order to grow.

For underrepresented educators, psychological safety takes on added value. I would hate to think certain students were uncomfortable talking about race relations because they were afraid of what reaction they might receive. Psychological safety is a necessary element for maintaining a space where open conversations and collective growth are possible. Psychological safety aligns with our humanistic approach by empowering students to bring their whole selves to the learning process without fear of being castigated or ostracized. Humanity comes first; we must accept students as they come, be gracious and understanding, and commit to enabling a nurturing learning experience.

Social Identity Leadership and Teachers as Team Leaders

When I was younger, I was obsessed with becoming an elite wrestler. I still consider my experiences on the wrestling mat as the most formative chronicles of my life. When I think about higher education and the classroom, two features of my athletic career stick out. First, I treated my teammates like family members. I would do anything for them. Those bonds transcended differences in other traits that could divide us. Teams can be powerful units. With the right team culture, features of chance—characteristics of your existence that the universe has thrust on you—are the least interesting elements about any given individual. Second, I had great coaches who would stand up for me, who helped me identify my goals, and who modeled the type of person I hoped to become. They led the way by creating communities of "we-ness." The group was greater than the sum of its parts. As teachers, we too must create a sense of "we-ness" in our classrooms to encourage social cohesion, to promote vulnerability and communication, and to remain resilient amid a constantly shifting landscaping of higher education delivery.

Teachers must lead their classes in the cultivation of knowledge, the development of skills, and the growth of their students as people. Social identity leadership proposes an informative model, as well as strategies, to help teachers be more effective leaders. Social identity leadership is a vein of research that investigates how the psychology of identity and social dynamics begins to shape how we self-categorize ourselves as members of groups and how these memberships shape our behaviors, values, cognitions, and so on.[8] Building groups with a positive shared identity can be a powerful ally in promoting knowledge and empowering resilience in uncertain times.

Social identity leadership can help us build better classrooms by creating more functional groups. To be an effective leader in the classroom—and consequently a more effective teacher—we can use two ideas from the social identity leadership literature to enhance our practice as educators. Social identity leaders must emphasize communalities instead of differences, as well as be engineers of identity and group goals. Leaders emphasize commonalities as opposed to differences.[9] Not long ago, I suspect this idea would have been laughed at; leaders were defined by their superiority, separated by an array of traits that made them exceptional. What we know today suggests the opposite. Effective leaders are skilled at identifying what connects individuals within an in-group rather than what sets them apart.

Underrepresented educators must recognize the importance of commonalities. Imagine two scenarios: In the first classroom, I, a Black man, walk in every day doing my best to point out all the ways that I differ from my students in an attempt to prove to them that I am worthy of respect. I intend to acknowledge all of the things that I have accomplished and all the traits I possess that separate us from one another. But in the second classroom, I, a Black man, walk in every day trying to convince every student that we are more alike than different. I intend to acknowledge that I have sat where they now sit and that we are connected via similar experiences and interests. Which approach do you suspect works better?

Humans have uniquely evolved social learning mechanisms that amplify our ability to learn from others. We learn much better from models we identify with as opposed to individuals we struggle to connect with. Teachers who can effectively identify commonalities with their students will have an easier time teaching than those who seek to highlight differences. For underrepresented teachers, if those commonalities do not exist naturally, then it may be important to engineer a shared identity in the classroom.

Teachers as team leaders are engineers of identity.[10] We craft the set of features that define our groups. Using the resources available to us, we can define a shared vision of the future for our classes and build the social, behavioral, and sometimes physical infrastructure to bring that shared vision to fruition. Teachers must be both the architects of what is and what will become of the group. This composition of shared identity and shared goals should be an emergent property of the group. The process should be a collaboration with students.

In my classroom, every year, I notice students yearning for content missing from the undergraduate curriculum, such as how to prepare for the job market or finding the right mentor. So, every year, my students and I put our heads together to decide what extra content they would like integrated into the course for the semester. Each year, the content is different and reflects the needs of the students. Through this process, I am putting the power in the hands of the group. We use resources to construct goals and activities the group members find to be in their own self-interest. The process and outcomes of this practice consequently lead to stronger perceptions of group cohesion, a higher sense of self-categorization as a member of the group, and the removal of demographic barriers. This can have a profound effect on someone who does not stereotypically fit the criteria of what students expect of a professor and academic expert. I, as someone who could be viewed as an outsider, am not seen as a separate entity but rather a canvas that reflects the educational needs of the whole class. Teachers as leaders champion solidarity.

Appreciating Systems of Influence and the Science of Change

I reflect frequently on the best teachers in my life. The influence of this collection of teachers, mentors, and coaches is what makes me, me. One may say the ultimate feature of the assortment is the diversity—different ages, ethnicities, religious creeds, political affiliations, gender, origin country, etc. In some cases, the similarities to my identity are what I value. For example, the experience of learning from a Black faculty member, someone who looks like me, can bring a sense of admiration. The teachers I remember most are the ones who helped me achieve the changes I wanted to see in my life, whether that be the acquisition of a skill, helping me learn valuable lessons, or providing the frameworks and models I would need to improve the way I moved through the world. My favorite mentors empowered me to change my behavior.

What I loved about my collection of sages was not the way they looked or where they came from but what they contributed to my journey. When I consider tools that may be helpful when seeking to make an impact as a marginalized professor (or any professor for that matter), I think about what any teacher can do to alter the trajectory of a student's life for the better. Education is in part a behavior change endeavor. To achieve the goals we seek in higher learning, we need students to learn about the world and be able to use that knowledge in their lives. The process of learning is psychological. The process of applying that knowledge is behavioral. To improve our practice as teachers, we must understand why students do what they do. This has become overpoweringly clear as the coronavirus pandemic forces disruptions and changes to pedagogy. Students need the agency to make changes that suit their educational needs. Teachers need evidence-based tools to empower students.

Behavioral sciences offer a useful toolbox of theories and strategies that help us understand and change human behavior. By using this toolbox, perhaps we can become better equipped to connect with students and help students become better versions of themselves. We all learn. We all behave. The science of how we learn and how we behave can connect students and teachers in profoundly positive ways.

Models of Change

Understanding students is difficult on the best of days. Fortunately, pioneers of psychological and behavioral sciences have spent decades refining modern models of behavior to help us better understand our motivations and actions. Behavior change models are structural frameworks made up of discreet and interconnected constructs. Think of constructs as building blocks and the whole model as a house. Individual constructs and whole models are useful when seeking to explain or change more complex student behaviors. The classroom, technology, and the obstacles we face in delivering education in universities seem to change every year, but the psychology that drives us is a little less erratic.

Let's take a simple yet powerful model, the capability, opportunity, motivation, and behavior system model (COM-B model) of behavioral motivation to demonstrate how this might look. The COM-B model is made up of three components that lead to behavior: capability, motivation, and opportunity.[11] I'd like to know why some of my students are completing a weekly online assignment and why some aren't. First, we investigate capability. Behaviors can appear on the surface to be easy enough but can often mandate a string of behavioral steps that may be confusing. To complete the weekly online assignment, students must log in to a portal, follow the steps to another link, enter data, and then save the completion receipt. Are the instructions clear enough? Second, we look toward motivation. It is only worth one point after all. Is the incentive structure right for this online experiment? Finally, there is opportunity. There is a slim window to complete this task. Some students may find the scarcity of time to be overwhelmingly restrictive. If any of these components is perceived as too arduous, consequently, the task does not get done.

We could use the same model as a catalyst to fix low completion rates. We can use more behavioral science tools such as the Behavior Change Wheel that builds on this model to help us design and implement strategies to remove the barriers listed earlier.[12] The science of behavior change can transcend demographics to help students and teachers achieve preferred outcomes. While differences may exist on the surface, creating ecosystems of transformative change, increasing enabling factors of change, and removing obstacles to change can help students become the individuals they want to be. Science-based approaches to teaching and learning are our allies; educators should use evidence-based behavioral science tools to understand and empower students to make the changes that matter most to them.

Adapting Behavior Science Principles for Online Learning

The coronavirus pandemic is probably the most disruptive event in higher learning this generation has encountered. Nevertheless, higher learning educators have been charged with making adjustments and delivering quality education. The restrictions the coronavirus places on learning present a unique set of challenges: all students are facing immense and novel threats to their health and well-being; the spaces we occupy to learn are different under social distancing guidelines; and it is difficult to make connections or adapt behavior for conducive learning when we feel like we have such little control over our circumstances.

Fortunately, online spaces present us with opportunities to apply our three principles. With the infusion of creativity and in the spirit of innovation, we can identify solutions for nonstereotypical faculty members. First, time should be invested in online spaces to understand the wants, needs, and aspirations of students beyond classroom content. Further, steps and activities should be done to encourage a sense of collective culture and shared leadership of the learning journey. Finally, as educators, we should encourage students to apply best practice behavior change strategies in their own spaces to encourage healthy learning habits. Despite all our efforts to work within the parameters of online spaces, we must remember as educators that humanity comes first. It is imperative we maintain our patience with students and ourselves, as well as do our best to guarantee all students are treated with grace and dignity.

Conclusion

My grandparents may not understand fully what I do, but I'd like to think that they are proud of me. Alas, it was the sacrifices they made that allow me to pursue a fulfilling career as a college professor. Though we have come a long way, we still have much further to go to create higher learning environments that are representative and inclusive, as well as agile and resilient enough to adapt to ongoing global challenges. I like to think of the higher learning landscape as another complex problem. With a dash of passion, a lot of hard work, and a commitment to growth, we can make our higher learning institutions bastions of diversity, growth, resiliency, adaptability, and self-actualization for students and faculty alike. Humanity comes first. As I've shown in this chapter, we can use principles of humanistic psychology to shape our pedagogy. Social identity theory can help us connect with students, and behavioral models and systems aid the learning and growth process in the classroom.

Teaching Takeaways

- Avoid the fundamental attribution error and build rapport by seeing students holistically and remembering that humanity comes first.

- Teachers are team leaders who must promote solidarity in the classroom.
- Use evidence-based behavioral science tools to understand and empower your students to make the changes that matter most to them and to facilitate their learning.

....

ERIK SIMMONS is a postdoctoral research fellow at Boston College and a former lead researcher on international World Bank projects who has taught at universities and led professional training workshops around the world. His research explores the interdisciplinary nexus of behavioral sciences, health, technology, and education, and his current project examines how to sustain childhood development interventions to improve the lives of families in Rwanda. His research has been published in media outlets, peer-reviewed journals, and books.

Notes

1. Harriet Schwartz, *Connected Teaching: Relationship, Power, and Mattering in Higher Education* (Sterling, VA: Stylus, 2019), 1–11.
2. Abraham Maslow, "A Dynamic Theory of Human Motivation," in *Toward a Psychology of Being* (New York: Simon and Schuster, 2013), 26–47.
3. Abraham Maslow, "A Theory of Human Motivation," *Psychological Review* no. 50 (1943): 370–96.
4. Abraham Maslow, "Some Educational Implications of the Humanistic Psychologies," *Harvard Educational Review* 38, no. 4 (1968): 685–96.

5. Edward Jones and Victor Harris, "The Attribution of Attitudes," *Journal of Experimental Social Psychology* 3 no. 1 (1967): 1–24.

6. Amy Edmondson, "Psychological Safety and Learning Behavior in Work Teams," *Administrative Science Quarterly* 44, no. 2 (1999): 350–83. See also Amy Edmondson and Zhike Lei, "Psychological Safety: The History, Renaissance, and Future of an Interpersonal Construct," *Annual Review Organizational Psychology Organizational Behavior* no. 1 (2014): 23–43.

7. Alexander Newman, Ross Donohue, and Nathan Eva, "Psychological Safety: A Systemic Review of the Literature," *Human Resource Management Review* 27, no. 3 (September 2017): 521–35, https://doi.org/10.1016/j.hrmr.2017.01.001.

8. Alexander Haslam, Steve Reicher, and Michael Platow, *The New Psychology of Leadership: Identity, Influence and Power* (New York: Routledge, 2010), 1–23.

9. Haslam, *The New Psychology of Leadership*, 77–106.

10. Haslam, *The New Psychology of Leadership*, 165–92.

11. Susan Michie, Maartje van Stralen, and Robert West, "The Behaviour Change Wheel: A New Method for Characterising and Designing Behaviour Change Interventions," *Implementation Science* 6, no. 1 (2011): 1–12.

12. Michie, van Stralen, and West, "The Behaviour Change Wheel," 1–12. See also Martin S. Hagger et al., eds., *The Handbook of Behavior Change* (United Kingdom: Cambridge University Press, 2020), and Susan Michie and Robert West, "Behaviour Change Theory and Evidence: A Presentation to Government," *Health Psychology Review* 7, no. 1 (2013): 1–22.

PART THREE

ANTI-RACIST PEDAGOGY

Strategies for Increasing Equity

....

CHAPTER 10

BEYOND MAKING STATEMENTS

The Reflective Practice of Becoming an Anti-Racist Educator

. . . .

M. Gabriela Torres

The practice of becoming anti-racist in pedagogy and inter-personal outlook is inherently reflective work. This chapter explains the logic behind the eight concrete reflection steps featured in a web-based resource and interactive workshop I developed at Wheaton College in the wake of George Floyd's murder. I devised eight steps of reflection that worked as entry points or ramps into anti-racist iterative practice. The eight steps of reflection are drawn from literature in cultural studies, social sciences, and scholarship on teaching and learning (SoTL), as well as my own reflective practice as a Latinx scholar in educational development. This chapter empowers readers to transform individual classrooms and institutional agendas by thinking through the value of these eight steps: interrogating your position, examining the impact of Whiteness, learning about how racism shapes social worlds, acknowledging racial trauma, interrogating expectations of ideal students, rethinking course content, learning about anti-racist pedagogical approaches, and devising actionable and iterative plans. Moving beyond simply making statements or the completion of checklists of best practice to eight steps of reflection and action is a practice for educators to embrace anti-racism as their life's disposition.

I teach at a private, liberal arts, four-year undergraduate, primarily White institution. Even though more than 30 percent of our students are national and international Black, Indigenous, and People of Color (BIPOC), I have learned from advising many of them for the past fourteen years that their experience is a difficult one.[1] I have seen class after class of BIPOC students, including some who were Latinx like me, graduate with some degree of trauma. The problem of belonging for BIPOC students is not unique to my institution and has been well studied for higher education generally and for four-year colleges in particular.[2] While scholars often cite insufficiency of the content offered at most colleges and universities to reflect the experience of racialized students in the classroom, what I saw was much more than this.

As in other institutions, students I worked with sometimes felt that they couldn't be themselves in the spaces that many of my colleagues construed as neutral spaces meant for all. Many of the students I advised did not feel able to exist with the same degree of freedom or sense of belonging that some of their White peers clearly did. They were often expected to carry the weight of veiled or explicitly racist comments in class discussions and interpersonal microaggressions in silence for the benefit of an institutional "civility" that embraced and perpetuated a problematic view of "call-out culture."[3] At our institution, critiques of racially hurtful comments in the classroom and students' cocurricular lives became routinely dismissed as merely performative call-out culture. This dynamic effectively silenced much-needed conversations. Many of our BIPOC students felt that our institution disciplined them into particular ways of being that were foreign. Despite the claims of our marketing materials, these students did not regularly feel at home. They were required to code switch or, as Bonnie Uriciuoli describes it, they had to be "limited to an institutional defined set of self-presentation."[4] As they do at other colleges, even as they managed to bring diversity to our primarily White campus, BIPOC students desperately sought spaces, within the bounds that our college would allow, to be with others who shared similar backgrounds and with whom they could get a sense of the comforts of being in their communities.[5]

In spring 2020, I was a Posse mentor. The Posse Foundation program is a wildly successful national program where young people with exceptional leadership potential from primarily urban areas attend elite colleges and universities across the United States in cohorts through leadership scholarships funded by the institutions they attend.[6] At our college, a faculty member works with the cohort as a mentor advising and supporting them individually and as a group intensely throughout their four years. In the more than three decades of existence, the program has been documented to provide students with an oasis of belonging.[7] In February 2020, the Posse scholars I worked with collectively made a public plea to administrators and faculty and asked us to rethink our curriculum and our work with them in the classroom and advising. They pointed to microaggressions, their inability to see themselves in our curriculum, and the trauma of the experience of feeling that they had to fit themselves into a system that was not designed for them. This was the trauma that I had seen in years past, and it was troubling to see it again with a group I had worked to support.

In March 2020, as the pandemic took hold, my group of Posse scholars left the liberal arts college we affectionately call "the bubble" and went back to profoundly difficult situations in New York City. Most went back to neighborhoods that one of them aptly called the "epicenter of the epicenter" of the COVID-19 pandemic. Despite these obstacles, in May 2020, ten amazing undergraduate scholars I worked with graduated from college into a pandemic that made their futures uncertain. In addition, they also bore the weight of trauma our own institution had added. This end made clear to me that institutions like ours, far from unique in their treatment of BIPOC students, needed to do better to ensure equity and belonging for all students. Equity and the fostering of a multiplicity of perspectives needed to be central to the design of courses, the curriculum, and the services our institution provides students. We needed to learn how to walk the walk of inclusion and equity and not add experiences of trauma through microaggressions and other explicit, though perhaps unintentional, forms of exclusion. We needed to address head-on what Tia Brown McNair and colleagues refer to as "the hierarchy of human value" within higher education.[8]

Seeing these struggles year after year, I've felt morally implicated but have never quite managed to overcome my own racialization in the space we shared to be able to act. As a racialized professor in a predominantly White institution, acting to challenge racism, even in my own classroom, is always a balancing act between the richness of the teaching opportunity diversity issues afford and the personal emotional toll of leading students through discussions that inevitably bring to the surface preconceptions and worldviews that are hurtful to peers. When I transitioned to the role of educational developer teaching faculty and teaching assistants, an additional challenge to embracing diversity in the classroom surfaced: the learning gap to engage in difficult discussions on diversity matters is large. Inequities have been central to knowledge production across all fields, and as a result, faculty and TAs often require engagement with content outside of what they might see as their areas of expertise, such as learning new pedagogical tools and examining their own roles and long-held assumptions.

Making the Link between Institutional and Personal Change

The layered conditions of vulnerability that I witnessed for BIPOC students at my institution are also present in many of their communities. In 2020, it was not only the pandemic but also George Floyd's murder and the subsequent civic protests that shifted my approach to action in significant ways. The police violence that became hypervisible in 2020 allowed many colleagues to see more clearly what has been happening in the United States for centuries. It was a moment in which I saw in my institution for the first time an opening for change that was supported by the leadership. In the aftermath of the protests in 2020, our college made a clear commitment to action.

As a codirector of the Collaborative Center for Teaching and Learning, I took this call to action seriously. Our center's vision and mission direct us to build a diverse community of learners through evidence-based pedagogy. Taking this mission to heart, together with my colleagues,

I began work on a teaching and learning resource to encourage personal and institutional reflection and an accompanying workshop. I had seen many colleagues share websites or Google document digests that had pages and pages of resources. Even as a person who teaches about race, racialization, health inequities, and immigration, it was almost impossible for me to even know where to begin to access the resource, let alone translate the literature into action.

As stated in *From Equity Talk to Equity Walk*, I knew that "change must happen individually before it can happen collectively" because it is individuals who "drive change, lead change, and sustain change."[9] By creating a resource titled "Becoming an Anti-Racist Educator," I aimed to provide a beginner's guide to fostering individual change in order to fuel institutional change.[10] I designed it as an entryway to guide reflection and action. The resource presents eight sequential steps for reflection. I discussed this resource and the process that led to its development in an interview for the podcast *More and More Every Day*.[11]

The eight steps for reflection are divided into two categories. The first four steps focus on personal reflection about positionality and worldview. The next four steps are designed to elicit reflection on the educator's role.

One: Interrogate your position. This step requires reflecting our shared socialization into particular worldviews.[12] It asks readers to interrogate Whiteness and White privilege in their lives as a concern of the first order.[13]

Two: Examine the impact of Whiteness on institutional systems and interpersonal interactions. This step is focused on the way that racism shapes the experiences of faculty and students in higher education.[14] It encourages a deeper understanding of the experience of colleagues and BIPOC students so that change can be crafted in courses and campus culture.[15]

Three: Learn about how racism shapes social worlds. This step requires becoming familiar with the impact of racism on individual lives beyond the context of higher education to encourage rethinking in general education and disciplinary curricula.

Four: Acknowledge racial trauma. This step draws on Columbia University School of Social Work's study of trauma-informed pedagogy and the Boston College Institute for the Study and Promotion of Race and Culture's work on racial trauma symptomology. This step asks readers to acknowledge that racial trauma exists.[16] It asks readers, for instance, how have you built in reflection so that students who are going through trauma moments can have the bandwidth to really focus on the course material?

Five: Interrogate assumptions of the ideal students. This step requires engaging in the examination of normative expectations of students and exploring how these can carry implicit bias.[17] This step also asks readers to consider alternate grading approaches and inclusive strategies for feedback on student work.

Six: Rethink course content. This is a challenging step that requires acknowledging the impact of racism on knowledge production. In anthropology, the discipline I practice in, this point has been eloquently raised by the work of #CiteBlackWomen.[18]

Seven: Learn about anti-racist pedagogical approaches. This is a practical step that surveys key pedagogical approaches designed as anti-racist or which have anti-racist potential, including approaches such as bandwidth recovery and dialogue across difference.[19] This step asks how do you assess students in ways that do not violate trust?[20] In addition, it asks readers to question how they encourage students to show them their knowledge and whether the assessments that are selected for a course are the most equitable way to assess students' knowledge.

Eight: Devise actionable and iterative plans. This is a practical step that suggests to the reader that to make iterative change, a concrete learning schedule or actionable program is required.[21]

The resource assumes that even when we are not wanting to be racist, we might be enacting racism simply because of the systemic racism that shapes the context within which we work. In crafting the resource, I wanted to make the connection that teaching takes place in systems that are imbued with explicit racism. Much research has shown that university systems are not designed for BIPOC people and are not designed to address the discriminatory experience of racism in the United States, which rests on a belief in the hierarchy of human value.[22] Nevertheless, there is limited action to change the culture, worldviews, and practices that take place within university systems.

From Resource to Workshop: Embracing Anti-Racism as an Individual and Educational Development Practice Beyond Making Statements

To move beyond the idea of a hierarchy of human value, the resource engages anti-racism as a practice. It calls on becoming anti-racist not as a state of being but through a continually iterative acknowledgment of our own power and privilege as persons and as educators. Ibram X. Kendi boils the work of anti-racism down to three actions: identification, description, and dismantlement.[23] As actions, they require our taking explicit responsibility for how our power and privilege shape the classroom and ourselves.[24] Consequently, anti-racism requires the sort of self-reflection that has the potential to bring about the sort of discomfort that yields personal as well as institutional growth. It is empowering, capacity-building work that makes our practice as educators meaningful and gives us the confidence to engage with the central social issues of our contemporary world.

According to Condon and Young, an anti-racist agenda in education "offers an understanding or explanation of race, racism, and the particular racial formations that develop in and around the classroom or program in question."[25] Such an agenda engages with

> how racism tends to be a part of the structures and mechanisms of grading in writing classrooms, in teacher feedback, in the ways that the school admits and places students into classes, in how and what it values in writing and how those values are related to larger dominant discourses. It explains the particular brands of whiteness and whiteliness that occur in the classroom and in assessments.[26]

To engage colleagues at our institution in learning how to be anti-racist educators, we devised a 90-minute workshop that asked colleagues to fill out a shared document before attending the workshop. The workshop attracted seventy-five colleagues out of approximately two hundred at our institution who work on instruction to students. The document that accompanied the workshop had two prompts: "In my practice as an educator, I am thinking of making this change. . . ." and "As I plan for change, I am struggling the most with. . . ."[27]

The synchronous part of the workshop had four parts.

First, participants were introduced to key insights from our web resource and pedagogical strategies. Second, participants were given shared reading time to read what their colleagues wrote and find resonance with their own thinking and aspirations. Third, participants were separated into breakout groups to share their plans and impressions and asked to listen to their peers. Finally, participants were given individual working time to revise their action plan. The workshop concluded with a discussion of the broader curricular implications of incorporating anti-racism. Ultimately, the workshop began a process of thinking together through challenges and proposals for new initiatives at the course and general curriculum levels.

Conclusion: Who Takes on the Work of Creating Equity?

Creating equity from an anti-racist perspective is really a redistribution of the work of engaging with diversity. Today, many of us are actually expecting our students to do all the work of bridging difference and systemic inequality in primarily White institutions. Engaging in the work of creating real equity means that the work of translating difference needs to be shared. This is work that I have slowly become more conscious about doing in my own practice as a professor. As a result, I often ask myself what student am I assuming in the selection of content, assignments, and in-class activities and whether the language or modes of interaction that I use limit access. Assuming cultural, racial, and neurodiversity in the classroom and university writ large is a design question for educational and faculty developers, for faculty, and for administrators. Through this process, I have learned that to create equity, we have to engage in a redistribution of labor that goes beyond the assumption of shared experience, the need to have a singular reality, or the presentation of an ideal voice.

The anti-racist reflection steps in the web resource "Becoming an Anti-Racist Educator" reimagine higher education institutions and educators to enable a plurality of voices and ways of being through reflective practice. Such a project has the potential to move us beyond pathologizing, tolerating, and othering difference with labels such as "underprepared," "marginal," or "minority." As we build toward change starting within our own pedagogical and institutional practices, we can begin to imagine what institutional projects that value and foster difference in the classroom might look like. Imagine, if you will, what would happen if we move beyond making statements to institutional and personal action? Could the ways that we subjectify or compel social and personal transformation in our students finally change? In this horizon of change, might more of us truly feel like the places where we learn and teach offer greater freedom and belonging through a design that is not just meant to tolerate us but also to enable our growth as scholars and persons?

Teaching Takeaways

- All of us are embedded in learning environments shaped by White privilege, racism, and racial trauma.
- Becoming an anti-racist educator is a values-driven disposition to engage with diversity and equity

through iterative personal reflection that can give us the capacity to impact social change.

- There are eight practical steps you can take to begin your practice as an anti-racist educator: interrogate your position, examine the impact of Whiteness, learn about how racism shapes social worlds, acknowledge racial trauma, interrogate expectations of ideal students, rethink course content, learn about anti-racist pedagogical approaches, and devise actionable and iterative plans.

....

M. GABRIELA TORRES is professor of anthropology and associate provost for academic administration and faculty affairs at Wheaton College, Massachusetts. Recognized as the most influential faculty member for three graduating classes, she was the designer and codirector of Wheaton College's Center for Collaborative Teaching and Learning. She is coeditor of *Marital Rape: Consent, Marriage and Social Change in Global Context* and *Sexual Violence in Intimacy: Implications for Research and Policy in Global Health.*

Notes

1. I use the term "BIPOC" not as a way to describe phenotypic characteristics or cultural categories of identity but rather to highlight the unique relationship to Whiteness that Indigenous and Black (African American) people have, which shapes the relationship with White supremacy for all persons racialized into the vague notion of "people of color" within a US context.

It is a term that suggests shared experiences of racialization, marginalization, struggle, and resilience.

2. Dwayne A. Mack, Elwood Watson, and Michelle Madsen Camacho, *Beginning a Career in Academia: A Guide for Graduate Students of Color* (New York: Routledge, 2014); Maithreyi Gopalan and Shannon T. Brady, "College Students' Sense of Belonging: A National Perspective," *Educational Researcher* 49, no. 2 (March 1, 2020): 134–37; Terrell Strayhorn, *College Students' Sense of Belonging: A Key to Educational Success for All Students* (New York: Routledge, 2018).

3. Jessica Bennett, "What If Instead of Calling People Out, We Called Them In?" *New York Times*, November 19, 2020, https://www.nytimes.com/2020/11/19/style/loretta-ross-smith-college-cancel-culture.html.

4. Bonnie Urciuoli, "Neoliberalizing Markedness: The Interpellation of 'Diverse' College Students," *HAU: Journal of Ethnographic Theory* 6, no. 3 (December 1, 2016): 203.

5. Beverly Daniel Tatum, *Why Are All the Black Kids Sitting Together in the Cafeteria? And Other Conversations about Race* (New York: Basic Books, 2017).

6. Libby Sander, "A Quarter-Century of 'Posses' Underscores the Power of the Cohort," *Chronicle of Higher Education*, October 28, 2013, https://www.chronicle.com/article/a-quarter-century-of-posses-underscores-the-power-of-the-cohort/.

7. Caralee J. Adams, "Posses Keep Students on Academic Track," *Education Week*, June 5, 2014, https://www.edweek.org/ew/articles/2014/06/05/34peerpower.h33.html.

8. Tia Brown McNair, Estela Mara Bensimon, and Lindsey Malcom-Piqueux, *From Equity Talk to Equity Walk: Expanding Practitioner Knowledge for Racial Justice in Higher Education* (San Francisco, CA: Jossey-Bass, 2020), 5.

9. McNair, Bensimon, and Malcom-Piqueux, *From Equity Talk to Equity Walk*, 1.

10. "Becoming an Anti-Racist Educator," Wheaton College, https://
    wheatoncollege.edu/academics/special-projects-initiatives
    /center-for-collaborative-teaching-and-learning/anti-racist
    -educator/ (https://tinyurl.com/anti-racist-educator).

11. South Phoenix Oral History Project, " 'Beyond Making
    Statements' M. Gabriela Torres," August 31, 2010, *More and
    More Every Day*, https://southphoenixoralhistory.com/more
    -and-more-every-day/more-and-more-every-day-gabriela
    -torres-8–31–20/.

12. Bree Picower, "The Unexamined Whiteness of Teaching:
    How White Teachers Maintain and Enact Dominant Racial
    Ideologies," *Race Ethnicity and Education* 12, no. 2 (2009): 197–
    215; Robin DiAngelo, *White Fragility: Why It's So Hard for White
    People to Talk about Racism* (New York, Beacon Press, 2018).

13. Stephen D. Brookfield, *Teaching Race: How to Help Students
    Unmask and Challenge Racism* (San Francisco: Jossey-Bass,
    2018).

14. Gabriella Gutiérrez y Muhs et al., eds., *Presumed Incompetent:
    The Intersections of Race and Class for Women in Academia*
    (Boulder: University Press of Colorado, 2012); Mack et. al,
    Beginning a Career in Academia.

15. Amy Harmon, "For a Black Mathematician, What It's Like to
    Be the 'Only One,' " *New York Times*, February 18, 2019, https://
    www.nytimes.com/2019/02/18/us/edray-goins-black
    -mathematicians.html.

16. Resmaa Menekem, *My Grandmother's Hands: Racialized Trauma
    and the Pathway to Mending Our Hearts and Bodies* (Las Vegas:
    Central Recovery Press, 2017).

17. Gina C. Torino, "Examining Biases and White Privilege:
    Classroom Teaching Strategies That Promote Cultural
    Competence," *Women and Therapy* 38, no. 3–4 (2015): 295, 307.

18. Lynn Bolles, "Telling the Story Straight: Black Feminist

Intellectual Thought in Anthropology," *Transforming Anthropology* 21, no. 1 (2013): 57–71.

19. Cia Verschelden, *Bandwidth Recovery: Helping Students Reclaim Cognitive Resources Lost to Poverty, Racism, and Social Marginalization* (Sterling, VA: Stylus Publishing, 2017); Patricia Gurin et al., *Dialogue across Difference: Practice, Theory, and Research on Intergroup Dialogue* (New York: Russell Sage, 2013).

20. David Scott Yeager et al., "Breaking the Cycle of Mistrust: Wise Interventions to Provide Critical Feedback across the Racial Divide," *Journal of Experimental Psychology* 143, no. 2 (2014): 804–24.

21. Corinne Shutack, "103 Things White People Can Do for Racial Justice," August 27, 2020, *Medium*, https://medium.com /equality-includes-you/what-white-people-can-do-for-racial -justice-f2d18b0e0234.

22. Gutiérrez y Muhs et al., *Presumed Incompetent*.

23. Kendi, *How to Be an Anti-Racist*.

24. Anneliese Singh, Derald Wing Sue, and Tim Wise, *The Racial Healing Handbook: Practical Activities to Help You Challenge Privilege, Confront Systemic Racism, and Engage in Collective Healing* (Oakland: New Harbinger Publications, 2019).

25. Frankie Condon and Vershawn Ashanti Young, *Performing Antiracist Pedagogy in Rhetoric, Writing, and Communication* (Boulder: University Press of Colorado, 2017), xvi.

26. Condon and Young, *Performing Antiracist Pedagogy*, xvii.

27. The "Becoming an Anti-Racist Educator" shared document asked participants to list their name, reflect on two prompts, and identify any resonance they saw with others' answers. For the prompt "In my practice as an educator, I am thinking of making this change . . . ," I noted, "This could be a change in course content, approaches to student meetings, assumptions about ideal student comportment and so on." For the prompt

"As I plan for change, I'm struggling the most with . . . ," I noted, "This could be access to resources, finding community supports, not knowing where to start, time or technology constraints, not knowing what is possible, and so on."

RIPPLING THE PATTERNS
OF POWER

Enacting Anti-Racist Pedagogy
with Students as Co-teachers

. . . .

Chanelle Wilson and Alison Cook-Sather

The two of us are located differently on several continua: age (under thirty-five and over fifty-five), professorial rank (assistant and full), and ethnicity (Black and White). But we are both small-statured, female faculty who teach in an institution built on the premises of White supremacy culture, which we labored under and unintentionally perpetuated for years. Like most faculty (and students), we came up through schooling built on these premises, such as perfectionism and power hoarding. Also like most faculty (and students), we experienced the trauma of having to prove ourselves accomplished and authoritative within this culture. Because of these schooling experiences, all of us, faculty and students alike, carry certain conceptions of what is possible in the classroom and who looks as if they belong there. If we are not vigilant, we can get stuck in a cycle of falling into performing according to White supremacy culture expectations rather than building and engaging in relational practice.[1]

Working in partnership with students helped us to develop the courage, confidence, and capacity to engage in more empowering, relationship-based teaching and learning; to, ultimately, engage with students as co-teachers; and to undertake what la paperson describes in *A Third University Is Possible*: "The witch's flight is the ripple in the patterning of power."[2] As we've shown elsewhere, teaching and learning can be a partnership, not a performance; power can be shared, and we can work in community rather than in competition with one another.[3] Such ripples in the "patterning of power" in higher education are an example of "the witch's flight"—Keeling's term for the "transgressive path of the Black Femme" that leads to "a more radical elsewhere."[4]

In this chapter, we are inspired by these concepts as they inform anti-racist pedagogies. We draw on our shared and respective, ever-evolving commitments to anti-racist pedagogies as they play out in Advocating for Diversity in Higher Education, a course we have both taught at Bryn Mawr College with students as co-teachers.[5] While we have been committed to anti-racist work for years, the intersection of the global pandemic and the Black Lives Matter movement intensifies our urgency, illustrating how racism is structured into society's institutions and practices. These must be systematically dismantled and rebuilt for progress toward equity. If we are not disrupting practices of White supremacy, then we are complicit in upholding it.

In this chapter, after briefly defining anti-racist pedagogy and our students-as-co-teachers approach, we summarize anti-racist practices we, and our student co-teachers, have enacted. We also offer recommendations to encourage you to ripple the patternings of power in your own courses.

Defining Anti-Racist Pedagogy with Students as Co-teachers

Drawing on George Dei's anti-racism definition, Jennifer Phillips and colleagues explain that the term "anti-racist" is an "action-oriented strategy for institutional systemic change that addresses racism and other interlocking systems of social oppression." Anti-racism, they continue, "explicitly names the issues of race and social difference as issues of power and equity, rather than as matters of cultural and ethnic variety."[6] Anti-racism aims to institutionalize anti-racist policy and practice, seeking "institutional transformation through changing structures and processes which militate against equality of access, process, and outcome."[7] Anti-racist pedagogy is "grounded in honing the critical exploration of racial inequality and White privilege so as to take direct action against injustice."[8] Kyoki Kishimoto argues that an anti-racist pedagogical approach:

1. Challenges assumptions and fosters students' critical analytical skills
2. Develops students' awareness of their social positions
3. Decenters authority in the classroom and has students take responsibility for their learning process
4. Empowers students and applies theory to practice
5. Creates a sense of community in the classroom through collaborative learning[9]

We organize the discussion of our course and our recommendations in relation to these five commitments, combined with a co-teaching approach.

Both of us began teaching with students by first working with students who were not enrolled in our courses but who took on roles "as co-learners, co-researchers, co-inquirers, co-developers, and co-designers."[10] Underpinned by the premises of respect, reciprocity, and shared responsibility, these are forms of partnership through which all participants "have the opportunity to contribute equally, although not necessarily in the same ways, to curricular or pedagogical conceptualization, decision making, implementation, investigation, or analysis."[11] While our institutional context encourages and supports critical engagement, many students, enculturated in White supremacy, doubt and even resist taking the witch's flight. Students are accustomed to hierarchy, clearly defined roles, and passive learning. Students arrive at our classes uncertain about and even suspicious of destabilizing any of these schooling norms.

Sometimes also called co-creation, a co-teaching approach produces stronger learning relationships that promote empathy and trust, improved disciplinary learning (students) and learning about teaching (teachers), more confidence as learners or teachers, a shift in identity toward more shared responsibility for learning and teaching, and a stronger sense of belonging to a learning community within the university.[12] Co-teaching is an extension of co-creation approaches, including co-facilitation with students not enrolled in our course, and it embraces what Catherine Bovill calls "whole-class approaches to co-creating teaching and learning" through which all enrolled students become co-teachers.[13]

Anti-Racist Pedagogy and Student Co-Teachers in "Advocating for Diversity in Higher Education"

We teach at Bryn Mawr, a selective liberal arts college traditionally for women located on the land of the Lenni Lenape, fourteen miles outside of Philadelphia. The Education Program we teach in draws a group of students diverse in ethnic/racial backgrounds, socioeconomic status, gender identities, sexual orientation, citizenship status, religion, and regions of the world. The school is a historically and dominantly White institution, where a four-year undergraduate degree is priced at over US$200,000.[14] In keeping with anti-racism's commitment to institutionalize anti-racist policy and practice, we aim to create an environment that distinguishes oppressive power structures with the explicit goal of establishing equity. Our course, Advocating for Diversity in Higher Education, facilitates understanding, critiquing, envisioning, and advocating for spaces responsive to the presence of diversity. We discuss below the ways in which we draw on Kishimoto's dimensions of anti-racist pedagogy, with students as co-teachers, in this class.

Anti-racist pedagogy "challenges assumptions and fosters students' critical analytical skills." Inviting student co-teachers to draw on their own knowledge, experiences, and perspectives and incorporating the different intersections of their identities counters hegemonic notions of objectiveness and absolute truth. Positioning a student as a leader in the classroom directly challenges the normalized perception of a teacher. Likewise, sharing power over decision-making with all students and seeing everyone in the space as a resource for deepened learning are ways that we relinquish the pretense of control created by oppressive structures.

This challenges what counts as legitimate content and incorporates nontraditionalized ways of accessing information. For example, we invite students to draw on their own lives as experiential data and to value it as course content.[15] To push back against the culture of White supremacy and worship of the written word, we use songs, podcasts, and various creative and artistic media as content.[16] We engage with students in critical analysis that requires all of us to ask and respond to hard questions, lean in to uncomfortable moments, and contribute to the learning process. During discussions, we specifically ask whose voices and perspectives are left out, and as a group, we consider other ways of thinking and knowing. We organize student opportunities to understand, challenge, and critique the structure of higher education, and we complicate the institutional structures that have been normalized.

Anti-racist pedagogy "develops students' awareness of their social positions," which begins with faculty developing awareness of our own fluid, contextual, social positions and reflecting on how those are both socially constructed and lived. Anti-racist teaching creates opportunities for students to engage in the same processes of raising awareness and engaging in self-reflection. All our undergraduate student co-teachers have been women of color, which disrupts the exclusion of this social location in leadership and positions students as legitimate sources of knowledge and authority.[17] Students in the role of co-teacher can share dimensions of identity with other students that, as instructors, we do not, and student co-teachers understand the experience of being students at the institutions where we teach in ways that we, as teachers in a different social position, never will.

Our class attracts a diverse range of students because of its focus. Many enrollees are from marginalized groups and come to the course with a heightened awareness of their social position. The course invites and validates their experiences, making it part of the course content, and it challenges all students, and particularly those in dominant positionings, to develop an awareness of other students' social positioning. We, and our student co-teachers, construct assignments that scaffold and invite reflection on social positions. For instance, for one assignment, students interview students who are not enrolled in the course about their experiences with the goal of creating "a forum for marginal voices to be heard and respected by putting them in a place where they can inform classroom pedagogy and student learning."[18] Their interviews become course content. We also develop students' awareness of their social positions by inviting them to reflect on how they are situated in relation to others within the course (e.g., in the whole-class sessions, in small-group sessions) and within larger contexts. These include the private liberal arts colleges at which we teach, which constitute a different context from, for instance, a large state school, and the historical and social contexts beyond the particular institution.

Anti-racist pedagogy "decenters authority in the classroom and students take responsibility for their learning process." In a hegemonic educational system, faculty assume ultimate authority in classroom spaces, stunting an instructor's own continued learning and growth, and if students view the instructor as all-knowing and all-powerful, they may disconnect from offering contributions that can push forward their own and others' learning. This top-down approach impedes students' responsibility for their learning, as they have been socialized to require external validation. Enacting anti-racist pedagogy requires sharing power in classrooms while acknowledging and reframing systemic authority. When we co-plan and co-facilitate with students, we decenter authority from the single faculty of record and open space for power to be renegotiated between members of the learning community. We encourage student responsibility for learning and responsibility for others' learning through weekly readings students select independently and for which they are responsible for posting an annotation online for everyone else to read. Similarly, everyone in the course receives feedback from peers on their work. In this way, faculty are not the only authority in evaluating and encouraging students. Further, we create opportunities for students to share their work publicly (beyond the class) rather than simply reaching the end of the semester, receiving a grade from the instructor, and moving on.

We also ask students to self-assess, using a parameter breakdown of different elements of the course (journal reflections, annotated bibliographies, research papers, and portfolios). We offer feedback on submissions throughout the semester, but in their final portfolios, students revisit their Course Commitment Form and offer a rationale for the score they've assigned themselves in each section. This is a difficult concept for students to grasp at first. We field many questions about penalties for late submissions and how we expect students to make decisions, but we work through these challenges with them. Self-assessment purposefully distributes power and authority back to students. It also helps to support co-teachers because they only give feedback and don't take up the awkward position of assigning grades in the way a teaching assistant might.

Anti-racist pedagogy "empowers students and applies theory to practice." Hegemonic educational systems and approaches conceptualize education as apolitical and ahistorical, whereas anti-racist teachers create opportunities for students "to apply theories to practice through problem-posing and dialog and figure out solutions or ways to improve their everyday lives."[19] The position of student

co-teacher itself is empowering and creates a different institutional location. Inviting women of color to fill these
roles situates historically excluded students to mobilize
their identities to effect cultural change and to redress epistemic, affective, and ontological harms that students from
minoritized groups experience as a result of the inequitable
and unjust structures and practices in postsecondary education.[20] Students experience the microcosm of the social
world that is the classroom and the institution to "actualize
changes in a bounded space," which provides students "with
the tools to create change in the 'outside world.' "[21] Thus,
students link theory to the practices they enact within the
course, as well as application through assignments that
often produce actionable reports and recommendations for
the wider college community.

Anti-racist pedagogy "creates a sense of community in
the classroom through collaborative learning." By countering "individualistic, competitive learning styles," we
strive to create with students a sense of community in
the classroom.[22] Sharing the leadership of an educational
space with a student co-teacher inherently models collaborative learning for enrolled students. As instructors and
student co-teachers, we learn about and from each other
as the course unfolds. By developing and enacting trust,
we and our student co-teachers model the type of relationship building that promotes a communal responsibility for
learning.

As a class we draw on Access Needs Forms that students
complete to intentionally create classroom guidelines and
to envision an ideal space that accounts for all the differences and similarities along with learning goals and activity preferences of the particular people in the classroom.[23]
We prioritize students knowing each other's names and

participating in different small groups so that people feel comfortable sharing with as many classmates as possible. We start with daily check-ins to prioritize building relationships on a human level, and then we share this responsibility with our student co-teachers and enrolled students. We have even used Google Forms to take enrolled students' suggestions of background music to play while people are arriving to class, so students decide how to set the tone.

We find midsemester feedback from enrolled students essential in sustaining and informing classroom community and collaborative learning. At the midpoint, we explicitly solicit anonymous student feedback on course goals, community guidelines, pedagogies, and students' perceptions of their learning. We share these responses with the entire class. Together, we analyze these informal data to decide how to move forward and what changes need to be implemented, and we rearticulate our commitment to supporting the community's learning and growth.

Recommendations

"To challenge assumptions and foster critical analytical skills," we urge you to recognize that everything is and should be open to critique, even the things you love and hold dear. We urge you to challenge assumptions regarding who can teach and who needs to learn by engaging a student as a compensated co-teacher, or at minimum a co-planner, in course development, and inviting enrolled students to co-create your courses with you. Recognize that you as the teacher of record are not the only one with valuable resources to be shared and that students will best develop critical analytical skills by working alongside you to generate resources for the course.

To "develop students' awareness of their social positions," you first need to recognize that social position is relevant to teaching and learning, regardless of the discipline in which you teach. As a faculty member, be aware of your own social position, be explicit about it, and recognize that it impacts the way you approach the classroom. Create assignments and activities in every course that affirm all identities and productively challenge enrolled students— and yourself as a teacher—to continually explore how social position intersects with course content.

To "decenter authority in the classroom and make space for students to take responsibility for their learning process," invite students to draw on their expertise and participate fully in developing the process and content of what they are learning, and make space for students to choose how they demonstrate their learning and how their work is assessed. To work toward distributing power in a space and rejecting hierarchical notions of authority, embrace student collaboration in all areas of structured and unstructured learning. Students will rise to the occasion with sufficient guidance and coaching. If self-assessment feels too radical, you might invite students to actively reflect on and share their learning and take those reflections into consideration in your assessment.

To "empower students and apply theory to practice," create assignments and activities that invite students to link theory and practice within and beyond the classroom and have that linking count. Furthermore, create a classroom space where critical feedback is structured into the practice; students in the room can always be resources to and for each other, but they need to be recognized and positioned as such by the teacher.

Finally, to "create a sense of community in the classroom through collaborative learning," you and your co-teacher(s) can establish a community that values all of the members within it. It seems rudimentary, but knowing the names of students and facilitating them knowing each other, beyond the academic content, is essential. Use daily check-ins that invite all people into the space, each session, and invite the co-teacher and enrolled students to lead. Further, purposeful use of group work for the sake of shared learning and group progress gives purpose to an otherwise avoided form of classroom engagement. Group work is not easy, and you need to guide students to navigate group dynamics, but if students are operating from the basis of shared responsibility, they can overcome any obstacles. In short, recognize practices that lead to competition between students and dismantle them throughout the semester, support and normalize collaboration, and constantly revisit the idea and language of community and growth to ensure that it includes everyone and is dependent on every person's contributions and insight.

Teaching Remotely

All of the strategies we discuss here can be enacted in remote teaching contexts; indeed, we both taught our courses remotely during the fall 2020 and spring 2021 semesters. We have found working with a co-teacher beneficial in online contexts because we can share the more technically complex responsibilities of opening, facilitating, and co-creating the learning space. We find that in remote forums, it is especially important to acknowledge our own and students' awareness of their social positions since differently positioned people experience different access to, extent of, and comfort with technology. We also find that remote teaching is conducive to decentering authority in the classroom if we invite students to take responsibility for their and others' learning processes through, for instance, devoting the last few minutes of class to breakout rooms in which students meet with accountability partners. Finally, we find that providing more highly structured opportunities to apply theory to practice and create a sense of community in the classroom through collaborative learning is essential in remote forums, as in face-to-face classrooms.

Conclusion

Our course creates space for each of us—faculty, student co-teachers, and enrolled students—to become "reorganizer[s] of institutional machinery" that enacts decolonizing strategies within our institution. Anti-racist pedagogy is one form the witch's flight takes in pursuit of such decolonializing.[24] It supports students in recognizing and acting in their capacity as agents in their own and others' learning. It also allows teachers to continue to be learners without losing authority through making relationships the premise of teaching—partnership in community rather than for performance, power hoarding, and competition. We offer these examples of a students-as-co-teachers approach, assignments, activities, and assessments that strive to enact anti-racist pedagogical principles and recommendations to you who strive to contribute to rippling "the patterning of power" that has sustained White supremacy and disempowered students, in hopes that you will focus on building relationships in which everyone can be both a teacher and a learner, following the witch's flight to "a more radical elsewhere."[25]

···

Teaching Takeaways

···

- Developing awareness of one's own social position and how to work from it to dismantle White supremacist structures and practices informs how we challenge assumptions about who is a *knower*, foster students' critical analytical skills, and invite the application of theory to practice.

- Sharing power and authority promotes deeper engagement and learning. Decentering authority, co-creating knowledge and practice, and creating a sense of community through collaboration all work together to constitute anti-racist teaching approaches.

- Working toward equitable and just educational practices benefits all learners—students and teachers alike—and moves us toward making classroom and institutional spaces the more radical elsewhere.

························

CHANELLE WILSON holds a doctorate in educational leadership from the University of Delaware. She is an assistant professor of education at Bryn Mawr/Haverford College and the director of Africana studies at Bryn Mawr College. She served as a public school practitioner in the United States and around the world. Wilson's current scholarship focuses on race, anti-racism, and anti-colonial practices in education. She enjoys facilitating knowledge that encourages personal connections, promotes critical thinking, and necessitates justice.

ALISON COOK-SATHER is Mary Katharine Woodworth Professor of Education at Bryn Mawr College, director of the Teaching and Learning Institute at Bryn Mawr and Haverford Colleges, and author or coauthor of more than one hundred articles and chapters and eight books, including *Education Is Translation: A Metaphor for Change in Learning and Teaching* and *Promoting Equity and Justice through Pedagogical Partnership*. Her teaching, program facilitation, and scholarship focus on co-creation for engagement and equity.

Notes

1. Harriet L. Schwartz, *Connected Teaching: Relationship, Power, and Mattering in Higher Education* (Sterling, VA: Stylus Publishing, 2019).

2. la paperson, *A Third University Is Possible* (Minneapolis: University of Minnesota Press, 2017), 64.

3. Alison Cook-Sather and Chanelle Wilson, eds., *Building Courage, Confidence, and Capacity in Learning and Teaching through Student-Faculty Partnership: Stories from across Contexts and Arenas of Practice* (Lanham, MD: Lexington Books, 2020); Alison Cook-Sather, "Living and Learning from Partnerships in Teacher Education," in *Exploring Professional Development Opportunities for Teacher Educators: Promoting Faculty-Student Partnerships,* eds. Leah Shagrir and Smadar Bar-Tal (New York: Taylor and Francis, 2021); Chanelle Wilson and Mercedes Davis, "Transforming the Student-Professor Relationship: A Multiphase Research Partnership," *International Journal for Students as Partners* 4, no. 1 (2020): 155–61.

4.   paperson, *A Third University*, 64, xvii; Kara Keeling, *The Witch's Flight: The Cinematic, The Black Femme, and The Image of Common Sense* (Durham: Duke University Press, 2007), 137.

5.   In the spring 2021 semester, the course co-facilitators, in collaboration with enrolled students and recent graduates, renamed the course Exploring and Enacting Transformation of Higher Education.

6.   George Sefa Dei, *Anti-Racism: Theory and Practice* (Halifax: Fernwood, 1996); Jennifer Akamine Phillips et al., "Barriers and Strategies by White Faculty Who Incorporate Anti-Racist Pedagogy," *Race and Pedagogy Journal* 3, no. 2 (2019): 252.

7.   Shirley Anne Tate and Paul Bagguley, "Building the Anti-Racist University: Next Steps," *Race Ethnicity and Education* 20, no. 3 (2017): 295.

8.   Amy Verhaeghe, Ela Przybylo, and Sharifa Patel, "On the Im/possibilities of Anti-Racist and Decolonial Publishing as Pedagogical Praxis," *Feminist Teacher* 28 (2018): 79.

9.   Kyoko Kishimoto, "Anti-Racist Pedagogy: From Faculty's Self-Reflection to Organizing within and beyond the Classroom," *Race Ethnicity and Education* 21, no. 4 (2018): 540–54.

10.   Mick Healey, Abbi Flint, and Kathy Harrington, "Students as Partners: Reflections on a Conceptual Model," *Teaching and Learning Inquiry* 4, no. 2 (2016): 8–20, https://doi.org/10.20343/teachlearninqu.4.2.3.

11.   Alison Cook-Sather, Catherine Bovill, and Peter Felten, *Engaging Students as Partners in Learning and Teaching: A Guide for Faculty* (San Francisco: Jossey-Bass, 2014), 6–7.

12.   Kelley E. Matthews et al., "Enhancing Outcomes and Reducing Inhibitors to the Engagement of Students and Staff in Learning and Teaching Partnerships: Implications for Academic Development," *International Journal for Academic Development* 24, no. 3 (2019): 246–59.

13.   Catherine Bovill, "Co-creation in Learning and Teaching: The

Case for a Whole-class Approach in Higher Education," *Higher Education* 79 (2020): 1025.

14. Christopher S. Collins and Alexander Yun, *White Out: Understanding White Privilege and Dominance in the Modern Age* (New York: Peter Lang, 2017).

15. Gloria Ladson-Billings and William F. Tate, "Toward a Critical Race Theory of Education," *Teacher College Record* 97 (1995): 47–68; Tara J. Yosso, "Toward a Critical Race Curriculum," *Equity and Excellence in Education* 35, no. 2 (2002): 93–107.

16. Tema Okun, "White Supremacy Culture," in *Dismantling Racism: A Workbook for Social Change Groups* (Durham, NC: Change Work, 2000), https://www.dismantlingracism.org/uploads/4 /3/5/7/43579015/okun_-_white_sup_culture.pdf.

17. Alison Cook-Sather and Praise Agu, "Students of Color and Faculty Members Working Together toward Culturally Sustaining Pedagogy," in *To Improve the Academy: Resources for Faculty, Instructional, and Organizational Development*, eds. James E. Groccia and Laura Cruz (San Francisco: Jossey-Bass, 2013), 271–85; Alise de Bie et al., "Valuing Knowledge(s) and Cultivating Confidence: Contributions of Student–Faculty Pedagogical Partnerships to Epistemic Justice," in *Strategies for Fostering Inclusive Classrooms in Higher Education: International Perspectives on Equity and Inclusion*, eds. Patrick Blessinger, Jaimie Hoffman, and Mandla Makhanya (United Kingdom: Emerald Publishing Limited, 2019), 35–48.

18. Alison Cook-Sather, Crystal Des-Ogugua, and Melanie Bahti, "Articulating Identities and Analyzing Belonging: A Multistep Intervention that Affirms and Informs a Diversity of Students," *Teaching in Higher Education* 23, no. 3 (2018): 374–89.

19. Kishimoto, "Anti-Racist Pedagogy," 549.

20. Alison Cook-Sather et al., "Mobilizing a Culture Shift on Campus: Underrepresented Students as Educational Developers," *New Directions for Teaching and Learning 159*

(2019): 21–30; de Bie et al. "Valuing Knowledge"; Alise de Bie, Elizabeth Marquis, Alison Cook-Sather, and Leslie Luqueño, *Promoting Equity and Justice through Pedagogical Partnership* (Sterling, VA: Stylus, 2021).

21. Cook-Sather Des-Ogugua, and Bahti, "Articulating Identities," 384.

22. Kishimoto, "Anti-Racists Pedagogy," 549.

23. Alison Cook-Sather, "A Tool for Changing Differences from Deficits into Resources: The 'Access Needs Form.'" *The National Learning and Teaching Forum* 28, no. 5 (2019): 7–9 https://doi .org/10.1002/ntlf.30209.

24. paperson, *A Third University*, 55.

25. Keeling, *The Witches Flight*, 137.

. . . .

CHAPTER 12

BEYOND "GOOD WRITING"

Enacting Anti-Racist Policies in Academic Writing

. . . .

Jacinta Yanders and Ashley JoEtta

. . . .

No. It's Fine.

. . . .

Before we can dig into this chapter and unpack what it means for us to be Black women professors in the writing classroom, it's critical to acknowledge the circumstances under which we are expected to produce quality work as scholar-teachers in the academy. As of August 30, 2020, approximately 123 Black folks have been fatally shot by police in the United States in 2020 alone.[1] As of August 31, 2020, approximately 183,374 people have died from COVID-19 in the United States. Because racism is systemic, COVID-19 disproportionately affects Black folks compared to other races in the United States. Black Americans experience the highest actual COVID-19 mortality rates nationwide—more than twice as high as the rate for Whites and Asians. These two emergent events, on their own, would be exhausting, demoralizing, and defeating. In tandem, they create and perpetuate inequitable work and living conditions. We are tired and our tiredness looks quite different because of our Blackness.

As Black women, we're not often expected to be front and center in writing or English classrooms. Typically, when writing and English are conceived of as a practice or as a skill, we don't see many Black women elevated to the forefront as experts on language and writing processes. The writing and English classroom professor is stereotypically conceived of as the White, cisgender male—adorned in corduroy and the like—who pontificates on the musings of Emerson, Tennyson, Shakespeare, or perhaps even Hogwarts. Because of this stereotype, it's common for students to initially mistake us for peers. Part of this mistaken identity is no doubt because we are young academics. But it's also because the racial hierarchy depicts us as inadequate at skin level. Before we even open our mouths, we are met with opposition and resistance, which has been an ongoing experience in the classroom our entire lives.

A Bit about Jacinta

My first language is African American Vernacular English (AAVE). AAVE isn't just slang, nor is it "bad" English—a persistent view, despite the Conference on College Composition and Communication's 1974 assertion that students have the right to their own language. AAVE is a rich, ever-evolving language comprised of several dialects. It also influences popular language usage, especially on social media—perhaps reflecting the familiar pattern of capitalizing on Black innovation while simultaneously marginalizing Black lives.

I was raised in a Black American family, speaking a dialect of midwestern AAVE largely influenced by southern origins. My grandparents, like many other Black folks, moved north during the Great Migration. For us, AAVE remains natural, comfortable, and colorful in ways that aren't as easily transferable to so-called Standardized English. Yet, I realized early on that AAVE was not what teachers wanted from me.

My hometown is predominantly Black, but most teachers I had were White. They typically required my classmates and me to learn the *rules* of Standardized English and mimic them in our own language usage. The few Black teachers I had often spoke AAVE while also encouraging what I eventually knew to be codeswitching. They knew we were going to be judged unfairly and wanted to take one avenue of judgment off the table. It makes sense. But I didn't like it. I like it even less now.

See, AAVE has never prevented me from being able to communicate. Why was it such a big deal if I said or wrote, "I ain't got no money" versus "I don't have any money"? You understand what I mean in both instances, right? Yet, many a teacher would say the second is *correct* or *good* grammar, and ultimately, that is most important. It's about being understood, they might say.

But you do understand me. You just don't want to.

Throughout my academic life, I've often codeswitched. I was/am good at it, but I'd be lying if I said it didn't coincide with an identity crisis, as well as some particularly bad poetry (shout out to *Love Jones*). It took me much longer than I'd prefer to learn that not only was Standardized English not inherently better than AAVE but also that I had to be the person in front of the classroom who expressed this to my students.

A Bit about Ashley

According to the National Center for Education Statistics, as of 2018, of the 1.5 million faculty of varying ranks at degree-granting postsecondary institutions, only 3 percent each were Black men and Black women. There aren't a lot of us Black American women front and center in the classroom. I was the first Black American woman to graduate from my PhD program at Purdue University, and I only knew of two other Black American women students in the whole department. I am the only Black American woman teaching first-year composition at my current institution. I am often the only Black American woman attending my discipline-specific conferences (I say *often* only to politely hedge, but I've never met another Black American woman at my home conferences). There is no other Black woman in corpus linguistics (to my knowledge), and I only know of five other Black women professors in applied linguistics, TESOL (Teaching English to Speakers of Other Languages), and sociolinguistics. Throughout my entire graduate education, I never had a Black professor in my fields of study.

During my first year as a PhD student in 2014, I asked a White woman professor in my program, second language studies, "Where are the Black scholars?" She nodded her head toward me as if to answer, "*You* are the Black scholar." In later incidents, she either explicitly said I would succeed because I was Black (ya know, affirmative action) or insinuated it and followed up with statements like "Make sure you have the methodological and theoretical chops to hold your own and sustain your future position as a scholar." I would (will) succeed not because I'm good but because I'm Black.

Impostor syndrome is the voice that creeps in and molests academics and professionals (typically women, and more often those from marginalized groups) with fears of being found out to be a fraud.[2] It's the voice in your head that says:

I'm not really good enough.

I don't know enough.

I got here by mistake.

I tricked others into believing I know more than I really do.

I don't belong here.

I don't deserve praise or accolades.

At any moment, success can all be taken away; it was never mine to begin with.

The absence of representation exacerbates impostor syndrome. Being a Black woman, a young woman, a multilingual woman, and a woman who was once poor and homeless makes me hyperaware of my positionality of being Other in the majority of my professional and academic contexts.

When I think about representation and why it matters in the classroom, especially when we're engaging in conversations around equity, inclusivity, and anti-racist policies that uplift and support our historically marginalized and disenfranchised students, I think about the weight of being the first, of being Other. Often, our students of color are the first in their families to pursue a higher education, and they're looking for a familiar face to turn toward, a face that says *you've got this, and I've got you.* This absence of racial representation of minority groups at the college level has ripple effects impacting student success and retention, as well as the ways in which students feel they can and are invited to bring their whole selves to the classroom.[3] While undergraduate programs are becoming increasingly more racially diverse among the student body, there's been little forward movement in the racial representation of faculty. How many of our students walk around feeling like impostors?

As a writing and language educator, I spend most of my time in the classroom pulling at the threads that have wound my students into walking clews of anxiety, doubt, and fear. Learning has become a place of pain for them because so much of their education has focused on "fixing" them through an interwork of strands that criticize, demean, and disparage their personhood. My students come into the writing classroom afraid to be creative, afraid to take risks, afraid of being policed, afraid to not know something because they're afraid of not being good enough, afraid of another layer of Otherness, and afraid of being exposed as a fraud.

Anti-Racism in the Writing Classroom

Anti-racism is an important pedagogical framework because Black and Brown students deserve to be in a classroom where pain isn't part of the lesson plan and where fear of being found out to be a fraud isn't reinforced with racist writing pedagogy that favors one linguistic variation over another. Students deserve to be in a classroom where their whole selves are welcomed and celebrated, including their language choices. Anti-racism teaches us to focus on the needs of the student rather than the needs of systems of oppression.

In order to talk about anti-racism and what we mean when we say we're anti-racist educators, we need to unpack a few definitions. Like Paolo Freire, we believe that naming is a critical step in the transformation process; we cannot transform what we are unwilling/unable to name.[4] Similarly, Ibram X. Kendi emphasizes the importance of identifying and naming phenomena so that we can collectively begin examining and questioning said phenomena.[5] The process of identifying and naming a construct such as race is particularly important because so often racism happens behind the scenes. Kendi defines racism as "a marriage of racist policies and racist ideas that produces and normalizes racial inequity."[6] Racist ideas have a way of bleeding into our thought processes, empowering White people to support racist ideas or to beat down Black and Brown folks until we believe we are less than White people.[7] Racist ideas perpetuate racial inequity because they inevitably become embedded in racist policies.

For one to truly be anti-racist, it is imperative to focus not on people as problematic but rather on investigating the policies that ensnare them. We certainly cannot do this work from a race-neutral place; in fact, race neutrality is itself a racist idea because the only true way to dismantle racism is to consistently identify it and describe it. As Kendi writes, "The construct of race neutrality actually feeds White nationalist victimhood by positing the notion that any policy protecting or advancing non-White Americans toward equity is 'reverse discrimination.' "[8] When we start advocating for policies that promote racial equity, we see abhorrent clinginess to policies that promote the advancement of White Americans via language that sounds inclusive but is actually another act of erasure, such as #AllLivesMatter or #BlueLivesMatter.

Jeffrey Moro argues we should "abolish cop shit in the classroom," referring to practices such as tech surveillance and literally calling the cops on students, mimicking the worst of a world that always enacts harsh "justice" upon

Black and Brown people.[9] Notably, the educational impetus toward surveillance and policing has only grown more insidious in the COVID-19 world where we now debate whether students should be forced to have their cameras on despite evidence asserting that ongoing surveillance can contribute to the development of symptoms similar to post-traumatic stress disorder.[10] This, in addition to concerns about uneven student access to technology, ownership of student intellectual property, privacy violations, and racial discrimination in technology should be enough for us to refrain from increasing the presence of surveillance in our classes. Yet, corporations like Proctorio and ProcterU continue to flourish. What do we signal to students when we monitor how often they log into the learning management system and use the data to infer their level of commitment to the class? Black and Brown students enter our classrooms having familiarity with being policed by a racist society that perpetually sees them as deficient and criminal. But what if we didn't treat any of our students like suspects? What benefits to teacher-student relationships, student confidence, student engagement, classroom community, and more might we see if we imagined classes outside of the confines of mis/distrust?

If we want students to use their own voices in their writing (as we often say we do) and we want them to take chances in their writing (as we often say we do), then we must create classroom communities that allow for these possibilities. As Jesse Stommel succinctly asserts, we need to "start by trusting students."[11] Trust is important for all of our students, but, again, particularly for our Black and Brown students who have often—implicitly and explicitly—been taught they have to do twice as much to get half as far. If we approach student writing from a position of trust rather than skepticism, discipline, and punishment, we might create a learning environment in which fear—one of the primary driving factors for intentional plagiarism—does not win.[12]

As Black women, we understand that ceding control in the classroom brings about its own set of risks. We risk harsh evaluations from students, colleagues, and administrators. We enter into our decision to foster trust with an understanding that we will likely have to fight harder to see our pedagogical wishes fulfilled.

But we've always been fighters.

Even if/when we're tired of fighting.

That being said, we're not able to effectively carry this out on our own in a way that has a broad, sustainable impact. Everybody has to commit, not just to the label anti-racist but also to actually doing the work. Those who have some measure of power have to collectively put theory into practice and be willing to stay the course, even when our anti-racist approaches are—perhaps unsurprisingly—overly surveilled and policed.

This is especially true given that some folks such as graduate students and those precariously employed may find themselves unable to make changes and institute policies like the ones we're describing. They may not be allowed to change their courses, they may have specific assessments they're required to use, or they simply may not have the bandwidth necessary to make significant pedagogical changes. This reflects deeply entrenched systemic issues. If at all possible, we recommend incremental changes, perhaps once a quarter or semester. Even the smallest of changes can have a lasting impact.

The four strategies described next are not the only ones that foster an anti-racist writing classroom or approach to writing in any other classes. However, they are four that we consistently make use of in our classrooms. These approaches have involved a good deal of trial and error. For example, Jacinta has moved from rubrics to contract grading to labor-based grading over the course of about five years. Ashley has also moved away from the traditional grading structure and embraces the liberation that comes with not grading; rather than focusing on traditional grades, she instead emphasizes the drafting process and focuses on providing feedback and teaching students how to engage with feedback and the revision process. In Ashley's anecdotal experience, students find that not being graded gives them room to stretch, take risks, and learn without fear of not being good enough. There's no one-size-fits-all magic bullet here, but hopefully, some part of what we describe will be useful to you.

First, validate and celebrate language and writing diversity in your classes. Both of our lives were significantly shaped by educational systems that denigrated our language and ways of thinking. Because of our experiences, we intentionally work toward not reaping the same types of trauma upon our students. Ironically, in disciplines outside of English, it often seems unpopular to validate language diversity. But it is the right thing to do.

Second, make sure your syllabi reflect your commitment to and acceptance of language diversity in your classes. Syllabi are often the first point of contact that students may have with our classes, and they very much shape student expectations of both our classes and us. For us, it's critical to craft the desired impressions, especially given the stereotypes that we know might be surrounding us. For our students, it's evident that many of them come to English classes (and writing assignments) with the perspective that these are requirements being foisted upon them and with the belief that their own writing will never measure up. Explicitly acknowledging the importance of language diversity from the start helps to shape the norms of our classes, and it also helps to shift the broader paradigms that undergird how we think about language as a society. If we want to cultivate a culture in which Standardized English is not considered the gold standard, we have to build a new way of thinking into our classes that goes beyond the theoretical statements of the past. It's not enough to just say "students have a right to their own language." We have to prove it. Make your classes a place where the richness of language variation is celebrated, rather than denigrated, and we can—almost—guarantee students will feel more immediate ease, which translates into better writing experiences.

Third, be intentional about the materials you use in your classes. We imagine everyone has heard that they should diversify/decolonize/make inclusive the materials used in their classes. Some have taken this advice positively, choosing to break away from canons that are exclusive by design. Others have responded negatively, voicing a commitment to use only what is "best." Many fall somewhere in between. As a practical step, we believe it is crucial to widen the range of materials used in all classrooms. Existing literature includes a wide range of dialects and languages, but in many classrooms, those dialects and languages are either not represented at all or questionably represented (we're looking at you *The Adventures of Huckleberry Finn*).

If students never see language variety in the materials we use, then any overtures we make about language variation become null and void. The message we convey is that the Austens, Hemingways, and such are superior. Including the occasional *Their Eyes Were Watching God* or *The Color*

Purple is not enough. Furthermore, you might include writing from the *New York Times* in your classes, but what about writing from *The Root* or *Remezcla*? What about including materials like Jamila Lyiscott's "3 Ways to Speak English" or a chapter from Luvvie Ajayi's book *I'm Judging You*?[13] Show students that their language is acceptable in your classroom and has value in the professional world. Lest we get copies of anthologies chucked in our direction, we're not saying you can't teach anything canonical. But if you want to change the language and writing paradigms, we believe it necessary to be intentional about those choices.

Finally, but perhaps most radically, reconsider how you approach the grading and assessment of writing. Ungrading, specifications grading, contract grading, and labor-based grading are particularly relevant to writing assessment.[14] This isn't just because there's little likelihood of objectively assessing writing. It's also because grades tell students whether they have the freedom to experiment with language, integrate their own voices, and write outside of formulaic structures. We want our students to grow as *writers*, not as people who can match a particular template at will. We have to give them the opportunity to play with writing and not fail them for it, and we have to do that over and over again in various classes, not just the Freshman Composition sequence. Think about the signal you're sending when you give a student a C on a draft. What does that tell them about who they are as growing writers? Think about the signal you give when you privilege academic research papers over all other forms of writing, especially given that most students are not going to be moving forward in academia after completing their undergraduate degrees. What are you telling them by hyperfocusing on the type of writing that is the furthest away from who they are, how they might want to express themselves, and what they might be doing with their lives?

Conclusion

We'd like to leave you with a set of questions for self-reflection and to consider while developing and teaching any course, especially courses that involve writing assignments. We encourage radically honest answers rather than simply putting forth the answer that may seem most acceptable:

- What does "good" writing look like to me? How did I develop this perception?
- What does "bad" writing look like to me? How did I develop this perception?
- If I'm requiring my students to complete writing assignments, am I also spending time teaching them how to write? Why or why not?
- How do my background and identity impact how I teach?
- What do my course policies communicate to my students (both explicitly and implicitly)?
- How do the backgrounds and identities of my students impact how I assess their work?
- Toni Morrison once said, "I tell my students, 'When you get these jobs that you have been so brilliantly trained for, just remember that your real job is that if you are free, you need to free somebody else. If you have some power, then your job is to empower somebody else.' "[15] How can you empower students in your classes?

Does all of this mean we need to rethink how we think about "good writing"? Absolutely. Is it worth it? Absolutely. For us, as Black women in academia, there are risks to making these choices. We know that we may be judged harshly for them, but we also know that upholding oppressive structures is not the way. The harm done to us in classrooms is not something we're willing to reinscribe, and we hope that you aren't either. To paraphrase Stommel, everyone has to agree to do the right thing.[16] When it comes to writing in schools, doing the right thing is necessarily different than doing what has always been done, but it is ultimately the best way forward.

....

Teaching Takeaways

....

- Validate and celebrate language and writing diversity in your classes.
- Ensure your syllabi reflect your commitment to and acceptance of language diversity.
- Be intentional about the materials you use in your classes.
- Reconsider how you approach the grading and assessment of writing.
- Engage in ongoing and radically honest self-reflection.

....

JACINTA YANDERS is an assistant professor of English at the College of DuPage. She teaches classes in a variety of areas, including composition, film, and literature. Jacinta previously served on the steering committee for the Critical

Media Pedagogy special interest group in the Society for Cinema and Media Studies, and she currently serves on the teaching committee for EDIT Media (Equity, Diversity, and Inclusion in Teaching Media).

ASHLEY JOETTA holds a doctorate in second language studies from Purdue University and is an assistant professor in the school of interdisciplinary arts and sciences at the University of Washington-Bothell. She currently teaches First-Year Composition, Research Writing, and Interdisciplinary Inquiry. Her research focuses on corpus analyses of disciplinary writing, specifically in engineering; the application of corpus-based pedagogy for disciplinary writing instruction; and the development and application of anti-racist writing pedagogy for the composition classroom.

Notes

1. Statista Research Department, "Number of People Shot to Death by the Police in the United States from 2017 to 2021, By Race," *Statisa*, May 3, 2021, https://www.statista.com /statistics/585152/people-shot-to-death-by-us-police-by-race/.

2. Pauline Rose Clance and Suzanne Ament Imes, "The Imposter Phenomenon in High Achieving Women: Dynamics and Therapeutic Intervention," *Psychotherapy: Theory, Research and Practice* 15, no. 3 (1978): 241–47.

3. Carol A. Lundberg and Laurie A. Schreiner, "Quality and Frequency of Faculty-Student Interaction as Predictors of Learning: An Analysis by Student Race/Ethnicity," *Journal of College Student Development* 45, no. 5 (2004): 549–65.

4. Paolo Freire, *Pedagogy of the Oppressed*, rev. ed. (New York: Continuum, 1996).

5. Ibram X. Kendi, *How to Be an Antiracist* (New York: Penguin Random House, 2019).

6. Kendi, *How to Be an Antiracist*, 17–18.

7. Kendi, *How to Be an Antiracist*, 6.

8. Kendi, *How to Be an Antiracist*, 20.

9. Jeffrey Moro, "Against Cop Shit," *Jeffrey Moro* (blog), February 13, 2020, https://jeffreymoro.com/blog/2020-02-13-against -cop-shit/.

10. Kaleigh Rogers, "What Constant Surveillance Does to Your Brain," *Vice*, November 14, 2018, https://www.vice.com/en /article/pa5d9g/what-constant-surveillance-does-to-your-brain.

11. Jesse Stommel (@Jessifer), Start by trusting students. #4wordpedagogy, Twitter, April 30, 2016, 10:53 a.m., https:// twitter.com/jessifer/status/726424167420145664.

12. Council of Writing Program Administrators, "Defining and Avoiding Plagiarism: The WPA Statement on Best Practices," December 30, 2019, https://wpacouncil.org/aws/CWPA/pt/sd /news_article/272555/_PARENT/layout_details/false.

13. Jamila Lyiscott, "3 Ways to Speak English," February 2014, *TED*, https://www.ted.com/talks/jamila_lyiscott_3_ways_to _speak_english?language; Luvvie Ajayi, *I'm Judging You* (New York: Holt Paperbacks, 2016).

14. Susan D. Blum, *Ungrading: Why Rating Students Undermines Learning (and What to Do Instead)* (Morgantown: West Virginia University Press, 2020).

15. Elissa Schappell and Claudia Lacour, "Toni Morrison, the Art of Fiction No. 34," *Paris Review*, 128 (Fall 1993), https://www .theparisreview.org/interviews/1888/the-art-of-fiction-no-134 -toni-morrison.

16. Rebecca Koenig, "To Grade or Not to Grade? During Coronavirus, That Is the Question," *EdSurge*, March 19, 2020, https://www.edsurge.com/news/2020-03-19-to-grade-or-not -to-grade-during-coronavirus-that-is-the-question.

PART FOUR

TEACHING WITH OUR WHOLE SELVES

Strategies for Instructional Authenticity and Pedagogical/Professional Success

CHAPTER 13

THE SUPERPOWERS OF VISUAL AMBIGUITY

Transfiguring My Experience of Colorism and Multiheritage Identity for Educational Good

. . . .

Donna Mejia

My appearance is frequently unsettling. I am a woman with six known ethnicities and a greater number of unknown ingredients. My DNA gumbo manifests blue eyes, honey-colored hair, and brown skin. I am routinely confronted with the question, "What are you?" This and numerous other microaggressions I experience in the classroom and boardroom give me a distinctive vantage point that renders visible how profoundly wounded and compromised we collectively are in addressing the legacy of colonialism, slavery, genocide, and racism in education.

I have learned that trying to bypass my identity ambiguity is pointless, so instead, I've chosen to fly my freak flag sky high, embrace the relentless social confusion I provoke, and welcome the weirdness.

In this chapter, I will briefly summarize colorism within North America's African-descended communities and the colonialist legacy fueling the common reactivity to multi-ethnicity. Then I'll share some of the proactive tools and practices for mutual learning and dismantling bias that I have developed and adopted to teach effectively from my visually ambiguous, multiheritage vantage point.

The Positionality and Historical Context of My Identity: Beyond Binaries

I inhabit middle ground in the binary of Blackness and Whiteness, but even this is not fully representative. I was raised by multiheritage Creole parents from Louisiana and Mississippi. Initially poor, they uplifted themselves to middle-class citizenship. I am the first in my immediate family to achieve an advanced degree. I live in an area that supports freedom of religious/nonreligious, political, and sexual preference expression. As a cisgendered woman, I am never challenged on my heteronormativity and frequently remind myself of what my life would be like otherwise. My past includes experiences of domestic violence. I am demographically minoritized in my community, as most of my neighborhood, coworkers, and students are European American. To counter this geographic isolation, I frequently travel to locations inhabited mostly by people of the global majority.

In multiple career opportunities, I've learned my presence was often tokenized and passively aggressively unwelcomed. I've experienced reprimands and sabotage if I demonstrated ascendancy from my supposed place in the race/power hierarchy (another case of the "pet to threat" scenario).[1] In most situations, I've persevered.

There is a constancy to the aggressions I field from both White and Black students, colleagues, and public patrons as an educator and performer in the arts. Fortunately, I feel strongly supported in my work by a crucial number of colleagues and supervisors. The 2020 global amplification of the Black Lives Matter movement during a pandemic has been monumentally important because it exposes a hegemonically subordinated narrative: how pervasive inequity and racism remain. As a participant in this international movement, and as an educator, I am compelled to complicate this conversation by elucidating the middle zone within a continuum of Blackness and Whiteness. That "middle zone" in the United States was the result of a historical pigmentocracy: slightly or strongly favorable socioeconomic treatment for African blended peoples who possessed a lighter hue of Blackness because they were frequently the offspring of White colonizers and slaves, whether through rape, contractual agreement, or (rarely) consensual partnership.[2]

In my family, I was taught that in the 1700s, the multi-heritage citizens of New Orleans were called *Creoles*, a word derived from the Spanish verb *crear* (to create). The nomenclature *los Crióllos* (the created ones) came from Caribbean slave owners. African American Creoles were originally free people. Their African parents were not. Mixed women were often exotified and occasionally arranged into sexual servitude to White men, creating grave power differentials and injustice within African-descended families. Often raised by single mothers under great strain, Creole children were often unacknowledged and regarded as illegitimate by their White fathers. Creoles were also subjected to White women's hostilities, whose husbands begot children outside of their marriages.[3] In avoidance of the South's "one-drop" rule for Negro designation, some Creoles made extreme efforts to escape oppression by disconnecting from their families to pass for White, received as a painful betrayal in African-descended communities.

The legacy of such sexual violation and manipulation of African families still haunts the United States in substantial ways: the ambiguity of antiquated, unspoken social contracts creates emotional minefields.[4] African-descended communities haven't had a moment's rest to truly unpack the legacy of colonialism, genocide, slavery, and dehumanization. Our transgenerational trauma and interrupted lines of cultural transference manifest in multiple ways, but colorism is one of our most disorienting forms of internalized racism, interweaving classism and biological and cultural racism. It represents the unimaginable pain each family had to navigate, frequently with conflicting survival responses and defenses within a single generation of a household.

The slow legal acknowledgment of multiethnic citizens in the United States evinces a collective desire to avoid the sociopolitical and moral questions our existence provokes. It would take until 2000 for the census to account for multiple categories of ethnic belonging:

> From 1790 to 1950, census takers determined the race of the Americans they counted, sometimes taking into account how individuals were perceived in their community or using rules based on their share of "black blood." Americans who were of multiracial ancestry were either counted in a single race or classified into categories that mainly consisted of gradations of black and white, such as mulattoes, who were tabulated with the non-white population. Beginning in

1960, Americans could choose their own race. Since 2000, they have had the option to identify with more than one.[5]

Currently, the demographic acknowledgment of multiheritage citizens has not equated to a clarifying deconstruction of the stereotypes and caricatures they face.

A few examples of the daily aggressions I encounter will illustrate my ongoing confrontation of these caricatures. I've had a student's parent seek my dismissal as a university advocate because she disagreed with my self-identification as an African American woman. When invited to the *Donahue Show* in 1992 to speak about multiethnicity and colorism, I was ambushed by a string of guests who were eager to villainize a "high yellow" woman. In 1999, a group of angry women in a market began yanking at my locks and accusing me of wearing a wig (I wasn't) and I had to be protectively escorted out by security. I was called a devil by a screaming, nine-year-old boy in South Africa. A former leader of the Denver Urban League yelled at me in a board meeting, saying he didn't have to listen to a "redbone." As recently as September 2020, a White woman in my dance community who was decrying a lack of diversity awarded herself the agency to decide I was not Black enough to meet her threshold of non-Whiteness. In her subsequent apology to me, she wrote, "The opinion you quoted didn't originate from me, but rather my friends of color." If this is true, then I was doubly skewered in this instance by Black, Indigenous, and People of Color (BIPOC) *through* a White woman for not being Black enough. I certainly couldn't visually pass for White if I wanted to. My own 1969 birth certificate from California categorizes me as "Negro."

I am customarily claimed and disclaimed, beloved or challenged by various peoples and populations. The following classroom strategies are a response to pain points in my personal history but are more importantly fueled by an intense desire to *heal* the implicit bias, internalized racism, and hidden curricula plaguing our social landscapes and classrooms.[6] If my visibility as an educator and performing public figure can provide an opportunity to address this hidden history in our national and international conversation, then I'll unapologetically optimize the confusion my physical appearance evokes. People will, perhaps, catch themselves before making another assumptive deposit to the antiquated bank of identity stereotypes. As described in each of the three specific teaching strategies I share in the following sections, I aim to make my visual ambiguity a superpower.

Begin Each Course with an Assumption Index

In statistical research, the testing of assumptions and the search for a researcher's missing points and deficiencies is a must. I began including an assumption index in my learning spaces to elucidate students' presumptions of our subject matter and reduce their combativeness when those assumptions are challenged by me. I designed the progression of questions to reveal the ways we have been acculturated to a subject before we presume agency from a critical viewpoint. It is our first lesson in intellectual humility: the importance of evaluating one's social filters before educational arrogance distorts our perceptions and analysis.

An assumption index is a scaffolded step to understanding one's positionality. A researcher's personal perspective may be relevant information when analyzing a subject. This is best addressed by a positionality statement: a disclosure of self-identification, initial perceptions, beliefs, cultural, economic, and ethnicity in relation to the subject. An assumption index aims to excavate down to what we presume to be true before it interferes with our learning. It should be useful to novices and experts alike because implicit bias, and our social indoctrinations, can distort intellectual pursuits at any level, propagating perceptions, practices, and policies that, left unexamined, enshrine obstructions, power differentials, and barriers to inclusion.

The assumption index administered for the opening of my "Dance in Cultural Perception and Expression" course contains questions aimed at cultivating participant reflexivity to the topic, such as the following:

- In my life, dance is:
- The circumstances through which I learned about dance are:
- Who taught me about dance?
- Where is this dance done or not done?
- Are there observers for this dance? What is their role?
- In this dance practice, are there signature differences between the movements and expectations of participants respective to gender, age, economic class, or any other marker of identity in the community?
- Where and when did the dance originate?
- Who are some of the historical icons of this dance?
- Why is this dance done? What is its social function?
- What values does this dance embody or communicate?
- How would you describe the movements of this dance?
- What kinds of comments have you received from others about the dance you do (or do not do)?
- What kinds of dance (if any) have you been told *not* to do or been prevented from doing?

Perhaps your discipline seems too far removed from dance for this to be applicable, but all disciplines require creativity in the production of new knowledge.

Take physics for example. We can use an assumption index to help students address perceptions of identity in physics and social indoctrinations that confine thinking and limit the kinds of questions we conceive and investigate; the very things that block our creativity. We can ask, Why study physics? Who, have you been taught, are some of the pivotal figures in physics history? What kinds of things have you heard/observed physicists do for "fun"? A meme or a stereotype of a physicist customarily includes tropes such as (fill in the blank)? Who, have you learned, are some of the unsung hidden figures or oppressed voices in physics history? If applicable, who taught you about these hidden figures? What is the highest achievement one can make as a physicist?

The answers are revealing. To neutralize caricatures, use an assumption index to render them visible, then take inviting measures for all to feel affirmed for their interest in physics. This differs from examining these stereotypes only to negate them. Some participants may truly feel their experiences and activities reflect the descriptors and tropes, and these signifiers of physics culture may have been meaningful and formative in their passion for the discipline (Dungeons & Dragons games, summer science camps, sci-fi fandom, etc.). We can help those who've been bullied for reflecting the stereotype, and we expand our circle of belonging to include those who've not experienced alignment with cultural signifiers of the physics arena. As a first activity, we set the tone for new foundations of collaboration, letting students feel deeply seen and received for who they are to build confidence in skill development.

The following prompts may be useful for creating an assumption index for your own specialty subject. Participant answers to an assumption index should remain private. Discussion might yield amplified insights, but the examination alone is something that adds value to one's learning.

- The successful personal characteristics my field of study values are:
- The interaction of my political beliefs and educational studies raises these questions for me:
- The interaction of my religious/nonreligious perspectives and educational studies raises these questions for me:
- The interaction of my familial upbringing and educational studies provokes me to think about:
- In my field of study, my visual presentation prompts reactions such as:
- My socioeconomic background and current financial placement have had the following impact on my access to resources and opportunities:
- The ways I am comfortable expressing my gender identity have impacted my participation in the field in the following ways:
- The physical ability or differently abled abilities of my body have framed my involvement within this field of study in the following ways:
- My language and nationality have impacted my involvement in this field of study in the following ways:
- My sexual identity and enduring sexual affiliations have intersected with my participation in this field of study in the following ways:
- My exposure to this subject came from or was given to me by:

- In my pursuit of learning in this subject, I have encountered these pitfalls or advantages:
- What others have said to me about my involvement with this field of study:
- What intimidates me most about this field of study is:
- What fascinates me most, or what I am most curious about, in this field of study is:

An assumption index intends to help all classroom participants see their social programming and, by extension, engage the practice of seeing others more equitably. This collaborative lens to learning and teaching should not be wielded as a devaluation or shaming of any identity but rather a curatorial tool for communal awareness. All social vantage points have the capacity to serve as hindrances or superpowers, depending on either the neglectful or conscientious ways we situate ourselves to the subject of study.

Model Mutuality

We possess immense leverage over students' learning, and we control methods of evaluation. Acknowledging this, our next step is to be transparent about our high expectations for student achievement while removing the guessing games of those power differentials. We say, unequivocally, that we view students as capable, and who they are—the identity they possess—will not interfere with the educational exchange between us. By creating learning agreements based on mutual respect, we remind students that they have both rights and responsibilities in the classroom, to us, to themselves, and to their peers.

My syllabus pledge is my first offering of equitable exchange:

I will be encouraging and humorous in my offerings. I will explain thoughtfully and clearly. I will offer citations for what I have learned and concede openly what I have not yet learned. I will ensure a welcoming and inviting environment where counterpoint ideas can be exchanged diplomatically. Our discussion will welcome new ideas, worldviews, and perspectives. I will remain receptive to these lesson plans changing and transforming based on sound examination of your input. Please let me know if you perceive glaring holes in my research. I intend to give you tools to increase your conversancy, expand your boundaries, and nurture independence. I have no interest in telling you what to think. Rather, I am passionate about helping you ask better questions without interference from socially indoctrinated filters. Who you are and the life you've lived bring value to our educational experience. I will respect our differences in and out of this conversation. Your dignity and comfort are important to me, and in return, I ask for your courage, diplomacy, open-thinking, and active involvement. I will hold myself accountable to the same caliber and standards I am requesting of you.

The pledge is an offering of accountability and a model of what is expected in our treatment of each other. Clearly, students arrive at our learning space with their own baggage and habituated relationships with authority figures. I make the first offering in my pledge to reduce identity power struggles, framing students as valued collaborators, and then invite them into further shared explorations of project menus, occasional choose-your-own-adventure selections of closely related readings, grading contracts, and modes of self-assessment in partnership with my feedback.

"Fumble Forward"

There will still be messiness around your best efforts. Impositions of those who refuse to acknowledge the impact of cultural and ethnic difference impoverish us, and internalized racism is some seriously dirty laundry that perpetuates division within BIPOC communities. The sting of ignorant comments scrambles my mind and stops my breathing for a few seconds, and if I were to define myself by these offenses, I wouldn't have pursued my passions in education. My multiheritage experience has taught me that if the cultural collisions of my tributary lines can be harmonized within me, this reckoning can also be accomplished in the world at large. To help my students approach this identity complexity, I've created a special practice called "Fumble Forward."

"Fumble Forward" seeks to promote exchange, and most importantly, hit the pause button on conventional responses such as anger. To keep a space of inquiry open in a charged subject matter, students will preface their public commentary by saying "I'm about to fumble with my words." The community responds as a chorus with "Fumble Forward!" It is our social contract to let confusion be a part of our discourse. Perhaps a student is unsure of the terminologies needed to join a conversation. Perhaps they are unsure if their questions will be offensive. Perhaps they don't have fully formulated ideas and opinions yet. But for the next few minutes, we've all agreed to suspend judgment, lean in, and help each other clarify through a process of corrective, delicate, or clumsy verbal surgery.

"Fumble Forward" allows us to stay open and speak from the heart with diplomacy, even if our voices are trembling and we can't find confident, stable ground. It gives us a starting place to back away from sounding off on each other. We can diplomatically move toward true listening and communication.

It hasn't failed yet. I've been told by many students that the approach succeeds in challenging scenarios with their parents, roommates, partners, employers, and more.

....

Conclusion: Educators as Agents of Change

....

Ultimately, the emotional exhaustion of helping others become comfortable with my visual ambiguity fueled impatience: I needed to reduce the amount of time it took for us to wade through our identity filters and presumed power differentials. I would burn out and be perpetually re-wounded if I couldn't get out of the microscope curiosity of "what are you." I aimed to take the focus off of me and put it into the "we."[7] We now jump-cut past weeks of social negotiations, drop into relationship with each other, and get on with learning the juicy subject at hand., I've observed students empowered to consider the importance of their own socialization grow more quickly into critical thinking.[8] Notch another micro-healing for me and a powerful dimensionalization of their minds—a win-win.

Learning more about me inside of the we—unpacking the context of my multiheritage—inspired a fearlessness for infinite complexities when researching any subject. Relational analysis and interdisciplinary study are now deep nourishment, a welcomed change from the intimidation they bore on my early learning. The world is presently amplifying calls for justice *inspired* by the work of educators and theorists. Your collective efforts are shaking the ground. As we proceed, we must catch ourselves before enshrining new binaries and enact care to avoid the oversimplification of narratives. Rather than feel overwhelmed and paralyzed by increasing complexity, my multiheritage has demonstrated to me we are fully capable of unpacking our intersectional identities with precision and depth.[9] Whatever freak flag serves as the foundation of your own superpower, use it to heal the fractures that "othering" has cost us.

....

Teaching Takeaways
....

- Educators, drawing on our own rich experiences and personal and collective histories, can be agents of change.
- An assumption index and modeling mutuality are proactive teaching strategies for mutual learning and dismantling bias.
- Creating a class culture that encourages true listening and communication by normalizing "fumbling" gives everyone the opportunity to "Fumble Forward."

....

DONNA MEJIA is the Inaugural Chancellor's Scholar in Residence for the Crown Wellness Institute of the University of Colorado Boulder and tenured in theater and dance as a transcultural fusion dancer. She is a Carson Dance Library "Legend of Dance" and a 2021 Outstanding Graduate

Mentor. Her interdisciplinary research received the 2011 Selma Jeanne Cohen Fulbright Award for International Dance Scholarship. She is deeply committed to truth, embodiment, dignity, and compassion in education. Visit her at https://donnainthedance.com/.

Notes

1. Kecia M. Thomas et al., "Moving from Pet to Threat: Narratives of Professional Black Women," in *The Psychological Health of Women of Color: Intersections, Challenges, and Opportunities*, eds. Lillian Comas-Diaz and Beverly Green (Westport, CT: Praeger, 2013), 275–86.

2. Alice Walker, as cited by Kimberly Jade Norwood, " 'If You Is White, You's Alright:' Stories about Colorism in America," *Global Studies Law Review* 14, no. 4 (Winter 2015), https://openscholarship.wustl.edu/law_globalstudies/vol14/iss4/8/.

3. Emily Clark, *The Strange History of the American Quadroon: Free Women of Color in the Revolutionary Atlantic World* (Chapel Hill: University of North Carolina Press, 2013); Ronald Hall, Kathy Russell, and Midge Wilson, *The Color Complex: The Politics of Skin Color among African Americans* (New York: Harcourt Brace Javanovich, 1992); Sybil Kein, ed., *Creole: The History and Legacy of Louisiana's Free People of Color* (Baton Rouge: Louisiana State University Press, 2000); Shirley Thompson, *Exiles at Home: The Struggle to Become American in Creole New Orleans* (Cambridge: Harvard University Press, 2009); Isabel Wilkerson, *Caste: The Origins of Our Discontents* (New York: Random House, 2020). See also Arnold Hrisch and Joseph Logsdon, eds., *Creole New Orleans: Race and Americanization* (Baton Rouge: Louisiana State University Press, 1992).

4. For historical analysis and perspective, see Carol Anderson, *White Rage: The Unspoken Truth of Our Racial Divide* (New York

Bloomsbury, 2016); Robert Jensen, *Citizens of the Empire: The Struggle to Claim Our Humanity* (San Francisco: City Lights Books, 2004); Ibram X. Kendi, *Stamped from the Beginning: The Definitive History of Racist Ideas in America* (New York: Bold Type Books, 2016); Baratunde Thurston, *How to Be Black* (New York: Harper Collins, 2012); Mabel Wilson, *Negro Building: Black Americans in the World of Fairs and Museums* (Berkeley: University of California Press, 2012). On teaching, see Elizabeth Dutro, *The Vulnerable Heart of Literacy: Centering Trauma as Powerful Pedagogy* (New York: Teachers College Press, 2019). On family impact, see Haim Ginott, *Between Parent and Child: New Solutions to Old Problems* (New York: McMillan, 1965). On healing racialized trauma, see Resmaa Menakem, *My Grandmother's Hands: Racialized Trauma and the Pathway to Mending Our Hearts and Bodies* (Las Vegas: Central Recovery Press, 2017).

5.   Kim Parker et al., "Multiracial in America," Pew Social Trends, June 11, 2015, https://www.pewresearch.org/social-trends /2015/06/11/chapter-1-race-and-multiracial-americans-in -the-u-s-census/. See also Eduardo Bonilla-Silva, "From Bi-racial to Tri-racial: Towards a New System of Racial Stratification in the USA," *Ethnic and Racial Studies* 27, no. 6 (2004): 931–50; Nathan Glazer, *We Are All Multiculturalists Now* (Cambridge: Harvard University Press, 1997).

6.   Mahzarin Banaji and Anthony Greenwald, *Blind Spot: Hidden Biases of Good People* (New York: Bantam Books, 2013); Heather Horst and Daniel Miller, eds., *Digital Anthropology* (London: Bloomsbury, 2012); Robert Jensen, *The Heart of Whiteness: Confronting Race, Racism, and White Privilege* (San Francisco: City Lights Books, 2005); Ijeoma Olou, *So You Want to Talk about Race* (New York: Seal Press, 2019); Steven Pressfield, *The War of Art* (New York: Rugged Land, 2002); Sharon Strand Ellison, *Taking the War Out of Our Words* (Berkeley: Bay Tree Press, 1998).

7.   Philip Ferback, "The Knowledge Illusion: Why We Never Think Alone," (webinar, University of Colorado Boulder, September 22, 2020). See also Steven Sloman and Philip Ferback, *The Knowledge Illusion: Why We Never Think Alone* (New York: Riverhead Books, 2017).

8.   Stephen Brookfield, *Becoming a Critically Reflective Teacher* (San Francisco: Jossey-Bass, 2017); bell hooks, *Teaching to Transgress: Education as the Practice of Freedom* (New York: Routledge,1994); Rhonda V. Magee, *The Inner Work of Racial Justice: Healing Ourselves and Transforming Our Communities through Mindfulness* (Los Angeles: Tarcher Perigee, 2019); Nyma McCarthy-Brown, *Dance Pedagogy for a Diverse World: Culturally Relevant Teaching in Theory, Research and Practice* (Jefferson, NC: McFarland, 2017); Saundra McGuire Yancy, *Teach Students How to Learn: Strategies You Can Incorporate into Any Course to Improve Student Metacognition, Study Skills, and Motivation* (Sterling, VA: Stylus, 2015).

9.   Sirma Bilge and Patricia Hills Collins, *Intersectionality* (Cambridge, UK: Polity Press, 2016). See also Simone Hyater-Adams et al., "Deconstructing Black Physics Identity: Linking Individual and Social Constructs Using the Critical Physics Identity Framework," *Physical Review Physics Education Research* 15 (August 2019): 020115-1-16, https://doi.org/10.1103 /PhysRevPhysEducRes.15.020115; and Maria P. P. Root, "A Bill of Rights for Racially Mixed People," n.d., Safe House Alliance, https://www.safehousealliance.org/wp-content/uploads/2012 /10/A-Bill-of-Rights-for-Racially-Mixed-People.pdf.

. . . .

CHAPTER 14

SHARING OUR STORIES TO BUILD COMMUNITY, HIGHLIGHT BIAS, AND ADDRESS CHALLENGES TO AUTHORITY

. . . .

Sarah Mayes-Tang

In May of 2014, I sat down for coffee with a fellow first-year professor. I'm sure we started the exchange by asking each other how things had been going, and I likely gave my usual answer of "challenging but rewarding." As our conversation continued, we each slowly let our guard down. As we revealed more of our actual experiences, we discovered expanding common ground: students challenging our classroom authority and doubting our expertise; ridiculous appeals to the dean that were investigated; directions to act or dress more masculine so we would be taken seriously; dwindling class registration; being told that we needed—somehow—to build up our class numbers; being told that perhaps we just didn't "fit in" at our institution.

We thought that these had only happened to us.

That was the beginning of our version of a support

group. As we shared our stories, we reluctantly saw that this negative treatment could be attributed to the fact that we did not fit the stereotypes of a physical science or math professor. This conversation marked a pivotal moment in my career. I went from being ambivalent about the role of identity in my profession as a professor to making this issue one of the central concerns of my career. Sharing stories was key to helping me understand how gender, identity, institutional politics, and mathematics culture interacted to build my experience and inform how I reacted to them.

I use the word "story" purposefully. It encompasses a narrative as well as the interpretation and emotional response to the narrative. The role of the storyteller within the story is vital. Just as sharing stories first opened my eyes to the impact of identity on my career, sharing stories has also been the most effective tactic that I have found for responding to challenges in the classroom related to the fact that I do not look like what students think of when they picture a professor. In this chapter, I will share what we know about the images of mathematicians and how sharing stories with peers and students has helped me teach effectively.

What Does a Mathematician "Look Like"?

When asked to draw a mathematician, students' images change dramatically during the middle school years. Their pictures transform from kind and primarily female teacher-like figures to overwrought, physically unappealing, and primarily male figures who cannot teach. Some pictures show men who resemble Einstein or portray wizards with special math powers.[1] No example drawings have shaded skin, implying that most children's mathematicians are White. While we might hope that these are simply the images of uninformed children, the images that even undergraduate math majors hold of successful mathematicians are not markedly different. In interviews with female undergraduate math majors, Katina Piatek-Jimenez found that students believed being exceptionally intelligent, socially inept, and obsessed with math could make a person excel more as a professional mathematician.[2]

If these three traits are taken for granted, young women and all people of color are less likely to fit this role than White men. Even exceptionally high-achieving women have less confidence in their ability in math than men and are more likely to credit their success in math to hard work than to innate talent.[3] Furthermore, college-aged women are more likely to place strong importance on their future family roles than men and to experience tension between their worker and mother identities.[4] Piatek-Jimenez argues that these beliefs about an ideal mathematician may be particularly harmful to women: "The image of mathematicians portrayed by the media and internalized by many through means of socialization causes dissonance with the traditional 'female gender identity.' "[5] Even though all women in the study had taken classes with female professors and none of them believed that the mathematicians fit a particular mold, they still held this common view of an ideal mathematician. This stereotype also distances all students of color from picturing themselves in this role. The very idea of thinking of oneself as exceptionally intelligent can cause a conflict with a Black student's identity. Interviews with Black gifted high school students revealed that they believed that if they acted superior to others by "being too smart," taking advanced courses, or acting "stuck up," they would be "acting White"; furthermore, Black adolescents tended to have stronger ties to family than their White peers.[6]

The math community itself promotes a view of the "typical mathematician" as being antisocial, socially inept, and obsessed with mathematics. For example, *The Mathematical Experience* by Philip Davis and Reuben Hersh is a classical text on the mathematical community as a whole. In its 2012 revision, it paints an image of "the ideal mathematician— the most mathematician-like mathematician" as isolated, obsessed with math, and socially inept. For example, "*He* [emphasis added] spends all his days in contemplating it. His life is successful to the extent that he can discover new facts about it. . . . He finds it difficult to establish meaningful conversation with that large portion of humanity that has never heard of a non-Riemannian hypersquare."[7] This image is prevalent even in the mathematical spaces that I belong to. Last week, someone in my math diversity group told this old joke: "How do you know if a mathematician is extroverted?" Answer: "He looks at your shoes instead of his own."

Who Am I?

I am a petite woman. I wear my hair blonde in a straight bob cut. I love to wear feminine clothes, and bright pink is my signature color. I dress professionally and appreciate looking put together. I enjoy books, baking, piano, and crafts. I don't like chess, video games, or other "thinking" games. I care about my family and enjoy spending time with other people. I consider myself a thoughtful and dedicated friend. I hold a PhD in pure mathematics. My dissertation is in algebraic geometry and commutative algebra. I voluntarily and enthusiastically chose a teaching career after graduate school, but I am still involved in math research communities. I currently coordinate a major calculus program that enrolls over 2,500 students.

I am a math professor. But I don't look like what people picture as a math professor. The "standard" image of a math professor remains a cisgendered White man. While I am not a man, I am White and, because of this, I am afforded many privileges in the classroom, academy, and society. In the past, feminist teachers have discussed issues of power and authority in the classroom but have ignored the experience of Black, Indigenous, and People of Color (BIPOC) faculty. I will attempt to incorporate some research on the additional challenges that professors of color face while acknowledging that I cannot speak for them or their experiences.

The Impact of Shared Stories

Long before our universities existed, storytelling conveyed knowledge. But why is storytelling particularly well suited to sharing the experiences of those of us who do not "look like" professors? Jo Anne Pagnao proposes fiction writing as a response to student criticism of higher education because at its root, "story-telling is a moral act drawing audiences into a moral universe"[8] The act of telling stories places our experiences as educators—and the knowledge they generate—into a moral arena. Stories connect the storyteller to the audience and connect the audience members. Recent scientific evidence explains a biological mechanism behind this bonding. The so-called moral molecule oxytocin that stimulates feelings of trust and being trusted is connected with stories. Specifically, when people watch narratives with a dramatic arc—that is, narratives that we think of as stories—their blood shows an increase in oxytocin, which has a positive correlation with their feelings and actions of empathy for the people in the video.[9]

As a form, stories allow us to frame problems in a way that is customized to our own place, time, and context.[10] They access the subtle corners of a problem or situation that are difficult to frame or explain in generalities. Storytelling benefits the storyteller as well. It helps us digest what happened and make sense of the events. It opens up new conversations and connections with others. Sharing and listening to stories is a recommended strategy to maintain and regain mental health.[11]

Sharing Our Stories Is Difficult

Pagano offers this cautionary note: "Stories and questions are gifts, and gifts may be refused, or they may be used in ways which the giver never intended."[12] Talking about challenges related to our identities can cut us to our core. Thinking that someone is treating me negatively simply because of who I am has made me feel everything from embarrassed to angry to humiliated to wrathful. Faculty of color experience a myriad of additional challenges when they enter the classroom not faced by me, as a woman with White privilege. Jeremy Franklin writes of "racial battle fatigue" in Black faculty, a term that encompasses stress from facing racism, racial traumas, and racial microaggressions daily.[13] In addition, a lack of belonging, additional service work, and race work within a department can serve to increase unjust treatment and emotional reaction experienced by

BIPOC faculty. As Aruna Srivastava writes, the movements of female teachers of color are under such a microscope of scrutiny that no mistake can be risked.[14]

It is difficult to share our stories of mistreatment and abuse within the classroom and within the academy, even with those closest to us. Opening up takes time and is a gradual process. At first, it's one small insight at a time, perhaps a perceived nudge or piece of an incident that is nagging at you. Gradually, through the give and take that is inherent to any relationship, complete stories emerge and can build relationships.

Sharing Stories Builds Supportive Communities

Everyone who does not fit the stereotypical image of a professor needs a group of supportive cheerleaders who will listen to their stories and affirm their struggles and achievements. For example, at the end of a class, we should have a cheerleader we can call and relate an interaction with a disrespectful student. That cheerleader should be counted on to back us up and talk through feelings that come from disrespect and other challenges to our expertise. I cannot emphasize enough how important a group of cheerleaders has been in my journey, and the only way to create a group of trusted confidantes is to begin to share your stories.

While I prefer to call these kinds of positive, interpersonal interactions "cheerleading" to emphasize that it should be positive, growth-oriented, and approachable, the literature on this kind of relationship often refers to it as "mentorship." In Nakita Fuller's research on the success of minority female faculty, the most common factor for success mentioned in interviews was a group of mentors and supportive individuals.[15] Research also demonstrates that mentoring can be learned, creating less isolation, more institutional capital, more community service, and fewer diversity teaching burdens.[16]

I recommend the following four strategies for creating supportive communities. First, because colleagues in other disciplines can be great cheerleaders, use networking groups within your institution, including outside your department/program. If your institution has a teaching and learning center, get involved with workshops or activities to meet new people or ask to be matched up! Second, take the first steps. Invite someone out for coffee (virtual coffee counts). Share an experience that you would like support with this week and see how they react. Ask if they need support with anything. These steps can be scary and seem risky, but it's the only way to develop connections. Third, be a mentor and cheerleader for others. Mentoring conversations often lead you to tell your stories. Once you are comfortable sharing your stories in mentoring relationships, you might be more able to seek support from peers. Mentors frequently find this work rewarding, and a way to avoid stagnancy in their own careers.[17]

Finally, look for positive communities online, an especially important source of cheerleaders for minority faculty in small institutions and departments. A 2018 study showed that participants in Twitter's #EdChat developed bonds with other educators outside of their usual networks who brought valuable new ideas.[18] If you are on Facebook, I recommend that you look for a nonpublic group targeted to a minority group of scholars, with strict community standards, where you can feel safe sharing your experiences. If you are on Twitter, consider searching for the following hashtags for general academic threads, such as #AcademicTwitter, and #PhdLife. For diversity-related discussions, see #WomenInSTEM, #BlackInSTEM, #BlackScientists, and #BlackPhds.

Sharing Stories Helps Students See Their Biases

I saw the comparisons coming from the moment the university's teaching schedule appeared. I would be teaching a mandatory second-year course alongside a man who fit the stereotypical image of a professor perfectly. I'll call him Professor P, for "Perfect." I employed several strategies to prevent the negative comparisons I expected. I met with Professor P before the course to explain my concerns. We divided the curriculum into places where I had a natural leg up and could call on my subject authority. I discussed implicit bias with students and included readings about bias against faculty members in the curriculum.

Despite these efforts, after the first class, students lined up outside the registrar's office seeking transfers to Professor P's class. Students compared me to him daily, and they even talked about how they wished they were in the other class in front of me. Even more troublingly, Professor P undermined my authority in front of the students during joint sessions. I also noticed students' implicit bias against other women professors, such as when the students spoke about their interactions with potential thesis advisors (a major part of the class), they spoke with less respect, commented on their motherly qualities, and planned to ask more "challenge questions" to women professors.

One morning near the end of the term, students prepared to leave class to participate in a campus-wide class walkout as a feminist protest. I decided to point out the feminist issue shaping our own class by sharing some of my stories about working in the institution and teaching our class. Rather than simply recounting the facts, I told them the story from my perspective: how I anticipated the problems, how I worked to prevent them, and most importantly how I *felt* throughout all of this. I told them that I felt embarrassed and betrayed. I even told them that I cried. I went on to show my students quotes from their writing about different professors at the institution that spoke of the knowledge of male professors frequently and about how "nice" or "not nice" the female professors were. I read them quotes from my end-of-term evaluations. I told them about the desperation of feeling like I was playing a losing game and how I didn't think that the situation would ever resolve. I could not both be myself and be a successful professor at the institution.

Rather than making me weak, being vulnerable allowed me to claim some of the authority and strength that I deserved. The things that I was ashamed of were out in the open. Surprisingly, I felt in complete control of the class from that day forward. Students listened to me and really seemed to respect what I had to say. I received notes and comments from several students in the class about how impactful this moment had been. While they had considered themselves feminists, they realized that they were not checking their unconscious biases in their classes and with those closest to them at school.

I recommend the following three strategies for using stories to help students recognize bias. First, if you are in a situation where a large part of the class is undermining your authority, consider the alternatives to exerting your authority in a traditional manner and instead share stories of not fitting the mold of what a professor "looks like." Include not just the narrative but also the interpretation and emotional response to those stories. Ask them to reflect on what you are telling them.

Second, remember that although the risks of being vulnerable to students that you do not trust are great, the potential rewards are also significant. For minority faculty members who are already more likely to be exposed to damages and attacks, opening themselves up for *more* of it all can seem reckless. But emotional vulnerability involves allowing our true selves to be known, including our imperfections, weaknesses, and shortcomings, and there can be tremendous freedom in showing more of our true selves. Further, it can help to build rapport between ourselves and our students and decrease the *psychological distance* between us; such efforts have been shown to increase students' perceptions of teachers.[19] Indeed, students have surprised me with their empathy and care, but I want to acknowledge that there are real concerns and risks.

Finally, never forget that you are the expert. While your stories have a strong emotional component to them, you are relying on your academic training to guide your movements in the class.

Sharing Stories and Student Evaluations of Teaching

One of the most awkward moments each semester is right before I leave the room so students can complete their end-of-semester student evaluations of teaching (SET). It feels as though there is a gigantic spotlight on me as I gather up my papers, say an uncomfortable goodbye, and shuffle out of the room. If I'm feeling awkward and unsettled, my students are too, and that's not the spirit I want to leave them in. One approach that has helped me to take back ownership of my classrooms in those pre-evaluation moments is sharing my stories. The first time I shared a personal story before evaluations was completely off-the-cuff. I had prepared my usual presentation on "how to give effective feedback to professors" with some examples of helpful and nonhelpful feedback. But the presentation no longer felt authentic when the time came, so instead I walked into the audience of three hundred or so and spoke from my heart. I told students that "unhelpful" feedback could actually be hurtful and shared hurtful student comments that were seared into my memory. I also shared a story of how patterns of comments like these had jeopardized my career and almost led me to leave academia altogether.

This was hard for me: the negative comments I shared with students are things that I could barely stand to read, much less repeat to a class of hundreds. But when I spoke about the inappropriateness and uselessness of terrible comments, I was turning something that had the power to damage and hurt me into a tool for students to learn and hopefully prevent hurtful words not only in my evaluations but also in those of other instructors. My stories foster what Johnson and Labelle describe as authenticity in teaching, and students perceive self-disclosure like this as part of instructional authenticity.[20]

I recommend the following three strategies for using storytelling as part of SET. First, although student perception of instructor authenticity is important for effective teaching, we should only self-disclose as far as our personalities and placements in systemic power structures allow. I am a White woman, and I acknowledge that White scholars of teaching and learning have not taken into account the perspectives of BIPOC faculty.[21] Second, use others' experiences to provide context. For example, I have a ritual of starting one class per week with a slide of an important mathematician, usually one who doesn't look like a mathematician. I might present some comments that were said about one of these mathematicians twenty, thirty, fifty, or one hundred years ago and ask students if they thought that comments like that would be made today in their classroom. This can provide a door to talk about student evaluations in your own life and classroom. Third, trust your intuition. One of the most important lessons from this experience was that sometimes I need to put away my lesson plans and speak from my heart. When sharing your stories, you do not need a script. Remember, you are an expert, and you know what will work and what will not work based on your experience and expert training.

Conclusion

Students, faculty, staff, and the public at large need to see a diversity of knowledge makers and knowledge sharers. Therefore we—professors who do not look like stereotypical professors—play a vital role in the institution just by "showing up." By being visible as we engage in our work, we will challenge perceptions of what it looks like to be a professor. We have stories to tell that stem from our presence in virtual and physical academic spaces. Whether they are positive or negative, our stories are valuable, and through our stories, we can build supportive networks, empower ourselves pedagogically, and empower our students to recognize bias and increase equity in the classroom.

....

Teaching Takeaways

....

- Stories have power. Sharing stories with other instructors can help us build a support system of "cheerleaders."
- Sharing our stories isn't easy, and our ability to freely share our stories is impacted by systemic inequities in higher education.
- Sharing our stories can help students recognize biases, including those related to student evaluations of teaching.

....

SARAH MAYES-TANG is a math professor at the University of Toronto. She earned her PhD from the University of Michigan, where she began to build her career as a math educator. She has since guided everything from tiny classes of three students to large programs of three thousand. No matter what the setting, "You don't look like a mathematician!" is one of the most common phrases she hears upon meeting someone new.

....

Notes

....

1. Susan Picker and John Berry, "Investigating Pupils' Images of Mathematicians," *Educational Studies in Mathematics* 43, no. 1 (2000): 65–94.
2. Katrina Piatek-Jimenez, "Images of Mathematicians: A New Perspective on the Shortage of Women in Mathematical Careers," *ZDM* 40, no. 4 (2008): 633–46.

3.   Lesley Jones, "Confidence and Mathematics: A Gender
     Issue?" *Gender and Education* 7, no. 2 (1995): 157–66; Melanie
     Hargreaves, Matt Homer, and Bronwen Swinnerton, "A
     Comparison of Performance and Attitudes in Mathematics
     amongst the 'Gifted': Are Boys Better at Mathematics or Do
     They Just Think They Are?" *Assessment in Education: Principles,
     Policy and Practice* 15, no. 1 (2008): 19–38.

4.   Jennifer L. Kerpelman and Paul L. Schvaneveldt, "Young
     Adults' Anticipated Identity Importance of Career, Marital,
     and Parental Roles: Comparisons of Men and Women with
     Different Role Balance Orientations," *Sex Roles* 41, no. 3
     (1999): 189–217; Deirdre Johnston and Debra H. Swanson,
     "Cognitive Acrobatics in the Construction of Worker–Mother
     Identity," *Sex Roles* 57, no. 5–6 (2007): 447–59.

5.   Piatek-Jimenez, "Images of Mathematicians," 643.

6.   Donna Ford, Tarek Grantham, and Gilman Whiting, "Another
     Look at the Achievement Gap: Learning from the Experiences
     of Gifted Black Students," *Urban Education* 43, no. 2 (2008):
     216–39; Barton Hirsch, Maureen Mickus, and Rebecca
     Boerger, "Ties to Influential Adults among Black and White
     Adolescents: Culture, Social Class, and Family Networks,"
     American Journal of Community Psychology 30, no. 2 (2002):
     289–303.

7.   Philip Davis, Reuben Hersh, and Elena Anne Marchisotto, *The
     Mathematical Experience* (Boston: Springer, 2011), 34.

8.   Jo Anne Pagnao, "Relating to One's Students: Identity,
     Morality, Stories, and Questions," *Journal of Moral Education*
     20, no. 3 (1991): 260.

9.   Paul J. Zak, "Why Inspiring Stories Make Us React: The
     Neuroscience of Narrative," *Cerebrum* (February 2015),
     https://www.ncbi.nlm.nih.gov/pmc/articles/PMC4445577/.

10. Ansie Harding, "Storytelling for Tertiary Mathematics
     Students," in *Invited Lectures from the 13th International*

Congress on Mathematical Education, ed. Gabriele Kaiser et al. (Switzerland: Springer, 2018), 195–207.

11. Substance Abuse and Mental Health Services Administration, *Share Your Story: How-to Guide for Digital Storytelling*, n.d., https://www.samhsa.gov/sites/default/files/programs _campaigns/brss_tacs/samhsa-storytelling-guide.pdf.

12. Pagnao, "Relating to One's Students," 265.

13. Jeremy Franklin, "Racial Microaggressions, Racial Battle Fatigue, and Racism-Related Stress in Higher Education," *Journal of Student Affairs* 12, no. 44 (2016): 44–55.

14. Aruna Srivastava, "Anti-Racism Inside and Outside the Classroom," in *Dangerous Territories: Struggles for Difference and Equality in Education*, eds. Leslie Roman and Linda Eyre (New York: Routledge, 1997), 113.

15. Nakita Fuller, "Factors Affecting Minority Female Success as Professors in Higher Education" (PhD diss., Nova Southeastern University, 2013).

16. Ruth Zambrana et al., " 'Don't Leave Us Behind': The Importance of Mentoring for Underrepresented Minority Faculty," *American Educational Research Journal* 52, no. 1 (2015): 40–72.

17. Terese Stenfors-Hayes et al., "Being a Mentor for Undergraduate Medical Students Enhances Personal and Professional Development," *Medical Teacher* 32, no. 2 (2010): 148–53; Carole Bland et al., *Faculty Success through Mentoring: A Guide for Mentors, Mentees, and Leaders* (Lanham, MD: Rowman and Littlefield, 2009).

18. John Mark Coleman, "Educator Communities of Practice on Twitter" (PhD diss., University of Alabama Libraries, 2018).

19. Lisa M. Vaughn and Raymond C. Baker, "Psychological Size and Distance: Emphasising the Interpersonal Relationship as a Pathway to Optimal Teaching and Learning Conditions," *Medical Education* 38, no. 10 (2004): 1053–60.

20. Zach Johnson and Sara LaBelle, "An Examination of Teacher Authenticity in the College Classroom," *Communication Education* 66, no. 4 (2017): 423–39.

21. Dalia Rodriguez, "The Usual Suspect: Negotiating White Student Resistance and Teacher Authority in a Predominantly White Classroom," *Cultural Studies* 9, no. 4 (2009): 483–508.

....

CHAPTER 15

TEACHING UP

Bringing My Blackness into the Classroom

....

Celeste Atkins

The vast majority of college faculty are White, which does not reflect the diversity of the population they are teaching.[1] One important facet of encouraging diversity may be rethinking our ideas of professionalism. What does it mean to be a professional? I am a zaftig, outspoken, unapologetically Black, cisgender, mostly straight, queer ally woman who is the daughter of an interracial couple, and single mother to an amazing Black girl. Critical race scholars assert that the socially constructed meaning of "professional" is really White, middle-class, heterosexual, and, often, male. For those of us who do not fit in many, or any, of those categories, our careers depend on finding ways to be professional that may not feel reflective of who we are. Black Americans in the United States learn, through both formal and informal means, that to be successful one must adapt to the dominant society's way of speaking and presenting oneself. In contrast, a consistent theme throughout this research is that the best teaching approach is authenticity. In my teaching experience, students will not trust you if they do not feel that you are being authentic.[2] In this chapter, I suggest a paradigm shift to the definition of academic professionalism through the theoretical lenses of intersectionality, impression management, and funds of knowledge.

One cannot truly understand racial inequality without intersectionality or without exploring how race intersects with other social identities, such as sexual orientation, gender, ability status, age, and socioeconomic status, to affect the life chances and experiences of an individual.[3] Intersectionality is widely used as a theoretical approach; however, there is a lack of consistency in academia about how intersectionality is defined, conceptualized, and employed in praxis. I employ intersectionality to disaggregate Black faculty and explore variations in experience and approach to impression management.

Impression management is "one of the most vital skills in human social life."[4] It involves "presenting oneself effectively to others" and is "a vital aspect of . . . occupational and organizational success."[5] Impression management, particularly in certain situations, requires self-regulation that may be taxing on an individual.[6] In particular, being a token minority and having to speak publicly about racial topics places extreme demands on individuals similar to the effect of stereotype threat.[7] This knowledge combined with research that shows the "othering" of faculty of color in academic environments and how female faculty of color perceive their authority as limited by their race/ethnicity and gender implies that impression management is key for faculty of color.[8] Swencionis, Dupree, and Fiske found that people of color are stereotyped and represented as lower status, less intelligent, and less competent than the

White majority.[9] Faculty of color know this, viscerally, and, therefore, spend more time and effort on impression management, particularly when they are most vulnerable (i.e., pretenure, newly hired). [10] However, the following findings point to an alternative perspective on impression management that expands the notion of funds of knowledge.

Judy Marquez Kiyama describes the concept of funds of knowledge as "based on the foundation that people are competent, [and] have experiential knowledge that is valuable and developed through life experiences."[11] She explains that instead of assuming that poor and working-class children of color come to school with a deficit based on their family environment and upbringing, teachers should find ways to leverage the strengths that each family and culture has. In her own research, Kiyama found that the very real and effective work that parents were doing to increase their child(ren)'s learning was being ignored. She referred to this work as familial funds of knowledge. I argue that we can expand the idea of funds of knowledge to incorporate the unique perspectives, experiences, and insights of faculty who have been traditionally marginalized.

The participants here are ten sociology faculty who identify as Black or African American. Two of the faculty identified as men and the remaining eight as women, and all identified as heterosexual, with one identifying as "heteroflexible." They all participated in semistructured in-depth interviews that averaged around an hour and a half. This sample is a subset of a larger population of sociology faculty recruited through snowball sampling. I purposefully sought participants who teach in all areas of higher education (research universities, four-year teaching institutions, and community colleges), across different regions of the country, and who identified with a variety of religions, racial groups, ages, and genders. Additionally, participants represented a wide range of teaching experiences.

Most of the faculty talked about their Black identity and being a rarity on campus. Most felt that students, colleagues, and administrators had biases, prejudices, and preconceived ideas about them solely based on race and gender. Alchemy shared that for his students "I'm not even sure they're used to seeing [Blacks]. So, I think when they see me, the first is like, 'Oh, am I in the right place?' Who is this?' " For Ted, "there was the perception that somehow I wasn't as qualified. And those would come out in questions of do I have a PhD . . . and the presumption that I'm an athlete . . . those kinds of things." These experiences reinforce findings in the literature that faculty of color are "presumed incompetent."[12]

For the female faculty, Eleanor, a veteran faculty member who has faced extreme issues including death threats during her teaching career, explains that as "Black women, we experience anti-Black racism that has a gendered flavor to it, right? And so, the narrative around that is that we're intimidating and angry and hate White people." Eleanor's experience resonates with me, as I have dealt with similar accusations. Shamari, who has very light skin and hazel eyes, states that she "get[s] the White people pass until they realize that I'm Black, the *Black*, Black for real. And then they're betrayed and so deeply hurt and upset." Tutsy, another veteran faculty member states, "From the jump there, they don't respect us, anyway. Right? I mean there's less respect for Black women in the classroom . . . unless you plant your feet and assert that, yeah, I have a PhD." It seems that while responses from students were varied, lack of respect, qualification questioning, and stereotypes were common. The experiences of these faculty reinforce the current literature on problems facing faculty of color.[13] It also illustrates the need for what bell hooks refers to as "engaged pedagogy," which focuses on faculty well-being and self-actualization.[14] Student bias against female faculty and faculty of color is well documented but few attempts have been made to counteract that bias in terms of promotion and tenure and many campuses still depend heavily on student evaluations, which put already marginalized faculty at higher risk.[15]

Participants were thoughtful about the way that they dressed. Some attributed it directly to the college environment, others dressed a certain way from earlier in their lives. Alchemy wears a shirt and tie every day and that is his professional wardrobe; otherwise, he is in athletic clothes. In his words, "I have two sets of clothes, one extreme or the next." When pushed he admitted, that as a sociologist, "it could be on a subconscious level" a form of impression management, but insisted, "now, I do it for me . . . because I do, you want to be perceived in a certain way." Ted shares that he "can play the Black coolness. . . . I try to wear things that students are not wearing." However, one drawback from this form of impression management is that the students may perceive that because he's "cooler, dresses a particular way . . . he's not that serious a scholar." Mbali says, "I've always tried to dress nicely at work, because that is work. I grew up in an era where . . . I'm working in an office . . . I have to look a certain way. And I've continued to do that . . . you will never see me wear jeans on campus." In contrast, Shamari decided to distinguish herself from students by wearing "big chunky rings and earrings." She continues, "And that is my professional look; I feel like I very much look like a working race and gender sociologist when I go to work in that gear."

For several of the women, their dress has changed based on time, tenure, and age. Marie wears "what makes me most comfortable," stating that "I was kind of just too old to worry about stuff like that . . . by the time I got back into grad school." Tina shifted her dress and mannerisms deliberately: "When I first started out . . . I always dressed professionally in a more masculine way. Because I thought that that would make an impression . . . of like authority and . . . power." She explains that over time "I have definitely allowed more of like my authentic Black girl personality to come out. I wear funky earrings. Now I got my hair in all kinds of different ways. I am dressing feminine when I feel like it." Willie also went through a transformation: "When I first started my job, my female chair said to me, like you know, you look young, and you have like a jovial kind of personality. So, you should probably wear business suits to work." Willie dressed that way until she earned tenure:

> The day I got tenure . . . I think it was a Wednesday, I walked into class the next day, now you know, I'm a little LA, I was wearing a pair of designer jeans, a tank top, and a blazer. That is my uniform now. . . . I have not worn a business suit since and will not wear a business suit.

It is clear from this study that, for these Black sociologists, impression management is a key part of their andragogical approach. They are often one of a handful of Black professors, if not the only one in their department or at their institution. They have been socialized by a White supremacist society that to be professional one must erase cultural and socioeconomic markers from one's speech, attire, and mannerisms. Faculty at the beginning of their careers, often based on explicit feedback from supervisors and mentors, tend to dress in what is perceived as more stereotypically "professional" attire. This serves to both establish their authority and increase the respect given to them by students and peers. There also seem to be generational factors in that some, like Mbali and Alchemy, grew up in a time when professional attire was expected, and they'd feel uncomfortable in an academic setting without that attire. With time and experience, many found that they can be successful and still be their authentic selves.

I assert that students need to see differing gendered, cultural, and regional examples of professionalism to expand societal notions of professionalism. In academia, the focus is often on objectivity and impersonality. However, for these sociologists whose job it is to teach some of the most challenging and at times, controversial subjects, the trick was to strip away objectivity and share themselves.[16] As Ted said, "I . . . think that the discipline is about helping to reveal these other voices, to give power to those of us of color. [To enhance] our voices and create that kind of knowledge." Eleanor states one must "be clear on kind of who you are, as a teacher, how your teaching fits with the other aspect of yourself and your career because you have other things you're called to do." Tutsy agrees, saying, "You need to start with where you are, what are your experiences . . . talk about what your privilege is. I'm Black . . . but I speak Standard English. I'm light skinned, I'm thin . . . these are my privileges." Teaching through the lens of your personal perspective models not only intersectionality but also inclusion and reflective thinking to your students.

Additionally, there is a desire to show the strengths and pride of Blackness, such as Angie, who dresses to highlight her race: "I suppose if I dig deep down . . . I do wear my hair natural and in my Afro wig . . . [to] communicate that I am Black." This is echoed by Willie, who shares her personal journey: "And I'm unapologetically Black. . . . Honey, I wouldn't trade my hips, my skin, nor my hair for anything in the world now. But I had to go through that experience to really appreciate and value who I am now." But there is more to it; there is a sense of letting the students know that it is possible to travel from where they have been to where the faculty are.[17] Shamari deliberately breaks away the mystique of being a PhD: "I talk to them about how I am the same chick, who up until four years ago was in section eight housing. . . . I'm the same chick that I was two months ago. And now all of a sudden, I'm Dr. Somebody and people are treating me different."

Veteran faculty are already expanding the idea of professionalism. Eleanor, who was chastised by a Black man for her attire not being professional, remembers "looking down at my pants . . . kinda like an animal print form-fitting pant, which I looked good in . . . and I said, 'You know why it is? Because I'm a professional, and I'm wearing it.'" Tina addresses this idea even more explicitly:

> So definitely over time, I've . . . brought more of my authentic self, which is bringing elements of my culture with me to work. . . . I have made a conscious decision to bring my Blackness and my Black womanness to the classroom, really for them [Black female students]. So that they can see like you can be yourself and be professional . . . express yourself in ways that we do, in terms of like our head movements and our . . . hands . . . that is professional who's to say it's not? . . . I've made a more conscious decision to bring it so that they can know they can bring it and to bring it into the space so that it can start to be seen as professional.

How does this research inform your pedagogical approach? Overall, it seems that to be effective, as well as use the engaging pedagogy referred to by hooks, faculty need to bring their whole selves into the classroom. To me, this seems a natural expansion of the idea of funds of knowledge. I argue that we should strive to mentor new faculty to teach in ways that bring their personal and cultural knowledge to the forefront. I encourage faculty to *be authentic*. There are many ways to be an effective teacher in face-to-face classes, as well as online, so work from your personal strengths and funds of knowledge. Bring your culture, background, and experiences into the class and share them honestly with your students.

Moreover, I encourage you to *model cultural professionalism*. Whether it be long hair for Indigenous men, or an Afrocentric wardrobe or Afrocentric hair, or Mestizo jewelry, or a bit of LA swag, or hippie chic, find your own professional uniform that expresses who you really are.[18] Until we expand notions of "professionalism," we will remain trapped in the androcentric, Eurocentric definitions of what is professional. Willie suggests that you "be sincere because if not, you might feel like you sold your soul."

I also encourage you to *find your people*. Create a network of support, of individuals who understand or are willing to learn about the specific barriers and microaggressions you face. Create a safe space to vent, get your feelings validated, and possibly share ideas. If those individuals are at your institution, that's wonderful, but if not, find them somewhere. In the words of Marie, "Be true to yourself . . . or whatever is best for you in that situation . . . and . . . where there aren't spaces create them."

There is no single solution to increasing diversity and inclusion. Things need to change on many fronts; however, increasing the number of marginalized faculty is a vital step.[19] I argue that a paradigm shift from professionalism being equated with middle-class White heterosexual expression, to professionalism consisting of authentic gender, race, sexual orientation, and cultural expression would be profoundly helpful in the recruitment and retention of faculty of color and other marginalized faculty. Moreover, I posit that this will also improve the recruitment and retention of students from marginalized groups. I assert that faculty of color bring unique funds of knowledge to the college classroom and that the emphasis should be on expanding those funds of knowledge rather than focusing on a narrow class-based, race-based, and often gender-specific idea of professionalism. As college classrooms become increasingly diverse, we owe it to these students to provide mentors and role models who are also diverse and to provide an environment that embraces cultural knowledge, divergent perspectives, and diverse identities. In my personal experience teaching students who are largely not Black, students are often shocked by my candidness, but my sharing and being frank about my experiences as a voluptuous woman of color often sets the stage for them to share their own personal experiences as well. It also gives them a realistic glimpse of life from a different perspective.

This work also illustrates the need for better teaching evaluation methods. Student feedback, while important, should not drive faculty evaluations. Teaching evaluations should be based on objective measures and account for implicit biases that affect evaluations of faculty of color. Ferber and colleagues posit, "If racism, sexism, and homophobia are the result of a process of socialization, then mounting a public argument for equality and social justice from a forum such as the classroom can theoretically challenge students' racist, sexist, and homophobic attitudes, and potentially evoke individual transformation and effect social and political change."[20] The respondents from the study presented in this chapter use their classrooms to evoke social change and advocate for social justice, and their successes create more space for diversity and inclusion in the campuses where they work. Moreover, they stand as mentors and role models for their marginalized students by demonstrating alternative options for professional attire and ways of teaching.

This study expands our understanding of Black faculty, particularly when it comes to impression management; however, more research is needed. Much would be gained by focusing on other individual marginalized identities (i.e., Latino/a/x faculty, Asian faculty, Indigenous faculty, mixed-race/biracial faculty, and queer faculty). More importantly, we need an intersectional approach that seeks to tease out how our multiple sometimes contradictory group memberships, such as being marginalized as a Black woman but having cisgender and heterosexual privilege all intersect to affect pedagogy and impression management.

....

Teaching Takeaways

....

- Be authentic.
- Model cultural professionalism.
- Find your people.
- Advocate for better faculty evaluation methods.

....

CELESTE ATKINS holds a PhD in higher education from the University of Arizona (UA). She taught full-time for nine years, receiving teaching awards from both regional and national sociology associations and a diversity leadership award from UA. She transitioned into faculty development in 2020 and is currently the assistant director for faculty mentoring initiatives at UA. Her scholarship has been published in *Accessibility and Diversity in the 21st Century*, and *Gender, Race, and Class in the Lives of Today's Teachers: Educators at Intersections*. Visit her website https://atkinsc.com.

Notes

1. Joann Moody, *Faculty Diversity: Problems and Solutions* (New York: Taylor and Francis, 2004), 22; Saturnin Ndandala, "A Portrait of Faculty Diversity at Selected Elite Universities," *International Journal of Higher Education Management* 3, no. 1 (August 2016): 75–82.

2. Caroline Kreber, "Academics' Teacher Identities, Authenticity and Pedagogy," *Studies in Higher Education* 35, no. 2 (March 2010): 184–91.

3. Patricia Hill Collins, "Intersectionality's Definitional Dilemmas," *Annual Review of Sociology* 41 (2015), 1–20; Abby Ferber, Andrea O'Reilly Herrera, and Dena Samuels, "The Matrix of Oppression and Privilege: Theory and Practice for the New Millennium," *American Behavioral Scientist* 51, no. 4 (2007): 516–31.

4. Kathleen Vohs, Roy Baumeister, and Natalie Ciarocco, "Self-Regulation and Self-Presentation: Regulatory Resource Depletion Impairs Impression Management and Effortful Self-Presentation Depletes Regulatory Resources," *Journal of Personality and Social Psychology* 88, no. 4 (2005): 632.

5. Vohs, Baumeister, and Ciarocco, "Self-Regulation and Self-Presentation," 632.

6. Vohs, Baumeister, and Ciarocco, "Self-Regulation and Self-Presentation," 632.

7. Vohs, Baumeister, and Ciarocco, "Self-Regulation and Self-Presentation," 643.

8. Bridget Turner Kelly and Kristin McCann, "Women Faculty of Color: Stories behind the Statistics," *Urban Review* 46 (2014): 681–702; Caroline Turner, "Women of Color in Academe: Living with Multiple Marginality," *Journal of Higher Education* 73, no. 1 (2002): 74–93.

9. Jillian Swencionis, Cydney Dupree, and Susan Fiske, "Warmth-Competence Tradeoffs in Impression Management across Race and Social-Class Divides," *Social Issues* 73, no. 1 (2017): 175–91.

10. Angela Onwuachi-Willig, "Silence of the Lambs," in *Presumed Incompetent: The Intersections of Race and Class for Women in Academia*, eds. Gabriella Gutiérrez y Muhs et al. (Logan: Utah State University Press, 2012), 142–51.

11. Judy Marquez Kiyama, "Funds of Knowledge and College Ideologies: Lived Experiences among Mexican American Families" (PhD diss., University of Arizona, 2008), 26.

12. Onwuachi-Willig, "Silence of the Lambs," 146–47.

13. Ndandala, "Portrait of Faculty Diversity," 79.

14. belle hooks, *Teaching to Transgress: Education as the Practice of Freedom* (New York: Routledge, 1994), 15.

15. Anish Bavishi, Juan Madera, and Michelle Mebl, "The Effect of Professor Ethnicity and Gender on Student Evaluations: Judged before Met," *Journal of Diversity in Higher Education* 3, no. 4 (2010): 245–56; Onwuachi-Willig, "Silence of the Lambs," 146–47; Sylvia R. Lazos, "Are Student Teaching Evaluations Holding Back Women and Minorities? The Perils of 'Doing' Gender and Race in the Classroom," in *Presumed Incompetent*, 164–85.

16. Robin M. Boylorn, "Black Kids (B.K.) Stories: Ta(l)king (about)

Race outside of the Classroom," *Cultural Studies Critical Methodologies* 11, no. 1 (November 2010): 59–70.

17. Jessica C. Harris and Chris Linder, "The Racialized Experiences of Students of Color in Higher Education and Student Affairs Graduate Preparation Programs," *Journal of College Student Development* 59, no. 2 (March–April 2018): 141–58.

18. For example, I used to have cornrows only as my "summer" hair because I worried that it might not be considered professional. However, during a global pandemic, having cornrows is one less thing to worry about, and I am proudly rocking my Black professional look.

19. Paul D. Umback, "The Contribution of Faculty of Color to Undergraduate Education," *Research in Higher Education* 47, no. 3 (May 2006): 317–45.

20. Ferber, Herrera, and Samuels, "The Matrix of Oppression and Privilege," 521.

CHAPTER 16

EMPOWERED STRATEGIES FOR WOMEN FACULTY OF COLOR NAVIGATING TEACHING INEQUITIES IN HIGHER ED

. . . .

Chavella T. Pittman

This chapter is all about affirming, validating, and empowering women faculty of color (WFOC). Their status as faculty does not shield them from the negative impacts of race and gender inequities in their everyday lives outside academe and negatively impacts them "inside" higher education.[1] At this writing, the COVID-19 pandemic, racial reckoning, and US political turmoil have greatly increased those inequities.[2] Women of color are underrepresented in the number of full-time faculty in the United States. Specifically, White women represent 35 percent of US college faculty, while women of color faculty are only ~7 percent (i.e., Asian 3 percent, Black 2 percent, Hispanic ≤1 percent, Native American ≤1 percent), and these women exist primarily at the lower ranks, as contingent faculty, and at two-year institutions, community colleges, and minority-serving institutions.[3] When we look

at teaching in particular, WFOC more frequently face inequities such as teaching overloads; colleague and student
challenges to their teaching; biased, ambiguous, or negative
evaluations of their teaching; and contract renewal, tenure,
and promotion practices that amplify raced and gendered
inequities. WFOC spend more time on teaching preparation
than their peers in an attempt to offset these inequities, so
they have less time and energy to work on the scholarly prod-
ucts necessary for successful reviews.[4] Teaching inequities
thus lead directly to negative contract renewals, tenure, and
promotion reviews for women of color.[5]

All of this is so *exhausting*. Unsurprisingly, WFOC report
experiencing stress, burnout, disillusionment, lowered
morale, and negative physical and mental health outcomes,
and frequently consider leaving academia altogether.[6]
Teaching is the overlooked siphon in higher education that
derails WFOC from renewed contracts, tenure, and promotion. We need that to stop ASAP. In this chapter, I aim
to empower WFOC for less stressful and more successful
teaching reviews. I offer specific strategies for empowered
teaching, validating their experiences of the teaching inequities that derail their retention or tenure and empowering
them to proactively challenge the teaching inequities that
hinder success in their academic careers. These strategies
are applicable for faculty across instructional roles (e.g.,
contingent, nontenure track, tenure-track) and across
teaching modalities (e.g., face-to-face, hybrid, remote,
online).

Are you reading this but aren't a WFOC, yet you have
marginalized statuses? Keep reading. While I would not do
a disservice to diverse faculty by describing us monolithi-
cally, odds are that what follows is relevant for your teaching, and its link to your progress toward contract renewal,

tenure, and promotion. Don't belong to any marginalized groups? *Pay attention.* This is an opportunity for you to learn about teaching inequities so you understand how embodied statuses impact teaching practices and how your women of color colleagues cannot implement teaching practices in the exact same way nor with the same outcomes as their White or male privileged peers. Use this knowledge to act as an ally by sharing this chapter's research-backed information and strategies to retain women of color and other diverse faculty.

Strategy #1: Know and Internalize the Research about WFOC's Teaching Efficacy

Research shows that WFOC are more likely than (White and male) faculty to use innovative, evidence-based, and transformative pedagogies, such as active learning or collaborative teaching, measurably increasing learning for students; they also focus on higher-order cognitive skill instead of surface learning, including more assignments connected to diversity in the real world.[7] They tend to focus on the affective, emotional, moral, and civic development of students, facilitating deep understanding and a desire and ability to change the world.[8] WFOC teach students to think critically about new knowledge and to recognize and understand structural oppression, consistently setting student learning goals that improve academic performance.[9]

WFOC, to begin to enact this strategy, fill in the blanks to describe your pedagogy/ies and student learning goal/s:

My teaching is excellent because it is [fill in the blank] (i.e., pedagogy—learning centered, active, problem-solving based) and focuses on [fill in the blank] (i.e., student learning goal—deep learning, critical thinking, civic development).

Unfortunately, it is a common approach that something is wrong with the quality of women of color's teaching that must be fixed, but the research does not bear out this deficit approach.[10] WFOC, please internalize this truth: your teaching is awesome!

....

Strategy #2: Know and Internalize the Research about the Broader Benefits of WFOC's Teaching

....

WFOC's teaching helps campuses attain their institutional goals of preparing students for a global society, increasing student learning and transformation across several areas of development.[11] The vital representation and support WFOC provide increases success and retention of diverse students on campuses and helps students achieve broader learning goals, such as critical thinking, informed citizenship, and diversity engagement.[12] It benefits individual students, campus, and society at large.[13] To begin to enact this strategy, fill in the blanks with the benefits of your teaching to students, campus, or society from the research described earlier:

> My teaching is beneficial because it produces [fill in the blank] and [fill in the blank], both of which are essential to the campus mission and to society.

Not convinced just yet? Let's put all of the benefits that women of color's teaching provides in their specific campus context. Take a look at your university's mission, values statement, or current strategic priorities. Can you see all of the overlap, synergy, and congruence between what WFOC do in their teaching and your university's stated values? WFOC help their universities fulfill their most clearly stated priorities and cherished values, helping all of society as a result. So WFOC please internalize this truth: your wonderful teaching has an impact far beyond your individual classroom, to the campus and society at large.

Strategy #3: Know the Research on Teaching Inequities Faced by WFOC

Administrators assign WFOC heavier teaching loads, more new course preparations, and more service courses.[14] I remember when one of my institutional clients insisted that all faculty had the same 2–2 teaching load. I pointed out that WFOC taught mostly new preps and lower-division service courses with enrollments of 150 students each, while the White or male faculty taught mostly upper-division seminars on their area of expertise with enrollments of fifteen students each. That is simply *not* the same 2–2 load.

Furthermore, students actively resist and inappropriately challenge WFOC's authority and teaching.[15] They are twice as likely as White male colleagues to face student resistance when they teach about social statuses such as race, gender, sexual orientation.[16] For instance, one of my Black woman clients recounted a White male student yelling, "You're wrong!" before storming out of the classroom in the middle of her lecture on structural racial oppression. Students also harass and threaten these women's physical safety and careers.[17] Additionally, colleagues and peers resist and dismiss as biased WFOC's pedagogies and diverse content. White colleagues frequently do not support

WFOC's transformative teaching.[18] In my clients' experience, White administrators, instead of acknowledging and addressing student resistance, frequently advise WFOC to only lecture and to not teach "controversial" (e.g., race) topics.

Institutions use certain common procedures for contract renewal, tenure, and promotions, despite proven shortcomings and inequities. Most notably, universities over rely on student evaluations of teaching, despite their gendered and raced biases.[19] Roughly 60 percent of universities use classroom observations but without collaborative best practices.[20] White colleagues' resistance to nontraditional pedagogy and diverse course content is legitimated as objective feedback about WFOC's "poor" teaching quality.[21] Such institutional practices pave the way for gendered and raced teaching inequities to be *incorrectly* amplified as "evidence" against WFOC in their renewal, tenure, and promotion reviews.

To begin to enact this strategy, fill in the blanks to describe your teaching inequities:

> My [fill in the blank] (teaching overload, student or colleague resistance, negative student evaluations, or teaching observations) is/are consistent with the patterns of race and gender inequities found in the nationwide literature on women faculty of color's teaching experiences. That is, these negative teaching occurrences are not rare or the result of "bad" teaching. Instead, they are structural inequities in society reflected in higher education, on our campus, and in my teaching experiences rather than individual deficits.

WFOC face teaching inequities from administrators, students, colleagues, and, additionally, renewal, tenure, and promotion procedures that hinder and derail their academic careers. Frequently, they're silent about these inequities because majority group members blame them as bad teachers instead of recognizing the inherent gendered racism in these teaching dynamics. So WFOC, hear me: the research plainly shows that there is no reason for shame or guilt. You are not alone or doing anything wrong in your teaching. The negative teaching experiences you are having are patterned gendered racism phenomena in higher education.

....

Strategy #4: Craft an Intentional Narrative about Teaching as a Woman of Color

....

Administrators, colleagues, students, and renewal, promotion, and tenure reviews reiterate an uninformed and myopic narrative that WFOC's teaching is deficient, and any teaching problems they face are an individual issue. For this reason, women of color must know and write an intentional teaching narrative to validate their teaching experiences, efficacy, and awesomeness. The easiest way for WFOC to enact this strategy is to write a few sentences that link pedagogy, content, or classroom management to the literature on WFOC's teaching efficacy and broader benefits, along with a few sentences that link their experiences with the research literature on teaching inequities faced by WFOC.

This is exactly what women of color have already done by completing the prior strategies. To begin to enact this strategy, rewrite the completed statements of the prior strategies, compiling them into a paragraph or two of a narrative that clearly describes the excellent features of WFOC's teaching and broader benefits of their teaching while also identifying gendered and raced patterns of resistance to that excellent teaching. WFOC, do not wait to write this intentional narrative until you have a problem! Do not believe or take to heart the deficit perspective others have of your teaching. Take this opportunity to intentionally situate your teaching narrative in the relevant research. Doing so will help you feel validated in your teaching choices and see that negative teaching experiences are not about you as an individual. Moreover, this type of self-reflection improves both your teaching and evaluations of it.[22]

Strategy #5: Strategically Share Your Intentional Narrative about Teaching as a Woman of Color

An intentional narrative about teaching as a woman of color cannot be validation for WFOC alone. WFOC must share these narratives with others to rewrite the current deficit narrative about their teaching as a strategy in both casual conversations with colleagues and in formal reviews. WFOC, remember that the default narrative your colleagues and students have about your teaching is that it is deficient. You must take a proactive role in sharing your intentional research-backed narrative to challenge the inaccurate one circulating about your teaching and naming the inequities you face. To begin to enact this strategy, use the completed text of the prior strategies and edit it for your voice. Plug that edited text directly into your teaching review materials and use it as a script for the conversations you have with colleagues/administrators about your teaching.

The following is sample text that you could edit to share your intentional teaching narrative:

- The experience I had with [fill in the blank] (teaching inequities) was indeed troubling/interesting/perplexing/misguided/etc. [then one or both of the bulleted text that follows].
- Did you know that the [fill in the blank] (pedagogy) I use is what is in the literature as one of the most effective teaching methods? In fact, the research also shows in addition to producing greater student learning that pedagogy also provides [fill in the blank] (benefit/s) to our campus mission and society at large. Here are a few citations if you are interested in learning more about the effectiveness of that teaching method I use and the benefits it provides to students, campus, and society [add cites from earlier strategies].
- Did you know that experience is exactly what is in the literature on the racism and sexism faced by women faculty of color from [fill in the blank] (administrators, students, colleagues, or contract renewal, tenure, and promotion practices)? Here are a few citations if you are interested in learning more about the teaching inequities that negatively affect the retention of women faculty of color [add cites from earlier strategies].

Sometimes this strategy of sharing an intentional narrative grounded in the research on WFOC's teaching is enough to safeguard their progress toward renewal, tenure, or promotion. Once administrators and colleagues are familiar with and more educated about the effective pedagogies and benefits of women of color's teaching, alongside the patterned experiences of racism and sexism, they can recognize the effectiveness and benefits of WFOC's teaching without the murkiness of race and gender inequity. That is not always the case, which is why I also suggest the final strategy.

Strategy #6: Collect, Analyze, and Share Student-Learning Data

Given the inequities faced by WFOC, they cannot rely on the university processes to accurately document their teaching quality but must collect, analyze, and share both quantitative and qualitative data on student learning via their teaching.[23] Instead of waiting for their first teaching review, the first batch of student evaluations scores and comments to be returned, or the first teaching observation or evaluation, WFOC should proactively have a process in place to measure their teaching effectiveness, even during the last week of class or immediately before the next teaching review.

To begin to enact this strategy, use some simple ways to collect student-learning data, such as a short pre- and posttest quiz to measure student learning before and after teaching a class session/module/a specific concept/course; a single item (with quantitative or qualitative response options) that asks students to fill in the blank: "I have learned new facts/theories/concepts about [insert specific theory, course topic, discipline]"; or a summary of student learning (e.g., use of evidence, writing quality, application) demonstrated by changes between earlier and later student assignments.

Women of color, ignore anyone who discourages you from executing the aforementioned strategies! The practice of analyzing existing assignments or collecting additional student learning data to reflect upon and improve teaching quality is a core component of the teaching portfolio, a proven practice to help faculty assess, improve, and document their teaching.[24] Collecting, analyzing, and sharing this data in reviews ensures that you will document student learning in your course.[25]

Conclusion

I have strategies for administrators and allies but change in institutions is slow, and these WFOC's next teaching reviews will probably occur first. They shouldn't have to bear the burden of these institutional teaching inequities on their shoulders, but here we are. WFOC's teaching cannot be just about student learning but must also put them in a position to be renewed, tenured, or promoted despite teaching inequities. The strategies here do just that because they are grounded in research. I want WFOC who experience teaching inequities to know that you are not alone. These faculty need to be told that their negative teaching experiences are part of a larger pattern of gendered racism in higher education.

Ally colleagues and faculty developers should work more proactively to learn and incorporate research literature about marginalized social statuses into the scholarship and practice of teaching and learning. They should share the research findings and strategies in this chapter as a way to normalize and incorporate it into the mainstream narratives about teaching and learning. It is impossible to understand the best teaching practices without understanding their intersection with the bodies that are doing the teaching and learning. There is so much research that recognizes and examines the intersection of social statuses and interpersonal interactions more broadly.[26] There are many books, articles, and studies specifically about the intersection of social statuses of the instructor and teaching interactions.[27] Instead of using privilege to gate keep, silence, ignore, and invalidate those works, read it and learn it. Colleagues have everything to gain by having a fuller understanding of what it means to teach with a marginalized status and thus nothing to lose.

....

Teaching Takeaways

....

- WFOC's teaching is awesome: innovative, transformative, and effective.
- WFOC's teaching serves the campus mission and benefits society.
- Institutional practices, administrators, colleagues, and students contribute to teaching inequities that derail WFOC's academic careers.
- Until these inequities are addressed, WFOC must enact strategies to demonstrate their teaching effectiveness and protect their academic careers.

....

CHAVELLA T. PITTMAN is a professor of sociology at Dominican University. Her research expertise includes higher education, interpersonal interactions and marginalized statuses, research methods and statistics. She has a love/hate relationship with running, is a beer aficionado, loves to learn, and believes Black joy is resistance. She provides consultation, coaching, courses, and workshops to help individuals and campuses remove the teaching obstacles (e.g., student evaluations, teaching overloads, colleague resistance) to diverse faculty's tenure and promotion.

Notes

1. Stephanie Hatch and Bruce Dohrenwend, "Distribution of Traumatic and Other Stressful Life Events by Race/Ethnicity, Gender, SES and Age: A Review of the Research," *American Journal of Community Psychology* 40, no. 3–4 (December 2009): 313–32; Natalie Slopen, Michelle Sternthal, and David R. Williams, "Racial Disparities in Health: How Much Does Stress Really Matter?" *Du Bois Review* 8, no. 1 (2011): 95–113; Peggy Thoits, "Stress and Health: Major Findings and Policy Implications," *Journal of Health and Social Behavior* 51 (2010): S41–S53, https://doi.org/10.1177/0022146510383499; David R. Williams, "Racial/Ethnic Variations in Women's Health: The Social Embeddedness of Health," *American Journal of Public Health* 92, no. 4 (2002): 588–97.

2. Eduardo Bonilla-Silva, " 'Racists,' 'Class Anxieties,' Hegemonic Racism, and Democracy in Trump's America," *Social Currents* 6, no. 1 (February 2019): 14–31; Neeta Thakur et al., "The Structural and Social Determinants of the Racial/Ethnic Disparities in the U.S. COVID-19 Pandemic. What's Our Role?" *American Journal of Respiratory and Critical Care Medicine* 202, no. 7 (July 17, 2020): 943–49; Musa al-Gharbi, "Universities Run on Disposable Scholars," *Chronicle of Higher Education*, April 17, 2020, https://www.chronicle.com/article/universities -run-on-disposable-scholars; Abiola Farinde-Wu, "The Added Challenges of Dealing with Race and Gender Issues During a Pandemic," *Insider Higher Ed*, May 8, 2020, https://www .insidehighered.com/advice/2020/05/08/added-challenges -dealing-race-and-gender-issues-during-pandemic-opinion; Colleen Flaherty, "Undue Burden," *Insider Higher Ed*, June 4,

2019, https://www.insidehighered.com/news/2019/06/04
/whos-doing-heavy-lifting-terms-diversity-and-inclusion
-work; Colleen Flaherty, "The Souls of Black Professors," *Insider
Higher Ed*, October 21, 2020, https://www.insidehighered
.com/news/2020/10/21/scholars-talk-about-being-black
-campus-2020; Hailey Fuchs, "Trump Attack on Diversity
Training Has a Quick and Chilling Effect," *New York Times*,
October 13, 2020, sec. US, https://www.nytimes.com/2020
/10/13/us/politics/trump-diversity-training-race.html; Henrika
McCoy, "The Life of a Black Academic: Tired and Terrorized,"
Insider Higher Ed, June 12, 2020, https://www.insidehighered
.com/advice/2020/06/12/terror-many-black-academics-are
-experiencing-has-left-them-absolutely-exhausted; Courtney
Wright, "Dear DEI People: Your Black Colleagues Are Waiting,"
Insider Higher Ed, June 19, 2020, https://www.insidehighered
.com/advice/2020/06/19/administrators-who-say-they-support
-diversity-and-inclusion-arent-reaching-out.

3.   Martin Finkelstein, Valerie Martin Conley, and Jack Schuster,
      "Taking the Measure of Faculty Diversity," *Advancing Higher
      Education (TIAA Institute)*, April 2016, 18; Sekile Nzinga-
      Johnson, *Lean Semesters: How Higher Education Reproduces
      Inequity* (Baltimore: Johns Hopkins University Press, 2020); US
      Department of Education and National Center for Education
      Statistics, *The Condition of Education 2018* (Washington, D.C.:
      NCES, May 2018), 185.

4.   Walter R. Allen et al., "Outsiders Within: Race, Gender, and
      Faculty Status in U.S. Higher Education," in *The Racial Crisis
      in American Higher Education: Continuing Challenges for the
      Twenty-First Century*, eds. William A. Smith, Philip G. Altbach,
      and Kofi Lomotey (Albany: SUNY University Press, 2002);
      Octavio Villalpando and Delores Delgado, "A Critical Race
      Theory Analysis of Barriers That Impede the Success of Faculty
      of Color," in *The Racial Crisis in American Higher Education:*

Continuing Challenges for the Twenty-First Century, eds. William A. Smith, Philip G. Altbach, and Kofi Lomotey (Albany: SUNY University Press, 2002), 243–69.

5.   Sylvia Lazos, "Are Student Teaching Evaluations Holding Back Women and Minorities? The Perils of Doing Gender and Race in the Classroom," in *Presumed Incompetent: The Intersections of Race and Class for Women in Academia*, eds. Gabriella Gutiérrez y Muhs et al. (Logan: Utah State University Press, 2012), 164–85; Patricia A. Matthew, ed., *Written/Unwritten: Diversity and the Hidden Truths of Tenure* (Chapel Hill: University of North Carolina Press, 2016); Caroline Sotello Viernes Turner, Juan Carlos González, and J. Luke Wood, "Faculty of Color in Academe: What 20 Years of Literature Tells Us," *Journal of Diversity in Higher Education* 1, no. 3 (September 2008): 139–68; Bonnie TuSmith and Maureen Reddy, eds., *Race in the College Classroom: Pedagogy and Politics* (New Brunswick: Rutgers University Press, 2002).

6.   Corrine Castro, "In the Margins of the Academy: Women of Color and Job Satisfaction," in *Dilemmas of Black Faculty at U.S. Predominantly White Institutions: Issues in the Post-Multicultural Era*, eds. S.E. Moore and R. Alexander Jr. (Lewiston, NY: Edwin Mellen Press, 2010), 136–57; Roxanna Harlow, " 'Race Doesn't Matter, But . . . ': The Effect of Race on Professors' Experiences and Emotion Management in the Undergraduate College Classroom," *Social Psychology Quarterly* 66, no. 4 (December 2003): 348–63; Alison Schneider, "Insubordination and Intimidation Signal the End of Decorum in Many Classrooms," *Chronicle of Higher Education*, March 27, 1998, 12–14; Ruth Zambrana, *Toxic Ivory Towers: The Health Consequences of Work Stress on the Health of Underrepresented Minority Faculty* (New Brunswick, NJ: Rutgers University Press, 2018); Ruth Zambrana et al., "Workplace Stress and Discrimination Effects on the Physical and Depressive Symptoms of Underrepresented

Minority Faculty," *Stress and Health* 37, no. 1 (September 2021): 175–85, https://doi.org/10.1002/smi.2983.

7. Anthony Antonio, "Faculty of Color Reconsidered: Reassessing Contributions to Scholarship," *Journal of Higher Education* 73, no. 5 (2002): 582–602; Scott Freeman et al., "Active Learning Increases Student Performance in Science, Engineering, and Mathematics," *Proceedings of the National Academy of Sciences* 111, no. 23 (2014): 8410–15; M. F. Knowles and B. W. Harleston, *Achieving Diversity in the Professorate: Challenges and Opportunities* (Washington, DC: American Council on Education, 1997); George Kuh, Ken O'Donnell, and Carol Schneider, "HIPs at Ten," *Change* 49, no. 5 (2017): 8–16; Michael Prince, "Does Active Learning Work? A Review of the Research," *Journal of Engineering Education* 93, no. 3 (2004): 223–31; Benidiktus Tanujaya, Jeinne Mumu, and Gaguk Margono, "The Relationship between Higher Order Thinking Skills and Academic Performance of Student in Mathematics Instruction," *International Education Studies* 10, no. 11 (2017): 78–85; Turner, González, and Wood, "Faculty of Color in Academe"; Jennifer Lyn Ramos, Bretel Dolipas, and Brenda Villamor, "Higher Order Thinking Skills and Academic Performance in Physics of College Students: A Regression Analysis," *International Journal of Innovative Interdisciplinary Research* no. 4 (2013): 13; Paul Umbach, "The Contribution of Faculty of Color to Undergraduate Education," *Research in Higher Education* 47, no. 3 (2006): 317–45.

8. Antonio, "Faculty of Color Reconsidered"; Marcia Baxter Magolda, "Teaching to Promote Holistic Learning and Development," *New Directions for Teaching and Learning* 2000, no. 82 (2000): 88–98; Kathleen Quinlan, *Developing the Whole Student: Leading Higher Education Initiatives That Integrate Mind and Heart: Stimulus Paper* (London: Leadership Foundation for Higher Education, 2012); Lisa E. Wolf-Wendel and Marti Ruel,

"Developing the Whole Student: The Collegiate Ideal," *New Directions for Higher Education* 1999, no. 105 (Spring 1999): 35–46, https://doi.org/10.1002/he.10503.

9.   Dena Hassouneh, "Anti-Racist Pedagogy: Challenges Faced by Faculty of Color in Predominantly White Schools of Nursing," *Journal of Nursing Education* 45, no. 7 (2006): 255–63; Olivia Perlow, Durene Wheeler, and Sharon Bethea, "Dismantling the Master's House: Black Women Faculty Challenging White Privilege/Supremacy in the College Classroom," *White Privilege Conference Journal* 42, no. 2 (2014): 251–59.

10.   Lazos, "Are Student Teaching Evaluations Holding Back Women and Minorities"; Matthew, *Written/Unwritten.*

11.   Antonio, "Faculty of Color Reconsidered"; Patricia Gurin et al., "Diversity and Higher Education: Theory and Impact on Educational Outcomes," *Harvard Educational Review* 72, no. 3 (2002): 330–66; Ellen Barbara Stolzenberg et al., *Undergraduate Teaching Faculty: The HERI Faculty Survey 2016–2017* (Los Angeles: Higher Education Research Institute, 2019). See also Anna M. Agathangelou and L. M. H. Ling, "An Unten(Ur)Able Position: The Politics of Teaching for Women of Color in the US," *International Feminist Journal of Politics* 4, no. 3 (December 2002): 368–98; Perlow, Wheeler, and Bethea, "Dismantling the Master's House"; Umbach, "The Contribution of Faculty of Color to Undergraduate Education."

12.   *The LEAP Vision for Learning: Outcomes, Practices, Impact, and Employers' Views* (Washington D.C: Association of American Colleges and Universities, 2011).

13.   Gurin et al., "Diversity and Higher Education"; Jeffery Milem, "The Educational Benefits of Diversity: Evidence from Multiple Sectors," in *Compelling Interest: Examining the Evidence on Racial Dynamics in Higher Education*, eds. M. J. Chang et al. (Stanford University Press, 2003), 129–69; Patrick Terenzini et al., "Racial and Ethnic Diversity in the Classroom: Does It Promote

Student Learning?" *Journal of Higher Education* 72, no. 5 (2001): 509–31.

14. Allen et al., "Outsiders Within"; Flaherty, "Undue Burden"; Susan D. Johnson, John A. Kuykendall, and Thomas F. Nelson-Laird, "An Examination of Workload of Faculty of Color by Rank" (Annual Meeting of the Association for the Study of Higher Education (ASHE), Philadelphia, PA, 2005); Ana M. Martinez Aleman and Kristen A. Renn, *Women in Higher Education: An Encyclopedia* (Santa Barbara, CA: ABC-CLIO, 2002).

15. Diana Freedman and Martha Stoddard Holmes, eds., *The Teacher's Body: Embodiment, Authority, and Identity in the Academy* (Albany: State University of New York Press, 2003); Harlow, "Race Doesn't Matter, But . . ."; Juanita M. McGowan, "Multicultural Teaching: African-American Faculty Classroom Teaching Experiences in Predominantly White Colleges and Universities," *Multicultural Education* 8, no. 2 (2000): 19–22.

16. Diana B. Kardia and Mary Wright, "Instructor Identity: The Impact of Gender and Race on Faculty Experiences with Teaching," (occasional paper, University of Michigan Center for Research on Learning and Teaching, 2004).

17. Chavella T. Pittman, "Race and Gender Oppression in the Classroom: The Experiences of Women Faculty of Color with White Male Students," *Teaching Sociology* 38, no. 3 (July 1, 2010): 183–96; Lois Benjamin, ed., *Black Women in the Academy: Promises and Perils* (Gainesville: University Press of Florida, 1997).

18. Uma A. Jayakumar et al., "Racial Privilege in the Professoriate: An Exploration of Campus Climate, Retention, and Satisfaction," *Journal of Higher Education* 80, no. 5 (2009): 538–63; Turner, González, and Wood, "Faculty of Color in Academe"; Villalpando and Delgado, "A Critical Race Theory Analysis of Barriers That Impede the Success of Faculty of Color."

19. AAUP, "Observations on the Association's 1975 Statement on Teaching Evaluation," *Academe* 91, no. 5 (2005): 42–45; Elizabeth Miller and Peter Seldin, "Changing Practices in Faculty Evaluation," *Academe* 100, no. 3 (2014): 35–38; Kristin J. Anderson, "Students' Stereotypes of Professors: An Exploration of the Double Violations of Ethnicity and Gender," *Social Psychology of Education* 13, no. 4 (2010): 459–72; Anish Bavishi, Juan M. Madera, and Michelle R. Hebl, "The Effect of Professor Ethnicity and Gender on Student Evaluations: Judged before Met," *Journal of Diversity in Higher Education* 3, no. 4 (December 2010): 245–56; Richard L. Dukes and Gay Victoria, "The Effects of Gender, Status, and Effective Teaching on the Evaluation of College Instruction," *Teaching Sociology* 17, no. 4 (October 1989): 447–57; Daniel Hamermesh and Amy Parker, "Beauty in the Classroom: Instructors' Pulchritude and Putative Pedagogical Productivity," *Economics of Education Review* 24 (2005): 369–76.

20. John A. Centra, "Colleagues as Raters of Classroom Instruction," *Journal of Higher Education* 46, no. 3 (1975): 327–37; Nancy Van Note Chism and G. W. Chism, *Peer Review of Teaching: A Sourcebook* (Bolton, MA: Anker, 2007); Steve Drew et al., "Formative Observation of Teaching: Focusing Peer Assistance on Teachers' Developmental Goals," *Assessment and Evaluation in Higher Education* 42, no. 6 (2017): 914–29; Yiasemina Karagiorgi, "Peer Observation of Teaching: Perceptions and Experiences of Teachers in a Primary School in Cyprus," *Teacher Development* 16, no. 4 (2012): 443–61.

21. John A. Centra, "Colleagues as Raters of Classroom Instruction," *Journal of Higher Education* 46, no. 3 (1975): 327–37; Chism and Chism, *Peer Review of Teaching*; Steve Drew et al., "Formative Observation of Teaching: Focusing Peer Assistance on Teachers' Developmental Goals," *Assessment and Evaluation in Higher Education* 42, no. 6 (2017): 914–29; Yiasemina

Karagiorgi, "Peer Observation of Teaching: Perceptions and Experiences of Teachers in a Primary School in Cyprus," *Teacher Development* 16, no. 4 (2012): 443–61; Miller and Seldin, "Changing Practices in Faculty Evaluation"; Turner, González, and Wood, "Faculty of Color in Academe"; Miller and Seldin, "Changing Practices in Faculty Evaluation"; TuSmith and Reddy, *Race in the College Classroom*.

22. Chism and Chism, *Peer Review of Teaching*; Peter Seldin, *Changing Practices in Evaluating Teaching: A Practical Guide to Improved Faculty Performance and Promotion/Tenure Decisions* (Bolton, MA: Anker, 1999).

23. Pat Hutchings and A.A.H.E. Teaching Initiative, *The Course Portfolio: How Faculty Can Examine Their Teaching to Advance Practice and Improve Student Learning* (Washington, DC: American Association for Higher Education, 1998).

24. Peter Seldin, J. Elizabeth Miller, and Clement Seldin, *The Teaching Portfolio: A Practical Guide to Improved Performance and Promotion/Tenure Decisions* (San Francisco: Jossey-Bass, 2010).

25. Miller and Seldin, "Changing Practices in Faculty Evaluation."

26. Joseph Berger, "Status Characteristics and Social Interaction," *American Sociological Review* 37, no. 3 (1972): 241–55; Monica Biernat and Diane Kobrynowicz, "Gender- and Race-Based Standards of Competence: Lower Minimum Standards but Higher Ability Standards for Devalued Groups," *Journal of Personality and Social Psychology* 72, no. 3 (1997): 544; Shelly Correll and Cecilia Ridgeway, "Expectation States Theory," in *Handbook of Social Psychology*, ed. John Delamater (Boston, MA: Springer, 2006).

27. Shirley Hune, "Asian American Women Faculty and the Contested Space of the Classroom: Navigating Student Resistance and (Re) Claiming Authority and Their Rightful Place," in *Women of Color in Higher Education: Turbulent Past, Promising Future*, eds. Jane-Maire Gaetane and Brenda

Lloyd-Jones (Emerald Group Publishing Limited, 2011); Catherin Medina and Gaye Luna, "Narratives from Latina Professors in Higher Education," *Anthropology and Education Quarterly* 31, no. 1 (2000): 47–66; Christine A. Stanley, *Faculty of Color: Teaching in Predominantly White Colleges and Universities* (Bolton, MA: Anker Pub, 2006); Venice Thandi Sulé, "Restructuring the Master's Tools: Black Female and Latina Faculty Navigating and Contributing in Classrooms through Oppositional Positions," *Equity and Excellence in Education* 44, no. 2 (2011): 169–87; Turner, González, and Wood, "Faculty of Color in Academe."

INDEX

....

TEACHING AND LEARNING IN HIGHER EDUCATION

Inclusive Teaching: Strategies for Promoting Equity in the
College Classroom
Kelly A. Hogan and Viji Sathy

Teaching Matters: A Guide for Graduate Students
Aeron Haynie and Stephanie Spong

Remembering and Forgetting in the Age of Technology: Teaching, Learning, and the Science of Memory in a Wired World
Michelle D. Miller

Skim, Dive, Surface: Teaching Digital Reading
Jenae Cohn

Minding Bodies: How Physical Space, Sensation, and Movement
Affect Learning
Susan Hrach

Ungrading: Why Rating Students Undermines Learning (and
What to Do Instead)
Edited by Susan D. Blum

Radical Hope: A Teaching Manifesto
Kevin M. Gannon

Teaching about Race and Racism in the College Classroom: Notes
from a White Professor
Cyndi Kernahan

Intentional Tech: Principles to Guide the Use of Educational
Technology in College Teaching
Derek Bruff

Geeky Pedagogy: A Guide for Intellectuals, Introverts, and Nerds
Who Want to Be Effective Teachers
Jessamyn Neuhaus

How Humans Learn: The Science and Stories behind Effective
College Teaching
Joshua R. Eyler

Reach Everyone, Teach Everyone: Universal Design for Learning
in Higher Education
Thomas J. Tobin and Kirsten T. Behling

Teaching the Literature Survey Course: New Strategies for
College Faculty
Gwynn Dujardin, James M. Lang, and John A. Staunton

The Spark of Learning: Energizing the College Classroom with
the Science of Emotion
Sarah Rose Cavanagh